I0092357

PRAISE FOR *GAP PROSPECTING*

"Gap Prospecting *is legitimately one of my top 5 sales books of all time. It breaks down why your prospecting isn't working, the psychology of why buyers avoid us, how to sell intrigue BEFORE you sell interest, and how to use AI properly.*"
– Abram Langston, DIRECTOR OF BUSINESS DEVELOPMENT—
ARIZONA AT IN TIME TEC

"*This isn't a hype book. It's a manual for understanding why buyers shut down, how to get past their defenses, and how to build messaging that doesn't trip alarms... If you're in sales, enablement or leadership and outbound feels like a grind that never quite clicks, this book explains why and gives you a way out that isn't based on luck or volume.*"
– John Mason, CEO AT JOHN MASON CONSULTANCY

"*In my opinion, this new book is, by far, his best work yet...It is not for those seeking an easy solution; it is not a silver bullet and does not claim to be. Prospecting demands not just effort, but effective effort, and this book guides you in the right direction.*"
– Rodney Nottingham, COMMERCIAL ACCOUNT EXECUTIVE AT
PRESTO-X PEST CONTROL

"*It's one of the most practical and thoughtful explorations of prospecting that I've ever read...This book doesn't pretend this can be solved by better emails or more calls. Instead, it reframes prospecting as the starting point for rebuilding trust by slowing down, leading with problems rather than products.*"
– Steve Ward, ENTERPRISE ACCOUNT MANAGER—
AEROSPACE & DEFENCE AT SNOWFLAKE

"*In a noisy world where buyers are pissed and swamped with the amount of crap they receive in their inbox and phones—*Gap Prospecting *is a 'Must Read' for any sales professional...If you need help getting to know your buyer, the problems they face, how to target them—start here.*"
– Andres Ortega, FOUNDING ACCOUNT EXECUTIVE AT CLOUDCHIPR

"*If* Gap Selling *is the strategy for the finish line,* Gap Prospecting *is the manual for the starting line...It takes Keenan's problem-centric philosophy and moves it upstream, solving the hardest part of the equation: earning the right to start the conversation in the first place.*"
– John Thompson, HEAD OF PARTNERSHIPS AT IMERSIAN

"If you are new to sales, this book is pure gold. It provides a strong foundation, clear structure, and practical guidance that will immediately improve how you approach outreach…Like Gap Selling, *this is a book you will highlight, fold pages, and come back to."*
— **Doyle Baker,** Strategic Account Executive—Proactive AI Agents at NICE

"Implemented correctly with the team, Gap Prospecting *is a weapon."*
— **Sergey Patkovskiy,** Strategic Business Development at EMO Trans

"So many prospecting books still talk like it's 2014. This one is firmly planted in the world we actually sell in today…It's rare to find a book that fires you up and gives you the playbook."
— **Mark Mangal,** Director, North American Sales at Eptura

"One of the most practical and thoughtful explorations of prospecting that I've ever read."
— **Jeff Hansen,** VP Sales & Consumer Advocate at RateCraft

*"*Gap Prospecting *gives you the tools, processes and mindset to grow, change and be successful."*
— **Leonard Matlock,** BDR Manager at EnergyCAP

"Fans of Gap Selling *and breaking the mold of prospecting stereotypes, you will not be disappointed."*
— **Evan Roth,** Federal Account Director at UiPath

*"*Gap Prospecting *is one of the select few I'll be adding to my sales enablement collection…because it is brutally honest about what's broken with prospecting, and it's unusually disciplined about how to fix it."*
— **Anthony Doyle,** Director of Sales Enablement at Turnitin

"If Gap Selling *resonated with you…this one's worth a look."*
— **James Kenny,** Client Director at Sopro

ALSO BY KEENAN:

*Not Taught: What It Takes to Be
Successful in the 21st Century that
Nobody's Teaching You*

Gap Selling: Getting the Customer to Yes

ALSO BY WILL AITKEN:

*Three thousand LinkedIn posts, and at least seven cold emails
my mom said were book-worthy*

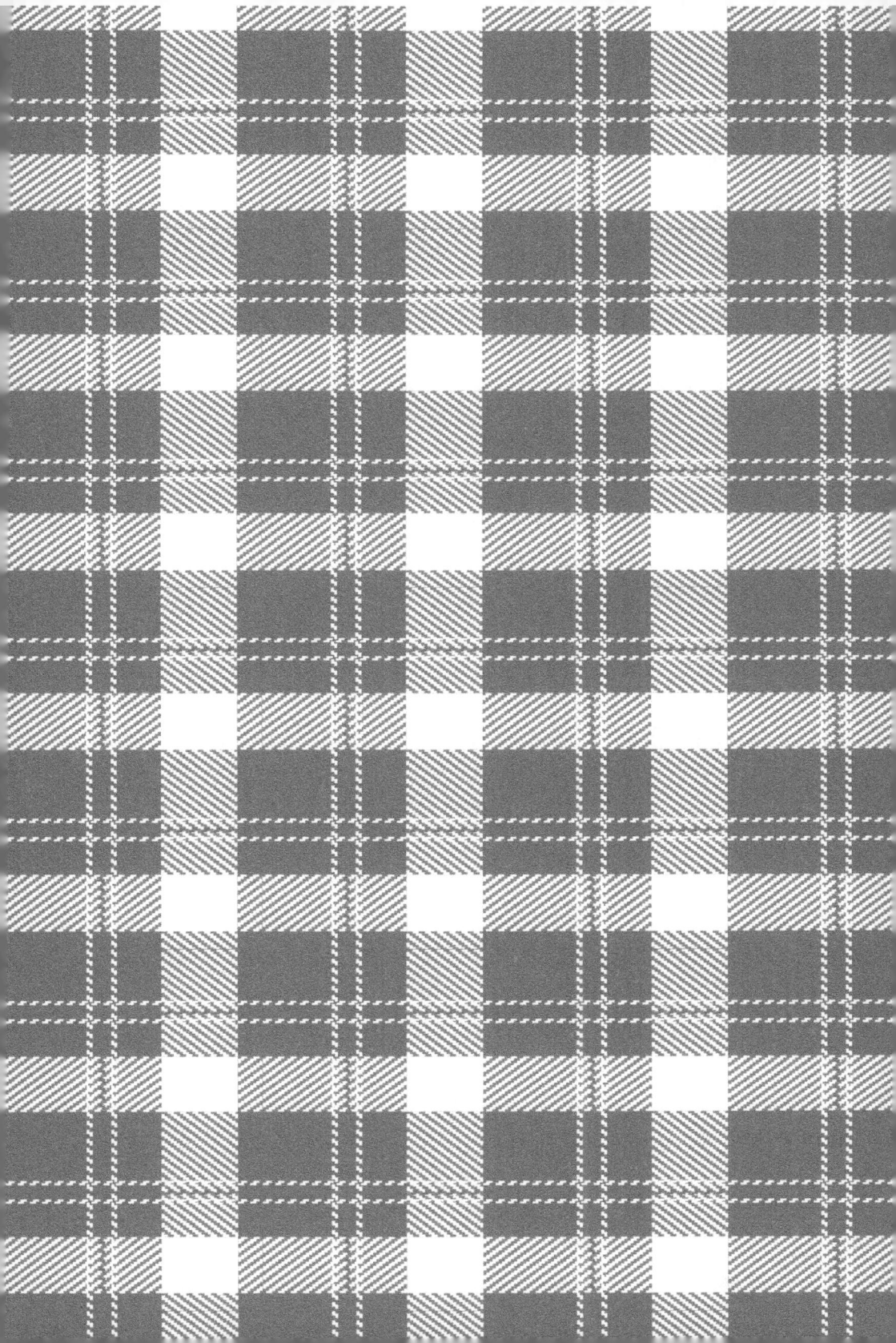

GAP PROSPECTING

GAP

PROSPECTING

GETTING THE BUYER TO ENGAGE:
HOW PROBLEM CENTRIC™ PROSPECTING
INCREASES PIPELINE BY CHANGING EVERYTHING
YOU KNOW ABOUT OUTREACH, PROSPECTING,
COLD CALLING, AND SENDING EMAILS

KEENAN & WILL AITKEN

SALESGROWTH.COM

GAP PROSPECTING

Copyright © 2026 by Jim Keenan and Will Aitken

All rights reserved. Printed in the United States of America. No part of this book may be used or reproduced in any manner whatsoever without written permission except in the case of brief quotations embodied in critical articles or reviews.

Requests for permission should be addressed to: info@salesgrowth.com

This book may be purchased for educational, business, or sales promotional use. For information, please visit amazon.com or salesgrowth.com.

FIRST EDITION

Edited by Heather Pendley and Eve Minkler.

Cover, infographics, and interior designed by ksrevivo.com.

Library of Congress Cataloging-In-Publication has been applied for.

ISBN 978-1-7328910-6-7

For my three daughters: Kenna, Elle, and Ava
—Keenan

For Emme and Archie, my two beautiful children.
For my father, Bill, who taught me consistency, effort, and showing up.
And for the mentors who invested in me along the way:
Dan, Scott, Mikey, Derek, and Tyler.
—Will

CONTENTS

GAP PROSPECTING

INTRODUCTION

Boom!

That's the sound the Yellow Pages make when they're dropped on your desk. For those too young to remember, the Yellow Pages were huge books, sometimes eight inches thick, printed on bright yellow paper, that listed the phone numbers and addresses for almost every business within a city or county. Businesses paid thousands of dollars to be included in them. They were the business hub of information before the internet, what we used to find anything and everything (to find people, you'd use its sister, the white pages). Everybody had one. The Yellow Pages for a major city could weigh several pounds, which is why I'll never forget the booming sound it made when my manager dumped one on my desk on the very first day of my very first sales job selling memberships to the Denver Metro Chamber of Commerce.

"Keenan, this is how you'll find your customers. Begin wherever you want."

That was about the extent of my training. I had no idea what I was doing, and was scared shitless, even if on the outside I acted confident bordering on cocky. But I was young, and after years of modeling, bartending, and living in glorious tourist destinations like Miami's South Beach and Vail, Colorado, I knew it was time to get my shit together. I was determined to make something of myself. I started dialing.

One year later, I was the company's top sales rep. Monthly, quarterly, yearly—I consistently beat everyone's sales records. How? I'd like to credit my high close rate to my natural charm and persistence, but really, it wasn't about the close. It was about what I did long before the close, before I even tried to sell. It was about the prospecting.

Every morning I'd start by opening up a customer relationship management (CRM) tool that I'd custom built for myself (without calling it a CRM, as I had no idea what one was). I used an old-school app like FileMaker Pro because software like Act and Goldmine were super new, and programs like Salesforce didn't exist yet. This is how I'd keep track of my lists of potential customers. I had lists of people I'd called, lists of people who'd agreed to let me snail-mail them brochures containing information about the chamber and how membership would benefit them, and lists of people to follow up with to book meetings. In every list, I made notes about what I'd said if I'd left a voicemail. Once I'd made it through all those lists, it was back to the Yellow Pages to continue making cold calls, just like I'd done on that very first day.

It was a killer prospecting routine, and I did it over and over. It was probably the first time in my life I'd been so disciplined. My technique couldn't guarantee that every prospect would convert into a paying customer, but it could guarantee that my sales funnel was well stocked at all times, which meant I always had opportunities to talk to people. And it worked because back then, people did something unheard of today: They picked up the phone.

Again, for those of you who can't remember the days before smartphones, let me break it down. The phone would ring, and though technology like caller ID existed, people would still answer, even when they didn't recognize the number. A ringing phone sparked intrigue. Who was calling? What did they want? We didn't call it that, but we'd experience some FOMO (fear of missing out) if we didn't answer. And in those few seconds between someone saying, "Hello?" and realizing they were talking to a total stranger lay a golden opportunity for someone like me to engage.

Back then, I could make 40-60 calls in one day and get a 70% connect rate (not that we talked about "connect rates" or used them as a metric; when almost everyone answers, you don't worry about who doesn't). When people pick up the phone 70% of the time, you have room to make mistakes. You can try different approaches and see what works best. If you stumble over your words or accidentally annoy someone, it doesn't matter because another live person is just a few dials away. Prospecting was a numbers game, and it worked in my favor. All I had to do was explain that the Chamber of Commerce could help them with the things they cared about most—getting more customers, influencing Denver's economic environment, and creating high-level relationships with the who's who of the city—and people were willing to talk.

That was 1997. I'd finally found my calling, so to speak. I eventually named my sales philosophy and strategy "gap selling"—because it uses problem-solving to close the gap between what a customer has or is now, and what they *think* they'll want to have or be in the future— and built a successful sales career and consulting practice with it. In fact, I published *Gap Selling* the book, which teaches salespeople how to use my problem centric™ approach to stop sabotaging themselves, earn customer trust, and improve their close rates. A short time after, a man I didn't know named Will Aitken moved to Canada and started a new sales job. I'll let him tell you what happened:

What happened is that once again, I heard the same question that had been repeated over the last five years: "Will, are you *sure* sales is the right career for you?" my dad had asked. My peers had asked. Now, my boss was asking. I couldn't blame them. From the beginning, my career, if you could call it that, had been a rollercoaster of inconsistent results. I'd have hugely profitable months followed by goose eggs, and big wins neutralized by disastrous losses. I'd never received any real sales training or coaching, and I didn't know what I didn't know, so I'd never taken it upon myself to do any research or dive into books, blogs, or podcasts by industry insiders. I was in sales because it was the job you could get when you had a pointless degree and an adventurous spirit that had taken you across four continents since graduation.

As far as I could tell, selling was a numbers game. If I could just talk to enough people and pitch enough stuff every day, with a little luck, I'd close enough deals to keep my job another month. Operating from this sense of constant panic and desperation was an exhausting, stressful way to live. I was newly married, and my wife and I had just moved from Australia, where we'd met, to her native Canada. It was time for a change. I couldn't answer with confidence that sales was, in fact, the right career for me, but I wanted one more chance to prove myself. To do that, I knew I'd need to switch companies and find a boss who'd be willing to invest in me and teach me to be a better salesperson. In exchange, I'd give the job everything I had.

The problem was that getting a gig like the one I wanted required a strong, consistent sales record and high-levels of experience. I had neither. To even get a shot, I was going to have to fudge my résumé a bit. I did, and it worked. An opportunity opened up at a local software company. I completed the online application, submitted my slightly embellished résumé, and landed an interview with the sales leader. To keep the focus off me and avoid saying too many untruths, I turned the tables on my interviewer and kept up a steady stream of questions. What was he looking for in a candidate? What methodologies did the team use? What customers were the best fit for their product? What resources did he recommend I study if I wanted to work successfully with him? *Gap Selling*? Never heard of it.

I made it through to a second interview, scheduled for the following week. That night, I purchased a copy of *Gap Selling* from Audible. I was immediately hooked on the concept of problem-centric selling. No wonder my sales results had been so inconsistent; I'd been doing everything wrong! When I was done, I started over from the beginning, this time taking notes.

On the day of my second interview, the VP of sales and the sales manager asked me to describe my sales approach. I recited almost word for word the formula I'd learned in Keenan's *Gap Selling*: Find the problem, identify the root cause, quantify the impact of the problem, and only then offer to provide a solution. It was everything they wanted to hear, and I got the job.

I felt guilty about bending the truth, but I silently swore I'd make up for it by taking all the coaching I could and applying to my work everything I'd learned from my new favorite book. My new bosses would be so impressed, they'd never have reason to suspect I wasn't the salesperson I said I was.

Nine months later, I was their star performer, breaking sales records and becoming the first account executive in their history to hit quota six months in a row. Later, during a long night of drinking, I admitted to my boss that I'd lied on my résumé. But by that time I was making them more money than any other sales rep working for them ever had. Today, we're still good friends.

I credit my performance to three things:

- I dropped my ego so I could absorb and apply every bit of coaching I received.

- I applied the gap-selling methodology to every one of my buyer interactions.

- I developed a killer prospecting routine that I repeated every single day, giving myself a fat, juicy pipeline that steadily fed me new potential customers to try to help.

Now, the year was 2021. I made cold calls, but with fewer people answering their phones, prospecting for new customers was increasingly done by email and social media DMs, especially LinkedIn. Most people hate prospecting, and at first, I struggled as well. But once I refined my messaging and saw what a massive advantage it gave me, I grew to love it and appreciate its power. Every outbound "call" was another at-bat, another chance to get someone's attention, another chance to apply gap selling techniques and get better at them. Most importantly, the resulting full pipeline allowed me to work from an abundance mindset, not scarcity and panic, which gave me the confidence to *not* pursue every customer. I could allow myself to disqualify anyone whose problems weren't suited for the solutions I had to offer, or whose problems weren't yet causing enough "pain" to compel them to make a change. This meant I could focus all my energy and time on the customers most likely to need my help and solutions. It was the difference between dropping a carefully targeted line into a pool teeming with hungry fish versus casting a net into a big pond that might yield a nice catch or two but was equally likely to dredge up a mess of algae and an old boot.

Since then, I've made hundreds of thousands of cold calls and sent an equal number of emails, while running sales teams and selling everything from software and media to advertising and merch. I started creating online content about what I'd learned about sales and what worked for me, frequently giving Keenan a shout-out for developing the philosophy and techniques that inspired me. My brand and profile grew, and I started getting hired to consult with other sales teams to help them improve their outbound results. Even today, I continue to make cold calls, not because I need to but because in a world of such rapid change, it's important to keep testing my strategies in the current environment to make sure they always work.

Keenan: Love that story, Will. It reflects much of what this book is all about. Ya mind if I wrap it up?
Will: By all means.

You surely see a theme in our origin stories. While we did a lot of other things right, both of us credit our highly successful sales careers to recognizing early that the probability of closing more deals hinged on the quality of our prospecting technique. And you've picked up a book on prospecting, which can only mean you're looking for advice on how to do it better. You've come to the right place. We're here to help. We know how hard it is.

WHY WE WROTE THIS BOOK

While Keenan addressed the issue of prospecting in *Gap Selling*, the main goal of the book was to outline the gap selling philosophy and show how it could radically improve the way you extract information from your customer during the discovery process and turn it into a sale. There just wasn't room to give prospecting the detailed attention it deserved. In the years since, however, as the sales landscape has changed dramatically, it became clear that gap sellers needed a strong foundation in gap prospecting—targeted, problem-centric prospecting—to ensure their success. Meanwhile, Will was out in the trenches, rigorously applying the fundamentals of gap selling to the prospecting process, working with over 30 sales teams in various industries, and seeing a 15.6% cold-call conversion rate, over triple the average. So, we teamed up to write this book. It gives Will a chance to share his expertise in the field with a broader audience and Keenan an opportunity to update and refine the prospecting approach he introduced five years ago, adjust it to the new sales realities of today's market, and expand on the processes that work best.

NOT JUST FOR SDRS

We're not going to say that every seller needs to prospect, but every seller should know how to do it and do it well. You just never know. Even if you're an account executive with a team of SDRs answering to you, even if you don't think you'll ever need to hunt for your supper, it's always better to be aware of the prospecting environment, what's working well, and what isn't. What if your SDRs suck? What if they quit, or you have to lay people off? What if you get a new job that has no SDRs or a powerful marketing team? Be prepared.

There's also an argument for prospecting even in good times. First, there's never a more confident salesperson than one with an overstuffed pipeline. Customers can smell desperation from ten miles away. They can smell confidence, too. When they sense that you're approaching them with an abundance mindset—selling because you genuinely want to help, not because you *have* to—it puts them at ease and builds trust.

Second, gap prospecting can be an important competitive differentiator. There's never a downside to having more leads in your pipeline than you actually need, with the end result of earning extra commission or growing your business faster than you thought you would. It protects you from any deals that fall through and allows you to be selective about where to concentrate your efforts when you're more confident about closing some deals than others.

Finally, keeping your gap-prospecting skills sharp helps keep all your other gap-selling skills sharp. The more you practice, the faster you figure out how to ask the right questions, the more in tune you are with your customers, and the more accurately you can diagnose their problems. Gap prospecting makes you a better gap salesperson all around, and probably a better boss to other salespeople.

What You'll Learn

Our goal is to take the ick out of prospecting. Prospecting today is complex, requiring multiple skills, approaches, tools, processes, and a solid understanding of what it takes to execute across all these elements—but when you're gap prospecting, it doesn't suck. We're psyched to introduce you to gap prospecting and finally give it the attention it deserves.

In Part I of this book, we'll make sure you fully understand how much the prospecting landscape has changed even in just the last few years, and most importantly, why. In our experience, most sellers are looking for a silver bullet, itching to get to the how but reluctant to slow down enough to understand the why. But the why matters a lot—don't skip it. And there's no such thing as a silver bullet; so, it's time we all stop looking for one. You'll be at a serious disadvantage if you don't understand why these gap-prospecting rules exist or work in the first place. We're all for listening to your gut, but if and when something unexpected sends you off course, if you don't know the rules, you'll be rudderless. Understanding why buyers respond to sellers the way they do, and why techniques improve selling outcomes, will keep you in the right mindset and make them easier for you to adapt, make them your own, and execute flawlessly, no matter what happens.

In Part II we'll get super prescriptive, offering detailed approaches on how to best execute gap-prospecting techniques. This isn't a high-level, check-the-box book covering outdated, overused clichés and tactics. We're going deep, and we're going to give you relevant, proven methods to get buyers to engage and work with you, covering topics such as how to:

- Develop a potent gap-prospecting mindset

- Accurately diagnose prospects' problems

- Use messaging that actually resonates with prospects

- Find better-fit leads that no one else can

- Make better cold calls

- Avoid and handle objections

- Leave voicemails that aren't a waste of your time

- Send incredible emails that get replies

- Record sales videos that aren't cringe

- Use LinkedIn in the right way to avoid burning your brand

- Know how and when to ask for referrals

- Follow up with sequences and cadences that convert

- Make the most of events and trade shows

- Convert inbound leads more often

- Ensure the meetings you book actually show up

- Use pattern interrupts that stand out

- Use technology that will help you be more effective

- Stay motivated and invest your time smartly so you can hit your targets while avoiding burnout

- Understand how AI will change the game and what to consider when using AI

We're not promoting gimmicks. Gimmicks won't hold up over time. What we offer are timeless strategies rooted in a foundational understanding of your customers, their status quo, their problems, and how you can make your message feel personal, timely, or relevant. As shared in *Gap Selling*, a salesperson's job is to help, not sell. Gap prospecting puts your buyers at ease. When prospects aren't forced into fight-or-flight mode (we'll talk about this later), they're more apt to let their guard down and engage with us. That's what we want. When we're perceived as a helpful resource and not a salesperson with an agenda, everything changes. Learning the strategies in this book will supercharge your gap-prospecting results today and allow you to adapt to whatever social or technical changes we see in the future.

"The more you interrupt people, the less they trust you."
—*Seth Godin*

PART I

IT'S BROKEN

PART I · IT'S BROKEN

Sales is broken—and we broke it.

In our effort to scale, streamline, and accelerate sales, we hardened buyers. We trained them to defend themselves. We eroded what little trust they had left. We replaced relevance with volume, insight with automation, and help with interruption.

We stopped trying to create value. We lost any real understanding of our buyers' businesses—their goals, objectives, constraints, and vision. We forgot that sales exists to help.

And when salespeople stop helping, they offer no value.

Buyers can't stand us.

They don't trust us.

They don't like us.

So they avoid us—emails ignored, calls blocked, messages filtered—and that outcome is on us.

Until we accept this reality, until we own the damage modern selling has caused, your ability to connect, engage, and earn access will remain fundamentally impaired.

It's time we wake up.

CHAPTER ONE
THE FUNDAMENTAL CHALLENGE

Oh, *man, what does he want?* Yvonne clocked the tall, lanky man in the blue polo from a block away. She saw him approach a woman in a sundress, who immediately moved away without turning her head or breaking her stride, making it clear she didn't want to engage with him. Right behind the girl in the sundress was a man walking his dog. The minute polo-man leaned in as if to say something, the dog walker put up his hand in the universal sign for "stop" and shook his head. Polo-man stepped back. *So annoying,* Yvonne thought, shifting her green workout bag to her opposite shoulder facing the street and out of reach, should the guy be looking to grab and run. *You can't go anywhere without someone bothering you.* By now she was just a few feet away from the stranger. She looked down at her phone, hoping that if she walked quickly and avoided eye contact, he'd leave her alone.

"Excuse me!"

Ugh!

"No thanks!" she said automatically, picking up her pace.

"Wouldyoulikeagiftcard? It'sfree!" Polo-man talked so fast his words were like Scrabble tiles spilling out of their bag.

Yvonne's instinct to be polite got the best of her, and she looked up from her phone. The guy had a pleasant expression and seemed harmless, and for a brief second, she considered pausing to see what he was holding out in his hand. Then she caught herself and kept moving to put distance as fast as possible between them. "Nothing is free!" she chirped, hoping to let him know that she, at least, was no pushover. Whatever he was selling, she wasn't buying. It was a relief to finally get far enough away that she could no longer hear polo-man accosting the next victim behind her.

"This sucks!" Trevor blurted under his breath. "I'm giving away money. How can this be so hard?" The stack of gift cards in Trevor's hands were feeling heavier by the minute. When his boss had told him the sales group would participate in an outbound workshop, he thought that meant sitting through another boring lecture about cold-calling scripts or email campaigns. But the sales coach who'd shown up that morning had a surprise for all of them. Instead of yammering from the front of the room, he handed each sales rep a stack of $50 gift cards. His instructions were simple: Give them away as fast as possible to passersby on the street. The first rep to give away all their gift cards would earn a $200 cash reward. Trevor was pretty sure his eyes had turned to dollar signs like in an old-fashioned cartoon. *Sweet!* he'd thought, trying not to look smug in front of his coworkers. *That money is mine.*

Out on the street, he wasn't feeling so confident. He may as well have been a half-torsoed zombie dragging himself across the sidewalk based on the level of revulsion, defensiveness, and skepticism people expressed at the sight of him. But with thoughts of what an extra $200 could buy dancing through his head, he put on his biggest smile and kept on, undeterred. Stepping forward to grab people's attention while making sure not to invade their personal space—don't they know it's unsafe to walk and text at the same time?—he tried to talk as fast as possible before they could get away so they would understand he wasn't some creepy slime-ball but was actually offering something they surely wanted. "Would you like a gift card? It's free!" But most kept walking as quickly as they could, pretending they couldn't see or hear Trevor holding out his gift cards. Some even gave him dirty looks. If they responded with a quickly muttered, "No, thank you," they also picked up their pace, like they knew that even a little bit of polite acknowledgment made them vulnerable to an interaction they didn't want to have. For a split second, he thought he might have an opening with a woman carrying a green workout bag, but the minute he made eye contact, she scurried to put more distance between herself and him while calling out, "Nothing is free!"

"This is!" he wanted to yell back, but he knew it would do no good. Everyone's body language screamed, "Ugh! Stranger danger! Stay away!" Trevor didn't want to take the time to check to see how many minutes he'd been out there, trying to give the damn cards away, but it was starting to feel too long. He wasn't in any danger should he fail to get rid of these cards, but the consequence wouldn't be fun. For while the first person to give away their cards was slated to win $200, the last person would have to make a live cold call in front of the coach and the other sales reps. As the minutes and the passersby mercilessly moved on, Trevor started to sweat. *I don't believe this*, he thought. *Buyers hate us sellers so much, we can't even give free money away.*

Will was the architect of this prospecting experiment and team-building exercise. You'll be happy to know that Trevor wasn't the last person to get rid of his cards, but he didn't win the cash prize either. The winner made it back empty-handed in two minutes. It took the last person ten minutes to get rid of their cards. But every seller was rejected at least once, and all reported that most people behaved exactly as you probably do when you're walking down a street and someone looks like they might try to get you to sign a petition, when you're at the mall and a vendor comes at you with a sample of perfume, or when you're at Costo and walk too close to the cell phone kiosk.

You might be wondering if the problem was the gift cards. Maybe they were for a new product or service no one had ever heard of, or something that wasn't all that popular. That's the thing—there were no strings attached. Trevor and his cohorts were giving away generic $50 Visa/Mastercard gift cards. They could be spent anywhere.

The people on the street were literally turning down free money.

Had these same individuals seen a $50 bill or gift card on the ground, chances are, they would have at least stopped to look a little closer. They might have picked it up to see if it was real, maybe while looking around for a hidden camera. They might have decided to leave the bill or card where it was. Regardless, they would have given it at least a few seconds of their time to determine if it was something of interest. However, these gift cards weren't on the ground. They were being proffered by salespeople, and everyone knows salespeople can't be trusted. It had to be a scam, right? The passersby didn't want to get suckered, and so, most passed.

Normally, Trevor and the other sales reps never prospected face-to-face; like most sales groups, they relied on lead generation providers and platforms, along with auto dialers, to reach out to buyers from the safety of their desks. By forcing them to see how prospects reacted physically to the in-person equivalent of a cold call, Will hoped to expose the fundamental challenge that has bedeviled sellers since selling became a thing: Even if we have something that could be of immense value to our prospects, most buyers' default response will be to reject it sight unseen. With that lesson learned, the class was now ready to seek solutions, and now so are you.

WHY BUYERS RESIST

Make no mistake, prospecting has always been hard. There are several reasons why humans are naturally resistant to strangers walking up to them for any reason, much less someone who's interrupting them and whom they suspect is trying to make a buck.

1. **It's biological.** We're naturally wired to avoid strangers, interruptions, and the unfamiliar in general. Lodged in our brains near the base of our skull, the almond-shaped amygdala—fun fact, the word comes from *amygdale*, the Greek word for "almond"—does its mighty best to protect us. Constantly scanning for threats, it helps manage our emotions and connects them to other parts of the brain responsible for memory, learning, and sensory experience.[1] For this reason, our brain's ability to perceive and interpret other people's intent, behavior, and emotions is influenced by a combination of factors, such as a person's individual tolerance for novelty, their gender, their previous experiences, their culture, and the environment or context in which they're having any given interaction.[2] Before we're aware that we've seen a face,[3] we unconsciously make snap judgments and threat determinants through facial recognition, as well as through body language, even from a distance[4], and even when we're not fully paying attention![5] In fact, body language is exceptionally good at spreading fear.[6] This explains why even from a block away, Yvonne was already picking up signals that Trevor was someone to avoid. While she didn't consciously register fear, her amygdala, responsible for triggering the body's protective fight-or-flight response,[7] had assessed the threat—uncomfortable but not dangerous, confrontation unnecessary, flight—the best option—and was compelling her to protect herself by moving her bag out of reach, picking up her

pace, averting her gaze, and generally steeling herself against an un-wanted interaction. Without knowing how to lower Yvonne's built-in defensive instincts, Trevor didn't stand a chance. HINT: Read that last sentence again; we're gonna come back to it. It's important.

2. **It's cultural.** The brain isn't irrational for being suspicious of sales-people. History is littered with charlatans whose exploits became permanent fixtures in the vernacular, from the original snake-oil salesman, Clark Stanley, to Charles Ponzi and his pyramid schemes, to George C. Parker, who repeatedly "sold" the Brooklyn Bridge, among other public landmarks he didn't own, to new immigrants,[8] inspiring the line, "If you believe that, I have a bridge to sell you." Throughout the 19th and 20th centuries, in literature, theater, and film, salespeople have been depicted as deceitful, aggressive manip-ulators, stand-ins for greed, and participants in a cruel "system of capitalism."[9] Every big story, like what you've read or heard about Enron, Bernie Madoff, and Wells Fargo, and every smaller story, like losing money on a fake Facebook Marketplace sale, reinforces the perception that sellers of all stripes are not to be trusted.

The skepticism runs so deep, sometimes buyers resist even when we try to sell them something they actually admit they need. Will once decided it would be a fun exercise to go door-to-door selling "No Soliciting" signs. He bought a few online and headed to a neighborhood not too far from his own. The people who opened the door would find a friendly guy wearing a white t-shirt that read "No Soliciting" in big black letters, and he'd say:

"Hey, I was chatting with a couple of your neighbors, and they told me they get a ton of sales reps knocking on their door, trying to sell stuff like pest control, solar panels, that kind of thing... Do you get a lot of that, too?"
"Uh...yeah," they'd say, reading his t-shirt, confused.
"How many would you say per week?"
"Three or four, I guess?"
"Wow, and does that disturb you? Get on your nerves?"
You could see the question in their eyes: *Where's he going with this?* But

many would reply, "Yeah, it does; I have a baby who naps," or "Yeah, I work nights, and I'm trying to sleep," or "Yeah, the dogs go nuts. It's annoying."

"A lot of folks on this block have posted signs that say 'No Soliciting' to try to prevent these interruptions. Is there a reason you haven't tried that yet?"

They'd usually say something about just not having gotten around to it. It's not the kind of thing you remember to put on the weekly shopping list.

Will would then say, "Well, that's why I dropped by. I spotted you didn't have a sign yet. Are you open to checking out a couple of the signs I've got?" Then he'd whip out a folder full of "No Soliciting" signs in various styles and colors.

One or two were incredulous. "Hang on. You're knocking on doors to sell...'No Soliciting' signs?"

"Yes!" Will would say, delighted they saw the irony. "I'm working myself out of a job here. Would you like one?"

Will thought the whole exercise was hugely entertaining, but not that many people laughed. Despite the fact that he was offering them something they'd just admitted they needed, most were so weirded out at having a stranger appear on their doorstep, they weren't really paying attention to what he was saying; they just wanted to shut the door. But not all. Will was able to override some of these buyers' baked-in resistance because he knew things about prospecting and human nature that Trevor didn't, all of which you'll learn in this book.

3. **It's at the cellular level.** (Or would it be sell-ular? Lol, yes, we're aware that's corny, and we're proud of it.) Bad puns aside, we salespeople trigger the resistance. Yes, us. The sellers. Even the majority of us, who would never defraud anyone. We spark it when we decide to believe that the path to a successful sales career is to sell as fast as possible and at any cost, and we fan the flames when instead of thinking of our buyers as partners, we treat them as prey. Is it any wonder they react to us, whether in person, by email, or on the phone, like we're predators? The amygdala responds to patterns, and most of the time, the pattern buyers see, consciously or uncon-

sciously, is that sellers aren't actually trying to help and aren't working in the buyer's best interest.

WHY THINGS GOT HARDER

The biggest obstacle to successful selling used to be that sellers didn't understand the fundamental rules of the selling game. Without a deep understanding of those rules, they couldn't land the first "yes" that leads to all the other yesses necessary to close a deal. That's where *Gap Selling* comes in. It exposes sellers' misconceptions and bad habits and lays out the rules, and people who fully embrace those rules and execute them find that they can build an efficient, effective practice, yielding predictable results. In other words, gap selling helps you sell more and better. But today, things are exceedingly more difficult, even if you've read *Gap Selling*, understand the fundamental rules of problem-centric selling, and execute beautifully (though we guarantee that the people who don't know the rules are struggling more than those who do, so if you haven't read *Gap Selling* yet, you should). It's because we lost access.

HOW WE LOST ACCESS

Thanks to a combination of social and technological factors, such as improved caller ID, call blockers, and society's shift toward communicating via text, the 70% connection rate Keenan enjoyed in his glory days has dropped to a not-so-glorious 3.9%. Of those 3.9% of people who pick up the phone, only 39% stay on the call for longer than 30 seconds. Of those who stay on the call for longer than 30 seconds, only 12% agree to a meeting. And of those meetings that get booked, only 50% of the prospects show up![10] So let us help you with the math: You need to make 1,000 cold calls just to set two meetings to get ONE opportunity. That's a LOT of calling to make your number. Eight in ten Americans say they won't answer phone calls if they don't recognize the number,[11] and Gen Z has decided it's rude to call at all, especially without texting first, with some using the phone as a phone so rarely, they've developed anxiety and "phone phobia."[12] Cold email conversion rates aren't much better. Depending on who you ask, they're just 1-5%. We've seen even lower.

Buyers invest in tools to avoid us and make our jobs harder, not just because they don't want to be scammed and spammed but also, in many cases, because they don't want to be sold to, period. Why should they?

If they have questions about a product or service, they can just look it up online. They can see how other customers like it and rate it. They can comparison shop. And they can do it in their own time, at their own convenience, without ever having to engage with us at all. They think they no longer need us.

They're wrong.

CHAPTER TWO
THE NINE TRUTHBOMBS
OF PROSPECTING

Hi, Burt, this is Mandi from Spendless Business Solutions, your go-to procurement platform, calling to tell you about—"

"It's Curt, and we're not interested. Thanks. Bye."

Click.

Mandi leaned forward and squinted at the screen in front of her. Sure enough, it said her contact's name was Curt, not Burt. She'd put off getting reading glasses for a few years now, but it felt like every month her vision got worse. Terrific. She could be the geriatric of the company, with I've-fallen-and-I-can't-get-up sales numbers to match her granny looks. For the umpteenth time, she wondered if she'd made a mistake leaving Blot, her Uncle Jim's print company. She hadn't been a sales star there, either, but she'd been handed a few steady accounts to manage and kept them reasonably happy. Seven years in, though, she was bored and had decided it was time to prove she could succeed someplace where there was no family-tied safety net. Today was her first day at her new job, and it wasn't going well.

But if there was one thing Mandi knew she had going for her, it was a belief in the power of positive thinking. *Next one is it; I can feel it!* She inhaled through her nose, shook her head to wake herself up, and plastered a smile on her face as she clicked the button that would connect her to her next call. She'd read that people could hear you smile through the phone and hoped it was true as she heard someone pick up on the other end.

"This is Kelsey."

"Hi, Kelsey! This is Mandi from Spendless Business Solutions, your go-to, all-in-one platform to streamline your procurement workflows.

And I'm calling today because I see you're the head of procurement over at TreeStar, so I wanted to see if you might be interested in an overview of how we help other procurement heads just like you."

"I don't have time for this." *Click.*

Mandi's smile disappeared. *Sheesh! So rude!*

The next two calls, she didn't get past her name before she was hung up on, so it felt like triumph when she finally reached someone who told her to email whatever she wanted to tell him, and he'd take a look. Score! Buoyed with renewed optimism, she thought she could smell success when she got through to a Dan in facilities, who allowed her to finish her introductory spiel.

"Hey, that sounds great," he said warmly, then he added, "But what we have now is working for us. And I have a meeting."

"Oh." Mandi thought about pushing back, but Dan didn't sound like someone who wanted to be convinced. "I totally understand how you feel. Another company in your space felt the exact same, but they found they were able to halve their expense processing times. Why don't I show you later this week?"

"Um, yeah, sure. Thanks again. Bye, now."

Click.

At least he was nice about it, Mandi thought. She looked up at the digital clock on the wall. It wasn't even lunchtime, and it already felt like she'd been on the phone for days.

We first met Mandi in *Gap Selling*, when she managed to piss off a CEO named Ted, who had promised his wife he'd get home in time to make dinner, then didn't because Mandi took up his time with an unnecessarily long-winded and wholly product-centered sales pitch. Unfortunately, she hasn't learned much since then to make her prospecting go any better than her selling. Maybe it's not her fault because she was never taught. But you, friends, won't have that excuse.

As in gap-selling methodology, there are nine indisputable truths about gap prospecting and what's really happening between buyer and seller when we prospect. If you don't understand these truths and keep them in the forefront of your mind every day, you'll be in for a world of hurt. Tape them onto your desk or your monitor and check yourself constantly to make sure you remember them on the occasions when you feel like you need to step back to lick your wounds. It'll help you take rejections less personally if you can remember that they're just the nature of the beast. They are:

1.   No One Gives a Shit About You

2.   People Are Insanely Busy

3.   People Hate Being Interrupted

4.   Your Prospect Doesn't Owe You Anything

5.   You Trigger Fight-or-Flight

6.   No One Ever Wants to Be Sold To

7.   Buyers Are Liars

8.   People Have Problems

9.   Prospecting Works

TRUTH #1: NO ONE GIVES A SHIT ABOUT YOU

Or your company. Or your product. Or your service. Or anything even tangentially having to do with you. This was a truthbomb in *Gap Selling* too, but it's even truth-bombier when you're prospecting. When you're selling, your buyer has given you some level of permission to approach. Not so in prospecting. They don't know you exist, and even if they do, they don't care. If they did, you'd have heard from them by now. It's not like you can't be found. In two clicks, they can look up your CV, company history, accounts and clients, and social media. If you're doing social right, in an instant they can know what books you're reading, what people you're talking to, what ideas you're most excited about, and what expertise and perspective you bring to the subjects that matter to them. But they haven't looked you up, or if they have, for whatever reason they haven't been compelled to reach out. Keep that in mind every time you send an email, phone call, or DM. The buyer will only care about you, your product, or your service when the time is right and when they believe you can move their current state into a better future state. Until then, they aren't interested in you. At all. So don't waste one nanosecond giving them information they didn't ask for, and focus on giving them the information they *need*. Later, you'll learn how to craft the perfect opener that grabs your buyer's attention and doesn't let go.

TRUTH #2: PEOPLE ARE INSANELY BUSY

The people you're trying to talk to are already overwhelmed with hundreds of calls, emails, Slacks, in-person meetings, online meetings, and LinkedIn outreaches per day. And somehow, they're also supposed to get their own work done, manage their teams, write their reports, and prepare their presentations. People barely have time to breathe, much less answer all the virtual knocks on their door. They wouldn't be able to even if they wanted to. But they don't want to. They want to get their work done, feel good about what they've accomplished that day, and go home. If they wanted to make you part of that, they'd have already reached out and put you on their calendar. They didn't, yet here you are. Which brings us to…

TRUTH #3: PEOPLE HATE BEING INTERRUPTED

According to a study out of UC Irvine, most people only work about 12 minutes before experiencing an interruption. Twelve minutes! In addition, after each interruption, they found that it takes, on average, about 23 minutes for people to recover and get back on track with what they were doing.[13] People are already struggling to stay on task, and then you come along, and by the very nature of cold outreach, you interrupt them again. When cold calling, you're breaking the social norm most of us grew up with that tells us that it's rude to interrupt people when they're busy. No one likes that. Is it better to send cold emails, maybe? People don't like those either. Over a decade ago, productivity expert Laura Vanderkam estimated that people could spend as much as 12 hours per year just deleting unsolicited emails. Even with improved filtering services, that number can only have gone up in the years since. Think about it this way: With every interruption, you're affecting your prospect's ability to do their job. No wonder they don't want to hear from you.

So that begs the question: Is there ever a time when people welcome an interruption, even if it gets in the way of their productivity? You can probably think of a few off the top of your head—like an emergency, a fire, or a dangerous weather report; for some of us, it's birthday cake in the conference room. Obviously, there are times when it's absolutely appropriate to interrupt. It's when the well-being, best interest, or peace of mind of the person you're interrupting will be immediately altered by information in your possession. (This seems a good place to remind you, on our knees, begging you please, to make sure you're contacting the right person who's qualified and authorized to make decisions about whatever it is you're selling.) And the only good reason to interrupt when you're prospecting is that you've identified, or suspect, your buyer may have a problem that's making them suffer, and you have a solution that will solve the problem. That's your best bet if you want to be met with intrigue and interest, not irritation.

TRUTH #4: YOUR PROSPECT DOESN'T OWE YOU ANYTHING

In another UC Irvine study, researchers found that people respond to interruptions with elevated levels of stress and frustration and an elevated sense of pressure.[15] Is it any wonder that after a while, they just don't have it in them to be polite to someone who, from their perspective, is calling to get something out of them? If you're reaching out uninvited by phone or email, your buyers don't owe you any courtesy or information. They don't even owe you the time it would take for you to get four words out. It's not nice to be rude to anyone, but cold callers have no grounds to complain if a buyer isn't nice, or if they get mad or hang up. You're the rude one, remember? You're interrupting.

It helps to remind yourself that we have no idea what our buyers are going through when our call comes in or our email lands. They could be worried about a family member, stressed out over a deadline, or hearing rumors about downsizing. Also keep in mind that when you show up on the phone or in their inbox, you're not there alone. You're one in a crowd of people, including competitors, clamoring for your buyer's time like fans mobbing Tyler, the Creator for a selfie. Try to have some compassion.

But also, get over it. You chose this work, remember? Consider yourself lucky if all the buyer does is hang up on you. You're on social media, so you know people can be awesome, and they can also be awful. As they say in elementary schools, you get what you get, and you don't throw a fit. If you can't handle the wide range of reactions you're likely going to get during outreach, you're in the wrong business.

TRUTH #5: YOU TRIGGER FIGHT-OR-FLIGHT

That rudeness you're met with is a symptom of the fight half of the human fight-or-flight response. If your buyer just hangs up without giving you a chance to talk, that's them taking flight. Later, we'll talk more about why salespeople trigger a part of the brain called the amygdala, which controls the fight-or-flight response, but for now, it's enough to know that your buyer is busy, and you're a stranger, so automatically they don't trust you. Any time they do give you is a huge gift. But if you lead with product and are disrespectful enough to get pushy, you're just going to intensify their fight-or-flight response. It's critical that you use whatever time you get to quickly disarm them and jolt them out of that reactionary stance. The best way to do that is by making sure they can immediately perceive you as helpful. If you can't disarm buyers' suspicions and distrust almost immediately, you'll struggle with prospecting.

TRUTH #6: NO ONE EVER WANTS TO BE SOLD TO

No one has ever sat down to work and thought, I hope someone interrupts me to sell to me today! But there's a caveat to this truth. No one ever wants to be sold to *badly*. No one minds being sold to when they're being sold something they want or need by someone they trust and who they believe has their best interest at heart. Earning that trust is the big challenge, the equivalent of running an obstacle course in the first three seconds of phone or email contact. But it can be done!

TRUTH #7: BUYERS ARE LIARS

We're taught that it's wrong to lie, but no one has ever gotten in trouble or suffered negative consequences for lying to a salesperson, and so people do it, and they do it often. It's often an act of self-preservation. Buyers lie because they're trying to avoid an uncomfortable situation. Take when a seller asks, "Do you have five minutes to talk?" Well, even the busiest person might have five minutes to talk…to their boss. To their spouse. To their kids or to people they *want* to talk to, like Girl Scouts during cookie-selling season. But do they want to talk to you? No, they don't. Not only because they don't know or trust you but also because they know that if they tell you the truth, they could be setting themselves up for an uncomfortable situation. It's uncomfortable to let a salesperson sell to you, only to have to tell them you're not interested, especially when you're fairly certain that the second you say you're not interested or what you have is good enough, the seller is going to try to talk you out of your decision. Humans will do almost anything to avoid feeling uncomfortable. Shutting down the conversation immediately with, "I'm busy," or "We're covered, thanks," allows them to avoid the unpleasantness altogether, guilt-free.

The thing is, if you're prospecting, your goal isn't to get to yes. It's to get to the truth. If a buyer hasn't given you a chance to explain the problems you see and the solutions you have to offer, they can't know for sure that they don't need what you're selling. If you really want to help them, you need to ask the right questions to find out for sure if they're right. That's because of Truth #8.

TRUTH #8: PEOPLE HAVE PROBLEMS

Buyers may not realize it yet, or they may not have gotten around to doing anything about it, but they do have problems they need solved. That's why sellers' hope should spring eternal—because buyers absolutely do want to fix their problems once those start causing them pain. If they're not feeling the pain yet, can you show them evidence that they're about to? Can you show them the crack in the pipe they hadn't noticed, just waiting for a tiny bit more pressure before it splits and creates a major flood? Can you show the weak link barely keeping their shit in place? Can you show them that they *are* feeling the pain; they've just been compensating for it and normalizing it for so long, they've forgotten how much better it would feel if the pain went away? Half the time, buyers insisting they don't need you have absolutely no idea that they're on the brink of experiencing some very real pain. Help them see it, and they'll do whatever they need to avoid it.

TRUTH #9: PROSPECTING WORKS

Reading this chapter could make you wonder why prospectors even bother. But if you talk to the right people and bring them solutions that make their problems go away, people buy. In fact, they love to buy! They love to buy products and services that help them get more leads, bring more visits to their website, help them move more products out the door faster, or keep their teams organized and productive. They love to buy whatever makes their lives easier and better. And they love buying from people they trust and who they believe are trying to help. If you prospect right and show buyers that you're that person, and that you're the key to that easier, better life, they'll open their door and welcome you in. Case in point, when Will went out selling "No Soliciting" signs, in less than two hours he'd knocked on 25 doors, had 12 conversations, and made three sales. That's a 25% close rate. We'll break down why his approach worked in Chapter 16. It's not easy, but when we put them and their needs first, and talk about problems instead of product, buyers will see us as peers, partners, collaborators, advisors, and consultants—people they can trust.

Getting a chance to show them you're that person starts with breaking through the noise.

CHAPTER THREE
IT'S A NOISY, NOISY, NOISY, NOISY WORLD

Have you ever sat down for a relatively early meal at a popular restaurant with someone you were looking forward to catching up with, only to find as the night progresses, more people fill the room, and the music cranks up to the point that you have to yell louder and lean increasingly farther toward each other for either of you to hear a word the other one says? Being a buyer today is like living 24/7 in that overcrowded restaurant, seated at a bad table near the kitchen, where you can hear bowls and spatulas clattering to the floor and the line cooks whooping in reaction to the soccer match playing on a phone they propped up on a shelf. Except in our case, the incessant, excessive, distracting, annoying noise isn't due to lots of people having a good time (or competing to be heard against some insanely loud sound music) or working hard.

So What's Causing It?

Two things. First, **oversaturation**. There was a time when the barrier to entry to building or selling a product was high. You had to build a product, launch a business and hire a sales rep or two who could handle all your selling needs, and as business grew, you brought on a few more. Today it's far easier because the barrier to entry is considerably lower as the number of vendors and products on the market has exploded. For example, in 2016, there were about 50 times as many items sitting on grocery store shelves as there were 80 years earlier.[16] Technology like cloud computing and pay-as-you-go services have made it much easier to launch new software.[17] Companies need a lot more salespeople to sell all that extra stuff. In addition, as conversion rates continue to crater, more and more companies are hiring sales teams armed with a sophisticated array of technology and automation tools that promise to maximize the efficiency, speed, and frequency with which they can reach prospects and new markets and drive growth. According to Dr. Howard Dover in his book *The Sales Innovation Paradox*, there was a 1,200% increase in the number of SDRs between 2015 and 2021. He calculated a 10-50x amplification of the total sales outreach that buyers receive from technologies and tools. Combined, these increases led to approximately 12,000% more shit landing in buyers' inboxes and phones.[18]

The second thing causing the cacophony is an increase in the **number of sales channels**. Everywhere buyers look, they're confronted with a sales pitch. They go on social media to look at cat videos, and they're assaulted with sales pitches. They see someone has reached out to them via DM, but it's not a friend; it's a stranger with a sales pitch. They open their email every morning to find a string of sales pitches waiting for them. Their phone rings, and nine times out of ten, when they check to see who it is, they see Mr. Scam Likely's name on their screen. Even if they ignore Mr. Likely, on the off chance they check their voicemail (who listens to voicemail anymore?), there he is again with a sales pitch. They're under constant assault. We're bombarding them!

Few sellers can fully comprehend just how bad the noise problem is unless they move up the sales org food chain, or become business owners like we did. Once we became buyers, we started getting hit up hundreds of times per day with random emails, cold calls, and DMs. *Hundreds of times.* If anything, seeing how other people prospect helped convince us how much a book like this was necessary. Every day, a flood of outbound messages vies for our attention, and unlike the rest of the world, we actually make a point to read or listen to a lot of them.

Ninety-nine percent of it is clichéd, generic, utterly forgettable, though sometimes laughable, crap. The pitches are self-serving. The cadence is overkill. The messaging is irrelevant. The targeting makes no sense. It drives us crazy! Every day, we're hit with a flash flood of garbage that interrupts our day, wastes our time, and clutters our inbox. We're subjected to messages that are crafted with so little attention to their recipients, we actually feel disrespected. It's clear that neither we nor our businesses matter to these sellers; all they care about is getting into our wallets.

Turning to mass-market, factory-style outbound to improve conversion rates had a paradoxical—and entirely predictable—effect. As the volume of outreach increased, the quality decreased. For many sellers, there just isn't time or room to craft a message with the personalization and care that might lead a prospect to pay attention and judge it intriguing and trustworthy. Think of it as wedding food. No matter how much money you spend, or how excellent the chef is, the food served at a big wedding is never going to be as good—or as memorable—as what that same chef could create for an intimate dinner party.

Now, you're probably thinking that while you know your prospecting might need some help, you're not *that* bad. Will hears it all the time. He'll be called in to help a team, but when he brings up this issue, they'll assure him that whatever their problem is, this isn't one of them; their outbound messaging is great. Then he'll take a look at their messaging for himself and have to tell them, no, it's definitely not. Based on how frequently we confront this mess in our own inboxes and with our clients, chances are very, very good that you *are* that bad. Your messaging is most likely just like everyone else's—intrusive, focused on your product, offering your buyer no compelling reason to engage with you, and showing little understanding of your buyer's business. And deep down, you must know it, because if you were writing emails and DMs that buyers wanted to read, they wouldn't be trying to hide from you, and you wouldn't be reading this book.

Any delusion you may suffer probably isn't all your fault. If you were trained at all, you were probably taught that whatever messages you're sending were the type that worked best. In many cases, management doesn't spend a lot of time evaluating and assessing the content their team members send out. Sometimes they're the ones who wrote the bad messages in the first place, and there's no protocol in place to let salespeople adjust and adapt as necessary. Or maybe it's not a human mistake at all but a poor AI system that simply asks you to hit the send button again and again like an obedient monkey.

It's a vicious cycle—the more buyers have tried to hide from the noise, the more we've resorted to bad sales practices to reach them, which has made them hate us even more.

CHAPTER FOUR
BUYERS ARE PISSED

We mean, really pissed! They're pissed about the number of phone calls, texts, and social media requests they get from sellers insisting they can make them more money or get them more clients, and making other promises they know better than to believe. They're pissed that sellers keep interrupting them, even though they're busy AF and at any one time dealing with a million different responsibilities, like hiring, firing, running the business, creating reports for their investors, updating their boss, holding one-on-ones, managing projects, and launching products. In fact, unless they work in procurement, only a tiny bit of their job is dedicated to evaluating and buying new products and services. They're pissed that when they do give sellers their time, in five seconds we reveal that we don't understand their business, what they do, or what they care about and why. They're pissed because we've become so self-centered and focused on ourselves, we don't really think about them at all. They're pissed because we don't see them as people but as quota.

WHY DO SELLERS KEEP DOING THESE SELF-DESTRUCTIVE THINGS THAT PISS OFF BUYERS?

1. **They don't understand prospects.** Most sellers don't really know what it means to be a real buyer. Salespeople tend to operate at a pretty low rung on the career ladder. They don't have much decision-making power, so not many people try to sell to them. That all changes as you rise up the ranks. Sellers just don't know what it's like to have people trying to get your attention all damn day and are therefore grossly disconnected from what's

important to buyers and how they want to engage in a buying process.

2. **They're at the mercy of sales leaders, who don't know what else to do.** Sellers may not know what it's like to be buyers, but sales leaders sure do. They're *constantly* dodging and deleting cold calls and emails. Will has even made cold calls to sales leaders who made sure to tell him how annoying they find cold calls...while they've got their teams making hundreds of cold calls. (Keenan finds this extremely frustrating, as it's the reason many sales organizations fail. A CRO refusing to take cold calls and rejecting cold outreach, even as they build a GTM outbound motion that relies on cold outreach, is the pinnacle of hypocrisy and lack of empathy. And as Keenan often says, empathy is foundational to selling.)

   As we already pointed out, managers themselves are often responsible for the terrible messaging and the poor cadence that sellers have to work with. In cases where sellers are free to create their own, managers frequently push activity—How many calls did you make today? Why didn't you make more calls today? How many emails did you send out? You didn't have enough activity today!—without actually reading the messages the team sends out or listening to their calls to make sure they're hitting the mark. Even when managers know there's a problem, many can't diagnose it because they were poorly taught themselves. They know what bad prospecting looks like, but they have no idea what good prospecting looks like. So they do the only thing they know, and double down on bad sales practices.

3. **Few know any other way.** Sellers frequently report to managers and sales leaders who learned to sell in a much different environment than the one we live in now (you know, like in the old days, the '90s, when that ten-pound book dropped on Keenan's desk), and who were promoted when they were high performers during a time when it was relatively easier to close a deal. It's common for a manager who comes up in good times to have no idea how to sell in tough times. They're in roles they don't un-

derstand, and they don't know how to adapt, so they push tactics that might have worked once upon a time but not today.

So sellers, sales leaders, and managers are pumping out all this noise that's driving buyers crazy and pissing them off. But it's not only buyers feeling these debilitating effects. You are too.

CHAPTER FIVE
THE BUSINESS IMPACT

The impact of poor prospecting practices and the noise it creates can be felt up and down sales organizations. Sixty-five percent of sales leaders say their customer acquisition costs (CAC) were up in 2024 compared to 2023.[19] When inefficiencies and costs metastasize, it ultimately makes a sale more expensive. Sellers are like squirrels whose survival depends on planning and expending their energy correctly. Normally, squirrels instinctively balance out their energy expenditure with food availability, guaranteeing that they'll have enough strength to forage and store food, as well as enough calories and fat to make it through the lean winter months. That's how they survive. But when they're hit with a stressor, like more competition[20] or habitat loss that forces them to spend more energy than they should to secure the same amount of food, it puts their survival at risk.[21] The same is true if a seller spends $60K to get a $70K sale. The more time and expense to gain a customer, obviously, the less profit. But in addition, inefficient spending leads to sellers feeling demotivated, burned out, overloaded, and anxious. Their stress goes up as they see the middling volume of prospects in the pipelines and worry, rightly, about making quota and earning enough money. And they can forget about qualifying for the President's Club and its associated perks, which might make playing this numbers game feel worthwhile. No wonder the average sales position tenure is only just over one year.[22]

Managers suffer, too, as they deal with longer sales cycles, higher customer acquisition costs, and the downstream effects of low win rates. To increase their reach, they'll hire gaggles of salespeople, but when they can't sustain the bloated sales teams, it's then a round of layoffs, which further demoralizes the sellers left behind. They spend fortunes on technology that promises to improve their reach and conversion rates, but nothing moves the needle.

The effects ripple out through the whole organization. Low-quality outreach means more emails go unanswered, more calls are ignored, and more meetings are left unbooked. Unable to count on their teams to bring in promising leads and book meetings through outbound, businesses are forced to rely more on the inbound leads generated by marketing. While those leads produce higher close rates, their unpredictability makes it hard for businesses to build reliable pipelines and accurately forecast. When those once-robust customer pipelines start to dry up, it further limits sellers' chances of closing, and revenue starts to fall. In response, businesses ramp up their outbound, flooding the world with calls, emails, texts, and DMs—many increasingly (and obviously) written with AI—in the hopes that someone, anyone, will respond. Yet as fast as they develop new ways to reach (or annoy) potential customers, new technologies like anti-spam software (like Spam Likely and spam filters) and apps like Robokiller that use AI to block calls and texts allow buyers to stiff-arm salespeople and avoid their messages.

Outbound effectiveness has been in decline for years, and it's only predicted to get worse. Again—outbound effectiveness has been in decline for years and it's only predicted to get worse. We can't keep doing what we're doing. We have to find a way to do better. And we can.

CHAPTER SIX
IT'S BAD, BUT IT'S NOT *ALL* BAD!

Here's the thing—your customers are out there, they need your help, and they do want to talk to you! Here are some more encouraging numbers than the ones above:

- 61% of buyers have purchased a product they didn't know they needed until they interacted with a salesperson. What this means is that buyers aren't always aware there are problems affecting their businesses, and salespeople can be an integral part in identifying and solving those problems.

- 95% of buyers have rescoped their problem after starting the buying process. This tells us that buyers aren't good at understanding the issues plaguing their organizations and therefore need help from salespeople to properly scope the problem.

- 58% of buyers have paid over budget for a product or service.[23]

Your customers have problems they need to solve, and you can be their conduit to relief. The terrain is rough, but it's not apocalyptic. While there's not much we can do about all the external forces and headwinds you're facing, we can absolutely do something about the way you navigate them.

THE SOLUTION IS GAP PROSPECTING

Gap-prospecting is the path to gap selling. Like gap selling, gap-prospecting is problem-centric, not product-centric. It works because it's not about touting your product or service—we're the biggest, the best, the fastest, the cheapest!—but about solving your customer's problem. That's where the similarities end. Gap selling is a two-way conversation, a Q&A process that allows you to figure out what the customer needs to close the gap between their current state—where they are now—and their future state—where they want to be. It's a conversation that's relatively easy to engage in when your customers are responding to inbound marketing, because you're capturing people who have already figured out they have a problem and are looking for ways to solve it, or who at least already think they have a problem and are interested in understanding it. Maybe it's just a tiny bit of interest, a mere blip in their subconscious, but it's there, and a skilled gap seller can run with that.

Prospecting, however, is the act of reaching out to someone who doesn't know who you are, doesn't care, and isn't even thinking about your product or service. They don't want to read your email, and they're not interested in your LinkedIn request. They don't want to know you at all. Read that again, and read it slowly. Your prospects don't care about you, your product, or your company. So when you're prospecting, the conversation is just one-way—until you say something to make the customer stop and think about something they weren't thinking about before. Skilled prospecting sparks curiosity, which is what will get the customer to stop and read your message, listen to your voicemail, or stay on the phone with you for more than three seconds. Curiosity can prompt the customer to ask their own questions. And when that happens, suddenly your one-way conversation is a two-way conversation. That's the goal. Gap-prospecting is the proactive path to discovery, giving you the ability to trigger your customers' curiosity long enough for them to give you the information you need to help them solve their problems, allowing you to close the gap and the deal.

Knocking on millions of real and virtual doors, just hoping to stumble across someone who needs your shit, is the Yellow Pages way, and it needs to be left in the Yellow Pages' days. Gap-prospecting pushes you to be more thoughtful, deliberate, and strategic, so you're not being annoying, nor wasting your breath on people who are never going to buy from you. For example, if an arborist showed up on your doorstep today and launched into a laundry list of why their tree-trimming services are superior to anyone else's, how many seconds would you wait before shaking your head and closing the door? Unless you were already planning on cutting some trees on your property, you don't give a crap about the arborist's business, and you're probably irritated that they interrupted the game you were watching, or the movie you were enjoying with the kids, or the wonderful dinner you were having with the family, by knocking on the door to tell you all about their great tree-cutting services. But what if the arborist recognizes that your trees could be sick and says, "Sorry to bother you, but there's a fungal infection that's spreading in this county. Not only does it kill trees, but it can also quickly spread to other vegetation and cost thousands of dollars to remediate. Have you talked to anyone about checking your trees for this fungus?" Well, now you are thinking about your tree, and you've probably got questions. The arborist did their research, figured out who needed their help, sparked curiosity, and created the need for a conversation. No matter what you're selling, the formula is the same. It works for everybody and anybody who has to go out and talk to someone who's not expecting them.

Without a deep understanding of that crucial element of problem-centricity, salespeople are the equivalent of an inflatable sky dancer, better described in *Family Guy* as Wacky Waving Inflatable Arm Flailing Tube Man. People drive right by Flailing Tube Man. Flailing Tube Man isn't problem-centric. He isn't personal. He certainly isn't proactive. Gap-prospecting gets customers to stop and pay attention. It exposes the problem customers often don't even know they have. It creates curiosity, interest, and inquiry. Get the customer to ask *you* a question, and you're halfway to the close.

LET'S FIX THIS

Initially, a gap prospector has two jobs:

1. Convince the buyer you're not a danger so they will read your email or stay on the phone and answer a few questions, and

2. Cut through the noise to get the buyer to act; i.e., agree to a meeting.

As we'll discuss later, that's how the winner of Will's gift card challenge beat out the other sellers. He managed to neutralize his buyer's threat detection system, connect in a meaningful way, and persuade the buyer it was in their best interest to engage. That's gap-prospecting. It requires immediately making your intent clear, offering value, and building trust. How you do that is what the rest of this book is about.

In these pages, you'll learn to make cold calls that don't get ignored, write emails that don't get trashed, and create LinkedIn posts that gain attention. You'll learn to build a brand reputation, build relationships, leverage networks, and other strategies. But not so you can sell. Rather, it'll be so you can make connections, facilitate introductions, and ultimately, access your target markets. Those who win the access game win it all.

If you're starting your emails by writing, "I hope this email finds you well," or if you're giving up too soon, or if you're targeting the wrong buyers, it's not technology that's keeping you from gaining access, preventing your emails from being read or your calls returned. It's that your message isn't compelling enough to break through customers' suspicion and business—the same issues that made it so hard for Trevor to give away free money—to believe there's value in speaking with you. You're not struggling for lack of effort. You're struggling because there's still a hole in your understanding of what grabs people's attention and what keeps it. Follow this book's practical, tactical steps, and you'll find yourself with a fat pipeline stuffed with clients ready to buy, share their positive experience with others, and drive even more business your way.

Now that you thoroughly understand the shifts, trends, and buyer psychology that make prospecting so challenging, you've got the foundation you need to start succeeding. To begin, gap-prospecting requires a mindset shift and knowing how to accurately assess the landscape. That's what you'll learn in the next part of the book.

Self-Interest is a poor teacher. —*Nassim Nicholas Taleb*

PART II
PUT THE BUYER FIRST

PART II · PUT THE BUYER FIRST

Great sellers help.

They don't pitch. They don't push. They don't diagnose or prescribe until they understand the problem.

They start by putting their buyer first.

They immerse themselves in their buyer's world—going deep into their buyer's business, their buyer's customers, business model, market, processes, tools, gaps, risks, and challenges. They understand their buyer's problems, the impact those problems create, and the root causes behind them.

The greatest salespeople can talk shop. They engage buyers as peers and consultants, not vendors. Why? Because they operate from their buyer's perspective—not their own self-interested, self-absorbed point of view.

They know their objective isn't to sell something. It's to understand how to help their buyer, how much that help is worth, and what it costs their buyer to remain where they are.

Selling doesn't come from pushing, telling, preaching, or pitching. It comes from putting the buyer, the buyer's problems, and the buyer's goals first—and becoming the person who understands those problems better than anyone else.

Put the buyer first. The rest takes care of itself.

CHAPTER SEVEN
GET TO KNOW YOUR BUYER

S o you've got a product or service to sell. What's your go-to move? For most sellers, it's to get out there and start talking about that product or service to anyone they think might want to buy it.

- We help people like you increase conversion rates by 50%!

- We provide industry-leading service and insights to grow into new markets!

- We help CTOs reduce their product time to market!

- We help you sell more on social media!

No. Stop. These are perfect examples of how NOT to reach out to prospects.

First, you're assuming your customer needs what you're selling. But if they thought they did, they'd already be looking for it, or they'd have already purchased it. People already interested in what you're offering represent a tiny percentage of your total market; finding them will be like looking for a needle in a haystack. If you're lucky and you do find them, you'll be facing an uphill battle. By the time you reach them, they've probably already done some research on it, poked around the internet to do some comparison shopping, and maybe already spoken to vendors. You're late, and now you're going to have to catch up, working against all the preconceptions they've formed.

Second, the buyers didn't ask, and they don't care. In an effort to capture existing demand, you're making a nuisance of yourself to people who *aren't* interested in what you're selling—and they're a much bigger group than the ones who are.

Stellar sellers know that the secret to success isn't capturing existing demand but creating demand where there was none before. It's about making people who don't care, care.

How? That leads us to the third and final problem with these email openers.

Look at the sentence structure of these pitches. Who is mentioned first?

It's not the buyer.

Creating demand starts when you stop thinking about yourself and your product and start thinking about your buyer and their problems first, only, and always.

Specifically, if you want to help people—as those pitches above say you want to do—you have to prove that you thoroughly understand their current environment or, to use a gap-selling term, their *current state*.

THE CURRENT STATE

We introduced the concept of the current state in Chapter 5 of *Gap Selling*. In its simplest terms, it's where your buyers are right now—their current environment, their current operating methods, their current culture, their current opportunities and challenges, and their current outcomes. It's the reality they're living in before you ever show up and let them know you, your product, or your service exists. Your mission will be to assess that current state with an eye toward understanding why it looks the way it does, what problems your buyer is experiencing within it, and how they feel about those problems. Therein lies the rub. There's reality, and there's how buyers *feel* about their reality.

No one changes things up when they're perfectly happy with their current state. However, people can be happy with their current state yet completely oblivious to brewing problems. People can be happy with their current state because the problems they're aware of haven't grown big enough to cause much pain. And of course, people can be happy-ish in their current state too. That is, they may be generally satisfied with their current state but also find themselves in various states of apathy, discontent, or irritation, depending on what the day has thrown at them.

(Honestly, don't these descriptions sound like some relationships you've been in?) The point is that many buyers only *think* they're happy with their current state until a seller exposes the cracks in their current state or at least empathizes and commiserates over issues the buyer knows they need to deal with. Give buyers a compelling reason to trust that your product or service could be the key to a better future state—that place where their problems are solved and they're enjoying the benefits—and they will willingly, eagerly give you their time and attention, the twin elements that make up prospecting gold.

But you're not there yet. First, you'll want to get to know your buyer really, really well.

BUYER IMMERSION

Before you even think about writing an email or a DM, or picking up the phone, you should be able to answer the following questions about your buyer:

- What do they do?

- What do they care about?

- Where do they spend their time?

- What are their responsibilities?

- What problems do they regularly run into (that you and your product can solve)?

- What metrics or criteria are used to gauge their success or failure?

- What are their KPIs?

- What determines whether they are hired, fired, or promoted?

- What technical language do they use, and how do they talk about their business?

- How do they make money?

- How does their business make money?

- Who are their customers?

- Why do their customers buy their products?

- What changes in their company or industry might be affecting them?

Does that sound like a lot? We're not suggesting that you need to go back to school to earn a degree or certificate in whatever is your buyers' specialty or field. We are suggesting, however, that you need to immerse yourself in your buyers' world. That's the only way you're going to be able to talk to them with the expertise and credibility necessary to prove that you understand what they go through on a daily basis. Knowing your buyer at that deep level will garner trust and keep you from making stupid mistakes that prove you don't know or care about your buyers. Will, who runs a sales coaching company and five-person video agency from home, not a trucking company, got an email from a trucking company asking to discuss his transportation and warehousing needs. Keenan, founder and owner of a sales training company, received an email offering to take his sales team "to the next level"—from a sales training company. Let that sink in. That's how bad it is out here. Take the time to know your buyers and the issues they care about, and they will notice, because you'll stand out from 99.9% of the outreach they receive (and automatically delete).

Okay, so how do you learn what your buyers care about? Research, research, research. You probably think you already do your research, but if you're not seeing the sales results you want, you're probably not doing enough, or you don't understand what you should be looking for.

Start with what you've got. For example, study your CRM to examine why people have bought in the past. You also want to go where the buyers are. Read their publications. Absorb their industry content. Analyze the macro trends happening in their industry. Attend the same events they attend. Listen to the lectures and watch the same videos they do. The deeper you understand the issues that your buyers face day in and day out, and the more of an expert you become, the better you'll be able to address their priorities. And in general, buyers don't prioritize what's going right; they prioritize what's going wrong.

Ask yourself this: Any time you've taken a new job, how much product training did you receive? How much time did your boss spend telling you all about the products' features, benefits, and technical specs and how it compared to the competition? A lot, right? Now, ask yourself: How much customer training did you receive? What did your boss or trainer tell you about the problems your customer might have had that the product could solve? Did you ever discuss what the ideal environment might be for the product? Did they inform you about the processes buyers were using to do the job your product could do or facilitate? Did they teach you what metrics your buyers used to gauge their success? If you're like most salespeople, you got little to no customer training. That's the whole problem.

Understanding your buyers' problems is much more important than knowing how your product works, because the problems are what buyers, especially those who aren't shopping yet, really care about. Come at them with features and benefits, and they're likely to tune you out. Come at them with understanding of why they're impacting the buyers' business, the root causes of those problems, how not solving them could be detrimental to the business, and a solution, and they'll tune in. Before you can help—and remember, you're a helper, not a seller—you need to know what problems they face, how those problems manifest, how they affect your buyers' outcomes and environment, the root causes of those problems, and how failing to solve those problems could be detrimental to the business. Once you've done that work, you can start mapping your product and the problems it solves to the things they care about, which will help you craft outreach that actually resonates and increase the likelihood that a buyer will stop and give you their attention.

CHAPTER EIGHT
MAP THE PROBLEM

Ask yourself this question: Why do people buy what I sell?

If we were to ask that question of a team that sells software that makes presentations interactive, they would probably say, "Well, duh, people buy our product because it makes presentations interactive." Maybe they'd say that it allows people to engage with their teammates, or it helps make presentations fun for the audience. But they'd be wrong.

Most sellers' default answer to this question is to list what their product or service does. They focus on the positive. But buyers don't buy to increase the positive in their life; they buy to lessen or prevent the negative. People buy because something in their world is bad or broken, causing them some level of pain and suffering or their business to lose money.

So in the case of a software that adds an interactive element to presentations, prospects won't buy it merely to increase participation and make their meetings more fun. That's aspirational. That's a "nice to have." Rather, they'll make the purchase because no one is participating in the buyers' meetings, and it's causing the buyer pain. They'll be inspired to buy, not because they want to make their meetings more fun but because their boring meetings are causing attendees to tune out, which means they aren't learning what they need to know. Consequently, the buyer's training scores stink, or their customer stat scores declined from 90% to 70%, or they're finding it impossible to get customers to sign up for events, or the completion rates for the program are below 10%. The prospect will buy a product that makes their meetings fun only when their boring meetings cost them in some way.

Too many sellers think they can seduce buyers with the possibility of experiencing something positive in the future, but that's not what motivates a sale. In fact, that's not what motivates most of our behavior. If the thought of positive gain in our future actually directed our behavior, imagining our future healthy, svelte selves would be enough to curb our late-night snacks and get us regularly to the gym. But you know what actually gets many people to eat healthy and to the gym? A heart attack. Not weight gain, not backaches, not pre-diabetes, not any of the slow-building, easy-to-get-used-to side effects of poor eating habits and insufficient exercise. Nope, many people have to feel like a giant metal safe is sitting on their chest, cutting off their air supply, for them to accept that they have to make some diet and lifestyle changes. The future is hypothetical; people will only make changes to what causes them the most discomfort in their current state. The same is true for buyers—they want help fixing the problems they're dealing with right now, today. The best salespeople get the buyers to feel that weight.

You've gathered data on your buyers. You know their challenges. Now it's time to organize that information so you can figure out your buyers' most compelling issues and how you can address them.

CREATE A PROBLEM IDENTIFICATION CHART (PIC)

Keenan developed the idea for the PIC in 2018, and it revolutionized the sales world by helping companies get better insight into their customers and by creating shorter sales cycles, better win rates, and more collaborative selling cycles. In *Gap Selling*, he introduced it as the first step to figuring out your customer's current state. A PIC is a simple yet powerful chart that helps you identify your buyer's biggest challenges, assess the impact of those challenges on your buyer, and diagnose their root cause(s). That diagnosis is key. Just as doctors can't prescribe treatments until they're sure they know what's causing their patients' symptoms, you can't offer a solution until you know what's causing your buyer's trouble. To push your "treatment" onto a problem when you're not sure the problem will respond would be irresponsible and unethical. Drafting this list of problems, impacts, and root causes will ensure that you stay focused and don't waste time asking irrelevant questions or confusing your customer as you try to find your entryway into their business.

Imagine living in a house where the doors and windows are invisible to outsiders, and how annoying, tiresome, and even scary it would be to hear someone knocking and tapping up and down the exterior walls while trying to find the front door. Don't do that to your buyer. Creating a PIC is like drawing a map that leads you to an unlocked entrance. It tells you what you're looking for and focuses your search before you ever introduce yourself to your prospect.

To create a PIC, you're going to draw three vertical columns. In the first one, you'll list all the problems your product or service solves. These are the problems your ideal customer profile (ICP) is experiencing before you reach out. Your buyer will have two types of problems: problems you can solve, and problems you can't. Don't worry about the latter. This is where all that product training comes in handy. If your buyer needs a Phillips head screwdriver because they're putting together furniture, and all you sell is tile, you're no help to them. You know what your product can and can't do, so don't waste your time on problems you don't solve.

In the second column, you'll list how those problems impact your buyer. Spelling this out helps you ascertain if a problem is big enough to compel a buyer to change. If a problem isn't causing your buyer significant discomfort, it's probably not one you'll want to target.

In the third column, you'll list the root causes of the problems. Maybe the buyer is working with the wrong vendor. Maybe they're working with outdated tech. Being able to pinpoint these details will help you shine. If you can open your initial outreach with the promise of relief and repair, your buyer will be all ears.

For more info on how to build a PIC, scan here

THINK PAIN, NOT GAIN

Take a look at that second column again, the one that lists the impact your buyers' problems are having on their business. We've already established that buyers are much more motivated by their desire to avoid pain than they are by their desire to pursue gain. It's a principle that behavioral economists call "loss aversion." A University of Pennsylvania study on how financial incentives affect people's motivation to increase their physical exercise reveals how it plays out. Just under 300 adults suffering from obesity were given the goal of walking 7,000 steps per day for 26 weeks. For the first 13 weeks of the study, participants were randomly split into four groups. The control group was given no financial incentive to meet their steps goal. The second group was given a gain incentive—they were promised $1.40 every day that they completed their steps. The third group was offered a lottery incentive—every day they could enter a daily lottery, with a potential prize worth an average $1.40 for every day their steps goal was met. The participants in the fourth and final group were given a loss incentive—at the beginning of every month, each was given $42; every day they did not take all their steps, they had to give up $1.40.

At the end of the 13 weeks, it was determined that the groups that received gain or lottery incentives performed no differently than the control group, which had received no performance incentive at all. However, the participants in the loss incentive group achieved their step goals twice as often as the control group.[24]

Pain is a greater motivator than gain. That's why people are more willing to take action to avoid losing what they already have than they are to disrupt the status quo—the current state—to gain something new. Losing what you have hurts more than failing to gain something that was never a sure thing anyway. So if you want to motivate a customer to consider disrupting their current state by buying from you, don't approach them by talking about how you could bring about some future state that could be better, maybe, some day. That's asking them to take a gamble. Instead, you'll want to highlight the problems that are causing them to feel pain right now, today, and ask for the opportunity to show them how the presence of your product can make that pain go away.

For example, here are some common household items you might own. If we list the pain and gain of each product, which triggers your emotions more?

DEODORANT
Pain: You smell so bad that people avoid sitting next to you at work.
Gain: You smell fresh and clean all day.

HIGH-END FLASK
Pain: Lukewarm coffee tastes like regret, and warm beer feels like a personal attack.
Gain: Keeps your drinks hot or cold for hours.

PREMIUM TOILET PAPER
Pain: Your butthole doesn't like being sandpapered.
Gain: Soft and strong for a luxurious clean.

FACE WASH
Pain: You look like a hormonal teenager mid-exam week.
Gain: Clear, glowing skin.

MATTRESS
Pain: You wake up with a back so stiff, you groan like your dad getting out of a Toyota Corolla.
Gain: Better sleep for better performance.

PHONE CASE
Pain: One drop on the floor=$900 mistake, and a screen that looks like it's been sandblasted.
Gain: Sleek protection with premium design.

AIR FRYER
Pain: You're too lazy to preheat an oven and too scared of deep frying.
Gain: Crispy food with less oil.

DISHWASHER PODS
Pain: Re-washing the same plate three times because your "eco setting" just misted it with steam.
Gain: Sparkling dishes with no residue.

NOISE-CANCELING HEADPHONES
Pain: Karen from accounting's non-stop chatting has you spiraling into madness before noon.
Gain: Total focus, anywhere.

Comfy Socks
Pain: One cold toe can ruin your entire goddamn mood.
Gain: All-day comfort and warmth.

As you read through these examples, did you feel it? Did you feel yourself respond more strongly to the pain than you did to the gain? If so, you're like most people, including your prospects. We're more emotionally susceptible to the negative, to the pain, than we are to gain.

We'll talk about how to craft "pain" outreach in Part IV: Doing the Work.

Now, buyers are going to be much more interested in speaking with you about a chronic or really uncomfortable pain than something minor that's easy to ignore. Don't waste your time on the latter. Turn back to your PIC. As we already explained, your buyer's pain can be felt anywhere—in the root cause, in the problem, and especially in the impact, which is where the worst pain usually lies—the one that hurts so much, it's likely to motivate your buyer to change. Your PIC reveals all of it. However, while you may think you know which pain is the worst of the worst—the problem your buyer is most motivated to solve—we propose taking one more step to ensure you're right. Like a masochistic masseuse, you're going to start pressing to find your buyer's biggest pain point.

The So-What System
Knowing that buyers are motivated by pain, not gain, we'll want to focus our messaging not on what we can help buyers do—that's gain language—but on what pain they're currently experiencing that's untenable or intolerable. The purpose of this exercise is to reverse engineer your service or product by examining how they suffer from the absence of you. To do this, you ask, "So what?"

For Example, Let's Say You Sell Software that Automates Invoices
What's the gain? Automating the invoices gets invoices out faster.
So what?
Buyers who do it manually take too long to complete the billing tasks and make mistakes.

So what?

Taking too long to create invoices extends the time to cash and extends projects; making mistakes can mean clients are not billed properly.

So what?

When projects are extended, timelines are missed, and clients are unhappy. When time to cash gets too long, it can lead to cash crunches, which can compel companies to use debt. When it takes too long to create invoices, the cost of acquiring the cash increases too.

So what?

When the cost of acquiring your cash (getting bills paid) is high, that cuts into profits, increases interest expense, and limits free cash flow for other investments. When invoices can't be collected on time, companies in essence become banks, lending money to customers without the benefit of interest. This can create shrinking profits, increased expenses, missed growth initiatives, and an inability to invest in new products or markets, thereby creating slow growth.

See what we did here? We found powerful motivations for an organization to change, and we did it by focusing on much more than just automating invoices.

LET'S TRY ANOTHER EXAMPLE, LIKE SOCIAL MEDIA MANAGEMENT SERVICES

The gain? Broader social media reach helps businesses grow online.

What does that mean to buyers who aren't using social media management services?

Low online growth. They're also probably spending too much or too little time creating engaging content.

So what?

If they're spending too much or not enough time creating engaging content, they're missing out on new followers and increased engagement.

So what?

If they're not getting new followers and increased engagement, they're not increasing their brand awareness and reach.

So what?

If they aren't increasing their brand awareness, then they are not penetrating their market and fewer people know who they are.

So what?

If fewer people know who they are, the fewer leads and inquiries they get.

So what?

If they're getting fewer leads, the less opportunities they will have in their pipeline.

So what?

If they are getting fewer opportunities in their pipeline, they will close fewer deals.

So what?

If they are closing fewer deals, they could miss quota, lose to the competition, be less profitable, experience an increase in CAC, experience a decline in growth, have to lay people off, or see a decline in stock price.

Again, we revealed severe potential consequences that are powerful motivations to change and big reasons a buyer would want to use social media management services.

FINAL EXAMPLE

Let's say you're selling industrial air filtration systems to manufacturing plants.

The gain? Cleaner air in the facility.

So what?

Without your filtration system, airborne particles build up from machining, welding, or sanding.

So what?

Workers are breathing in those particulates. That leads to more respiratory issues, more sick days, and potential workers' comp claims.

So what?

Increased absenteeism hurts productivity. Injuries or long-term illness spike insurance premiums and open the door to liability.

So what?

That means higher costs, lower output, and possible fines from regulatory bodies like OSHA or local health authorities.

So what?

Now the company's reputation takes a hit, retention becomes a problem, and they're losing skilled labor while struggling to hit production targets.

So what?

Missed production deadlines means lost contracts, delayed shipments, and pissed-off clients who start exploring competitors.

That's a clear, painful cascade. You're not selling clean air; you're helping your buyer avoid lawsuits, protect output, and keep their best people from walking out. That's the real pitch.

When you can prove that you understand the environment in which your buyers operate, and map a connection between their current state and your solutions, you've also drawn a map to your buyers' desired future state. That map will guide all your messaging from now on, no matter what channel you use.

UPLOAD YOUR PIC TO AI

Now you're going to take one more step. If you haven't already, open an AI account—ChatGPT, Claude, or the chatbot of your choice—and upload your PIC. With this move, you've set the foundation for a rock-solid, problem-centric launchpad that will help you generate creative, relevant, irresistible outbound. Keep reading, and we'll show you how.

CHAPTER NINE
TARGET YOUR BUYER

Imagine you run an ice cream truck. You want to increase sales. It's wintertime and nighttime, so you pile into the driver's seat and head out to a business park, slowly cruising the parking lot, playing that famous ice cream-truck tune.

Huh?

Right. That makes zero sense. But a lot of sellers are just that clueless when they decide who they're going to try to sell to.

Being able to clearly articulate who your buyers are, and their problems, automatically gives you an enormous advantage ahead of most other people selling in your space. But that knowledge won't do you much good if you try to reach every single buyer who might be experiencing those problems. That's inefficient and impractical and could take a lifetime. For example, if you're a recruiter, your potential buying pool is going to be everyone who hires and fires employees. That's, like, every company that has grown bigger than its initial founders. You'll never be able to be everything to everyone, and to try will inevitably mean diluting your messaging to the point that it isn't relevant to the people you could have reached with more personalized targeting. A better use of your time would be to target the people most likely to be experiencing the problems your solution is best suited to solve, spend your time in the areas where the most people are likely to be feeling those problems' effects, and reach out to the people most likely to be interested in your solution.

How do you find these buyers? Start categorizing them by:

1. **Firmographics**
Consider the characteristics and demographics of the businesses.

What type of industry are they in? What size are they? Do they exist in multiple locations or just one? How about geographic location—are there certain laws that make it more likely that business operators in one state might be dealing with problems at a different rate than in other states? What about international organizations?

2. Impact Sensitivity

Within these firmographics, who will care most about the problems you're able to solve? Who's most responsible for managing them? Who's going to get the brunt of the blowback if they don't get these problems under control? Notice that we didn't tell you to identify who has the most decision-making or purchasing authority. Especially in B2B sales, you're often dealing with teams that must come to a consensus before making any purchases. Successfully reach just one person in that chain, and they can give you access to everyone else you need to talk to or at least give you information that allows you to speak to those with political power. You don't want to spread yourself too thin, but you don't want to unnecessarily limit yourself either.

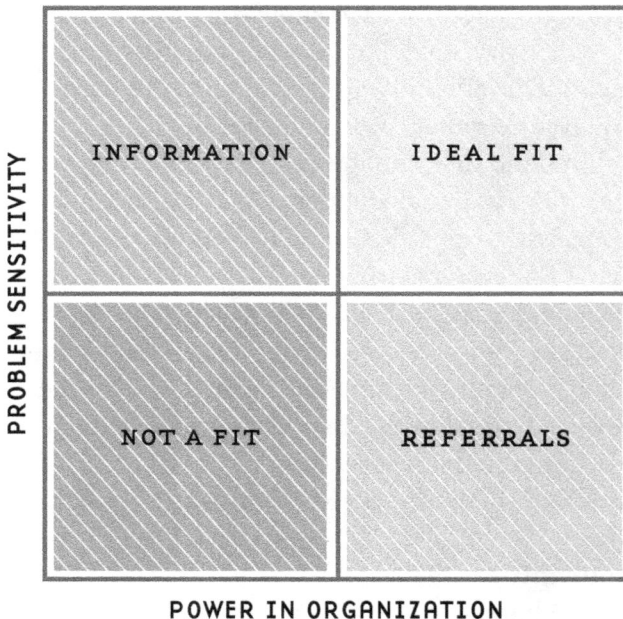

PROBLEM SENSITIVITY	INFORMATION	IDEAL FIT
	NOT A FIT	REFERRALS

POWER IN ORGANIZATION

3. **Intent Signals**
This is an inbound action, a metaphorical hand-raising. If someone downloads a tool from your website, it implies they're dealing with the issue your tool was built to improve. In many cases, however, the tool alone won't be enough to completely solve their problem, because the prospect doesn't have the expertise that you do and doesn't know how to best to use it.

4. **Viability**
It's just as important to eliminate poor fits as it is to identify good ones. If you know there are certain industries that don't normally struggle with the problems you solve, or suffer from the impacts of those problems, and are therefore known to be slow to adopt, take them out of consideration. Focus your energy on the industries, companies, and buyers where you're most likely to see success.

Our ice cream truck driver can't do anything about winter being a regular feature of their selling environment. But they can target their buyers using the same system we just outlined.

They know the problems they solve—hunger, sugar cravings, boredom, overheating.

Who suffers the impact of these problems in the middle of winter? Parents with children.

Where are parents with children experiencing hunger, sugar cravings, boredom, and overheating? It's not a business park, obviously. It's:

- Holiday markets
- Street fairs
- Winter carnivals
- Winter light trails
- Ice skating rinks
- Sports events

- Corporate family events

- Holiday parades

The vendor understands their buyers and their problems, so they'll have solutions in the form of peppermint- or eggnog-flavored ice cream, hot coffee to make affogatos (or to offer caffeine boosts for tired parents), hot fudge for sundaes, cocoa and marshmallows, and other winter-themed treats.

This is how you target the buyers who are most likely to want to hear from you.

Familiarity Plays

Firmographics, impact, and viability all matter, but we're going to insert an addendum here: If you have to start somewhere, start with the lowest-hanging fruit—the people you already know, or who know you, even if only kinda sorta. It stands to reason that when you're communicating with someone who already knows you a little, or knows someone you know or work with, you'll have an easier time connecting. It's trust by association. Familiarity overrides the biggest challenge of outbound: being a total stranger.

We're not saying send a message out to every person in your Insta feed. But as you're looking for buyers within those categories who might need your help, it would make sense to target anyone with whom you've already connected at some level, directly or indirectly. Humans are wired to trust what feels familiar. It's why we're willing to try a new brand if we've seen it in someone else's fridge, or why, when deciding between two identical items online, we'll choose the one we think we may have heard of. And it's why we're more likely to respond to:

- Someone who knows us personally.

- Someone who knows of our company.

- Someone who knows someone else we know.

- Someone who works with a company just like ours.

You can also increase your chances of making a familiarity play by building a strong brand and making sure your social media is on point, which will draw buyers toward you and even prompt them to engage. There are no better targets than the ones already exhibiting interest in you or showing potential signs of a problem.

There are lots of other ways to connect. If a buyer did business with your former employer or another rep who's now left the company, or has served on a board with your CEO, that's an indirect but solid connection. Heck, there's nothing wrong with reaching out to your Uncle Milt's pickleball partner whom you met at last year's holiday party, as long as you've determined there's a real chance they might need the help you're providing. By reaching out to someone with whom you've already established even just a casual connection, you're bypassing the biggest challenge to outbound and cultivating new customers—the human tendency to distrust strangers. But if the buyer is already familiar with you, whether through brand, interaction, or just association with other people they trust, you're not a stranger! And if you've got the sheen of trustworthiness, your cold outreach isn't cold at all. Like anyone dipping their toe into a pool of water, buyers are much more likely to jump right in if that water's already a little warm. With a familiarity play, you can invite buyers to be receptive to your outreach with signals that tell them you're not a stranger. For example, you can contact them through:

- **Your own network:** "Hi, Steve, we met at SXSW last year. Working with a handful of companies to solve [problem]. Have you run into this before?"

- **An exec's network:** "Hey, boss, how well do you know [exec] over at [other company]? Would you be able to make an introduction? I can draft you a message if so."

- **Your customers' networks:** "We're working with [customer] in your space to address [problem] and figured you might be running into that too."

- **Your customers' competitors:** "We're working with a company in [your space] to address [challenge] and figured this might be on your radar too."

- **Shared investors:** "Saw you're also backed by [VC]. We've seen a lot of companies in their portfolio solve [problem] with [solution]. Worth a conversation, or is that not something you're seeing?"

- **Competitor customers:** "Saw you're using [competitor]. Curious how that's working out on the [specific pain] side."

- **Tech integrations/ecosystem overlap:** "Noticed you're using [partner tool]. We usually show up when teams are looking to extend that into [outcome]."

- **Past conversations/old leads:** "Our teams connected a while back. At the time, you were running into [problem]. Is that something you were ever able to address?"

You don't need to know your prospects; you just need them to feel like they might already know you.

In all these examples, we're always tying back to something we know about the prospect to justify reaching out but still focusing on a common problem. If we haven't yet been able to identify their problem, we can turn to catalysts or symptoms.

SYMPTOMS AND CATALYSTS

Sometimes it's not obvious that a buyer or organization is struggling with a problem that you can solve, but you don't want to overlook a prospect just because you're not sure. To uncover these potential buyers, look for symptoms and catalysts.

A **symptom** is an external sign of the existence of disease. Jaundice is a symptom of liver damage. Swollen joints are a symptom of arthritis. In sales, a symptom is the external sign that a buyer is suffering from a problem. If it's one you can solve, that's a smart buyer to target. For example, a symptom of a company having a hard time hiring is help wanted ads open longer than a few months with no increase in headcount. So if your product or service helps people hire great teams, you'll want to note any company whose job opening announcements linger unfilled for a long time. A flood of negative online complaints about poor customer service—the symptom—would be a natural target for someone selling software that facilitates customer service (the solution). In the early days of Will's business, a video editor named Hansel Alvarez diagnosed Will with an "illness" just by looking at his YouTube channel. In his prospecting email, he pointed out that Will hadn't posted a video in several months, and that the videos Will did post weren't doing especially well. He went on to explain that low content volume and poor performance were symptoms of a problem the video editor had frequently witnessed—successful business owners finding it hard to make the time to edit and upload videos as often as they wanted to. And then he announced that his purpose was to help folks who wanted to grow their YouTube channels and drive subscribers to their business. Did this sound interesting? Will thought it did, and after a productive, informative meeting, he hired Hansel.

If you don't see any obvious symptoms, look for catalysts. You'll recall from high school chemistry that a **catalyst** is a substance that increases the intensity of a chemical reaction. In the context of sales, a catalyst is an event or other external signifier that can intensify whatever symptoms your buyer is suffering from, even if you (and sometimes they) can't see them yet.

For example, Will was called by a representative from a grant-writing company, who asked him to confirm that he was operating out of Nova Scotia. Yes, he was. And he'd been in business for a little over a year? That was correct too. Then they asked, "Are you aware that there are grants available to Nova Scotia small businesses once they've been in business for a year?"

As a matter of fact, Will was aware. But when he'd gone to the government website to investigate what he'd have to do to apply for the grant money, he'd gotten overwhelmed by the convoluted application process and given up. He was very busy, after all, and applying for grants takes time.

It sure does, and that's why this company was reaching out. There was money out there for Will, not just through the federal government but also through provincial and territorial agencies, as well as private organizations. The grant-writing company could take on all the research to find which grants he was eligible for and complete the complicated paperwork. They'd get paid when he got paid. Was he interested in talking? He was.

Will wasn't suffering from any obvious symptoms that could come from not having grant money, but the grant-writing company had done their research and knew that he was probably in a position where he should be thinking about how to access that money. That was the catalyst. All they had to do was confirm that Will's inability to apply for the grants was causing him pain—and it was, because it sucks to leave free money on the table—and offer a solution that could stop it.

Catalysts are great ways to expand your outreach while remaining focused on the likeliest prospects. Let's say you sell a bug tracking tool. Because you know that bugs frequently slip through the development and testing cracks, you might target companies that just launched a new product and ignore companies whose products are already well-established. Here's another example: You're a sales training company, and you find out that a business has just hired 20 sellers. You know that companies often face a big problem when bringing in new sales hires—they don't ramp up fast enough and miss their targets. Adding 20 new sellers at once is likely to intensify that problem. It's a catalyst, and it's a sign they could need your help.

Now, you could introduce yourself and offer to train their sales team so they get up to speed quickly, but you won't because you know that buyers are motivated by pain, not gain. How will your prospect suffer from the absence of you? Think about the problem you predict—new sellers ramping up too slowly and missing their targets.

So what?

The whole reason a company would bring on 20 new sellers is to drive more revenue.

So what?

So without you, these new sellers might not start generating revenue fast enough, and the prospect will miss their revenue goals and lose money paying unprofitable sellers.

That understanding gives you an opening to say to your prospect, "Would you be open to seeing how other teams have overcome issues with slow ramp times?"

Catalysts and symptoms are everywhere if you know where to look. You can put together a list of typical catalysts by examining your CRM data and talking to your current customers. Note the pain that prompted them to buy your product and compare it to how that pain manifested itself publicly. Some typical catalysts might be:

- Hiring increase

- Layoffs and firings

- Increase in number of job openings

- Poor product reviews

- Great product reviews

- Negative employee reviews

- Great employee reviews

- Relocations

- Geographic expansion

- Financial performance

- Website updates

- Rebrands

- Bad press

- Good press

- IPO

- Competitor activity

- Leadership changes

- Acquisitions

- Product launches

- Investments

- Changes in legislation

- Investor reports/call transcripts

- Priorities mentioned online by the CEO

- Awards

- A mention in an analyst report

Ultimately, symptoms and catalysts serve to help ensure you spend your time talking to prospects most likely to need your help and increase the relevance of your messaging because you can speak about the things they care about and not crap that they don't. That's how you turn a one-way conversation into a two-way conversation and bridge the gap between your buyer's current state and the future they would prefer

To find the most effective symptoms and catalysts for your buyers, you can play detective by looking through your historic data, likely available in your CRM. Typically, in the past, when companies bought from or showed interest in your offering, what changes recently happened that prompted them to try and solve the problem? If every company that has bought from you has been hiring freelancers, for example, that becomes your #1 catalyst/symptom for target selection.

In some cases, however, you may not have an existing customer base, or you may have already worked all the target accounts demonstrating symptoms and catalysts you know from your CRM. This is a good opportunity to use your PIC-infused AI tool. Prompt the AI with something like:

"Using this PIC, help me identify 50 catalysts (things/changes/events that can make these problems more frequent and/or severe) and symptoms (things/changes/events that suggest an account is already suffering from these problems) that I could observe online about a business as an outsider. This will help build a more engaged prospecting list and personalize my messaging to potential prospects."

You can get a list of new catalysts and symptoms to begin testing. Find the ones that are the easiest to observe as an outsider, then ask how you can go about efficiently finding this information when looking into an account.

The brain ignores what it does not find relevant.
—*David Eagleman*

PART III

THE GOAL OF PROSPECTING

PART III • THE GOAL OF PROSPECTING

Nothing happens until your buyer stops and says, "I need to read this."

More accurately, nothing happens unless your buyer is afraid not to engage.

If your outreach doesn't trigger concern, uncertainty, or a sense of loss, it won't register as valuable. Buyers don't engage because they're curious or polite—they engage because ignoring the message feels riskier than paying attention.

Getting a buyer to stop, look, read or listen and then act is not a superficial skill or a creative exercise. It's behavioral. It's neurological. There is a science behind attention, threat detection, and decision-making.

And if you don't understand that science—if you don't know how to trigger the right cues at the right moment—your prospecting doesn't just get harder. It fails.

This part is about mastering that moment.

CHAPTER TEN
LIGHT UP YOUR BUYER'S BRAIN

Lieutenant Commander Michael Riley looked at the screen in front of him and concluded that he was about to die. In his role as anti-air warfare officer on the HMS *Gloucester*, a British destroyer stationed off the coast of Kuwait during the last days of the Persian Gulf War, his job was to monitor the radar scope for incoming Iraqi attacks. As the Americans advanced toward Kuwait City, Riley knew that the Iraqi operators at a Silkworm missile site nearby were facing the prospect of losing their chance to use their weapons to attack ships near the coast before being overcome. And there was one ship in particular, the USS *Missouri*, that had been pushing to get as close to the coast as possible, making it a juicy target. That was one of the ships the *Gloucester* was supposed to protect. Within five seconds of spotting the blip on the radar announcing something in the air heading their way, Riley felt a chill. There was a chance it could be an American plane, but he was sure it was a Silkworm missile.

The problem was that as firmly as he believed his assessment, there was no way to confirm his hunch. On radar, Silkworm missiles looked exactly like the American A-6 planes that were also flying in the same region. They were the same size and shape and flew at the same speed. They did differ in the altitude at which they flew—Silkworms at about 1,000 feet, and A-6 planes anywhere from 2,000 to 3,000 feet or more—but the radar Riley was using, the one that could pick up blips at their earliest, only swept vertically, and therefore couldn't gather altitude data. A different radar system, called the 909, swept horizontally to measure altitude. But as the blip approached, the *Gloucester*'s weapons director had trouble feeding the 909 the tracking numbers it needed to read the object's altitude. For 44 excruciating seconds, Riley watched the unidentified object come closer and closer, sure that everyone on the destroyer would die if he didn't do something to stop it. Finally, the 909 spat out the altitude: 1,000 feet. Riley fired the Gloucester's weapons, and the object was destroyed.

It would be four hours before anyone could confirm that Riley had shot down an enemy Silkworm missile and not an American plane.[25]

Standing at the entrance to the Canyon Lake trail on an unseasonably warm late spring day, Ava felt like cheering for herself. True, if her New Year's resolution to spend more time outdoors had been a plant, it would have died of neglect months ago. But as her teenager liked to say, still made it, so it counts. Who would have thought overcoming inertia would feel so good? She hadn't even started moving yet, but she could feel winter's extra pounds evaporating, along with the sweat already starting to soak through her t-shirt.

Ava had only been walking for about half an hour before she started to wonder if she'd made a mistake. She'd thought the shade of the trees would keep her comfortable as she trekked, but there wasn't the slightest breeze, and the heat was oppressive. As her pace slowed and her water bottle got lighter, her thoughts were just starting to wander to the ice-cold beer in her fridge when she heard a rustle in the brush to her right. *Oh, shit, what was that?* She paused mid-step, turning her head in the direction where she'd thought she'd heard the sound. Everything was still. Ava shook her head, glad no one was there to see her freeze like a scared rabbit, and then took another step forward. Then she heard it again, a rustling sound. She stopped. This time, she thought she caught some movement out of the corner of her eye. She turned toward it, her eyes scanning the wild tangle of branches and leaves carpeting the forest floor. Something was moving low to the ground. *Oh, shit, is that a snake?* Ava's muscles started to tighten. Panic took over. Was she gonna die out here by herself, bitten by a poisonous snake? She thought about her daughter, her husband, and all the things she wished she had done as she waited for the still-invisible creature to strike at her ankles. Suddenly, she saw the tiny head of a chipmunk poke out from under a leaf. Ava relaxed and let out a relieved sigh. Feeling stupid at her overreaction, she called out to the little guy, "Hey, Alvin," as he scampered up the nearest tree. Ava briefly thought about continuing on to the end of the trail, but she'd had enough outdoors for one day. As she headed back in the direction of her car, she decided to call her friend Jill, who had a pool. It would absolutely be within the bounds of her New Year's resolution to spend her outdoor time floating in an inflatable lounger.

On the surface, the stories of the British Royal Navy officer and the reluctant hiker have nothing in common. Yet they revolve around the invisible workings of the human brain, so in that way, they're identical. Because whether it's on a warship or in the wilderness, the brain always works the same way. For our purposes, we're especially interested in the function of two complementary regions of the prefrontal cortex: the orbitofrontal cortex (OFC) and the anterior cingulate cortex (ACC). That's right, we're going to talk neuroscience again, though super simplified because neither of us is a neuroscientist.

The OFC—The Pattern Seeker

You already know that our brains are constantly on the lookout for threats, like Riley's constantly spinning radar antennas. One way in which it weighs those threats is by looking at patterns, because as the human species evolved over millennia, our brains figured out that identifying patterns was an efficient method for avoiding things that could get us killed. As early humans, it would have been impossible to, say, examine every tree or rock to make sure nothing was lurking behind it waiting to pounce, so our brains evolved to quickly and easily categorize everything that we see, hear, and smell as important and worth paying attention to, or unimportant and therefore safe to ignore. Today, though most of us live in modern environments where we don't have to fear wild animals stalking us unless we choose to enter their territory, our brain is still constantly on alert. Subconsciously, wherever we go and whatever we do, our brain, specifically the OFC, is constantly working in the background, checking for patterns and judging their value. If everything looks the way we would expect it to, even in unfamiliar territory, the OFC assigns it low current value and therefore not worth much, if any, of our attention. Category: Unimportant.

THE ACC—THE *OH-SHIT* CIRCUIT

Sometimes, something won't register quite the way your brain anticipated, which prompts the anterior cingulate cortex, the ACC, also known as the "oh-shit circuit," to spring into action. The ACC is the region of the brain that registers errors, conflict, or anything that deviates from expectations. When it picks up on something unusual or different, it sends out an alert: YO, STOP! LOOK AT THIS! IT COULD BE IMPORTANT! Like an internal alarm system, it draws your attention to the thing that doesn't fit your brain's expectations and forces you to focus on it so your OFC can gauge its value. Important or unimportant? Problem or not-problem? Because it's part of your stress response, it might also trigger a physiological reaction, like a sickening drop in your stomach or you breaking out in a sweat.

The ACC response is often completely subconscious. Michael Riley initially couldn't explain how he knew the blip on his radar was a missile and not an American plane; his best guess was ESP.[26] Only later, when the story was analyzed further, did he agree that it was possible he'd noticed that the flying object first registered on his radar screen much farther from the Kuwaiti coast than where planes usually appeared. The discrepancy was explicable only by the fact that Silkworm missiles travel at much lower altitudes than planes, which makes them invisible to radar until they've made it farther out to sea. As Gary Klein noted in his book *Sources of Power*, where this story originally appeared, Riley didn't save the *Gloucester* and the *Missouri* by recognizing the missile for what it was, but because subconsciously he saw a "deviation from a pattern."[27] In other words, his brain saw something unexpected—the unusual location of the blip—and his ACC compelled him to zero in and take a closer look. In the woods, Eva's ACC worked exactly the same way when it noticed something that didn't add up—a rustling noise on a windless day—prompting her to stop in her tracks and pay closer attention to her surroundings.

INTERRUPT EXPECTATIONS

Now, what the hell do the OFC and ACC have to do with prospecting? They work together to make people pay attention when necessary, even if for only a half-second longer than they normally might have. And what is the equivalent of gold to modern-day sales prospectors? Attention. It's everything to salespeople. Now, as we've already discussed, buyers have learned from a lifetime of experience—which the OFC has registered as patterns—NOT to give us sellers their attention. Their OFCs are primed to block us out completely. Before our buyers can even register our existence, we've been categorized as unimportant. A seller's job, therefore, is to interrupt the pattern their buyer's brain is anticipating. It has led them to believe you couldn't possibly have anything interesting to tell them. You have to prove them wrong. How? By inserting something unexpected into their OFC's path that will trigger their ACC to wave as frantically as a castaway spotting a ship on the horizon. HEEEEY! STOP! OVER HERE!

From the buyer's perspective, it might look like this:

Audrey leaned forward in her desk chair, one hand hugging her oversized coffee mug to her chest to warm her up against the arctic, air-conditioned chill of her office, the other hand poised over her mouse. In her role as chief information security officer (CISO) of a global manufacturing firm, she'd developed a strict morning routine: Coffee. Calendar. Crisis mitigation.

And Culling.

The day had started smoothly. The coffee didn't taste burnt. Her calendar didn't show wall-to-wall meetings. And no crises. There'd been a security alert, but as usual it had turned out to be a false positive. She made a note to talk to HR about setting up another security awareness training to teach people, for the love of all that was holy, to stop, read, and think before they clicked on any link sent by an outside source. Human error was Audrey's nemesis. Even with every security protocol in place, and a team as trained and vigilant as a pack of Dobermans, she never felt like she could fully relax. She tilted her head from side to side to stretch her neck, wishing she could treat herself to a massage, and clicked open her email account. Time for the cull.

There they were, waiting as always, stacked in a bolded, black-and-white row like piano accordion keys—about 30 unread emails, most of them from people and companies she'd never heard of, trying to sell her things she didn't want. Every day, the solicitations piled up like unfolded

laundry in her inbox, promising cybersecurity software and tools that offered "next-gen protection," "AI-powered defense," and "seamless integration." All buzzwords, no substance. She didn't even open them anymore, as she'd learned the hard way they rarely had anything interesting
to say. They were all the same—pitches telling her what she needed by
people who clearly didn't understand what she was up against, offering
generic solutions to her very real, very specific problems. As Audrey took
another swig of coffee, her tired eyes barely registered the subject lines
of the emails as she quickly clicked them one by one into the digital
garbage can.

Are you 100% sure your endpoints are secure?
Delete
Quick question about your firewall config.
Delete
Let's talk threat surfaces over coffee.
This one, Audrey noticed long enough to spot the inclusion of a
cutesy coffee cup emoji. *Cringe! Delete*
Delete
Delete
Dele...
Audrey's finger paused over her mouse.
Gaps your SIEM isn't catching.
Audrey had full confidence in her team and their systems and pro-
cesses, but this subject header made her pause. *Oh, shit.* Was it possible
there was a new threat she hadn't heard of? Something her team didn't
know?
She clicked the email open, expecting to quickly confirm that this
email should follow all the others into the garbage. This is what it said:

New Message   — ⤢ ✕

To   Audrey   Cc Bcc

Subject   Gaps your SIEM isn't catching

Won't pretend to know everything about your environment, Audrey. But I'll bet your team's pretty confident in their tooling. And still, there might be things they don't see.

We just helped a financial services client with a fully staffed SOC, SIEM in place, and routine vulnerability scans.

They still missed:

- Dormant accounts with expired passwords still holding privileges

- Two internal servers with RDP exposed over VPN

- Alert fatigue that buried a lateral movement signal for 11 days

These aren't zero-days, they're the mundane gaps that real attackers love, and they're invisible until you look at the problem differently. That's what we do—root-cause simulation that shows you how small misses become breach vectors that can lead to increased chances of breach and exposure to ransom, DOS and loss of data.

Would a 20-minute walkthrough of how we've seen these issues show up, even in well-tooled orgs, be useful?

Best,
Sam

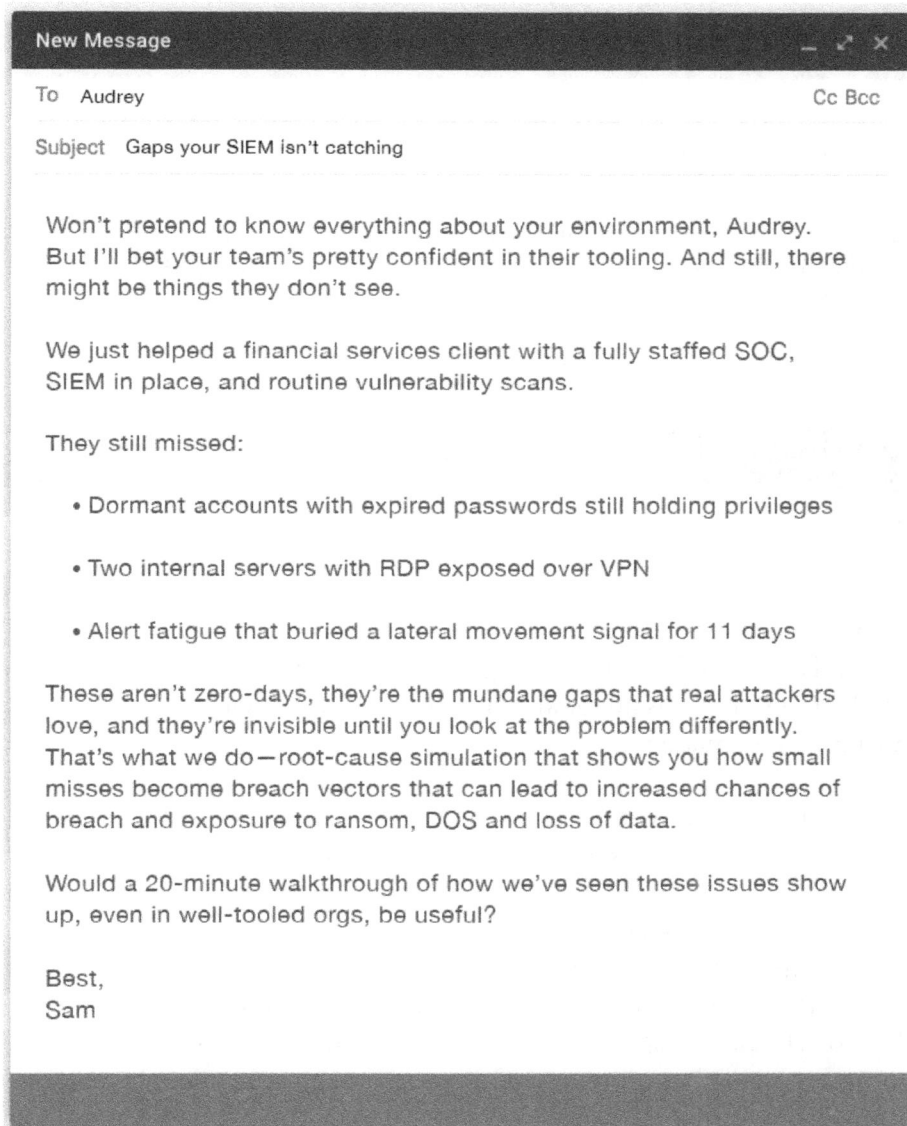

Audrey read the email again, then hit Reply.

New Message _ ↗ ✕

To   Sam   Cc Bcc

Subject   RE: Gaps your SIEM isn't catching

Hi, Sam. I'd be interested in hearing more about what you have to
offer. Would you be able to schedule a short call later this week?
Thursday afternoon looks especially open.
Best,
Audrey

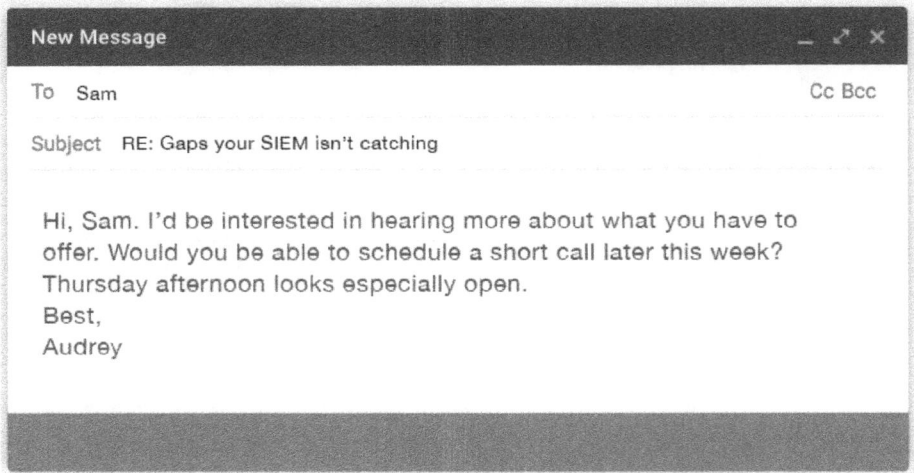

What just happened?

As Keenan said in *Gap Selling*, prospecting marks the first yes in a whole series of yesses necessary to get to a successful close. A yes is a sale. And Sam just made two.

A Tale of Two Sales
Every successful outreach consists of two sales.

Sale #1: Intrigue (Makes People Stop):
Behind the scenes, Audrey's OFC was humming along, scanning her emails and judging their value as harshly as Simon Cowell in the early days of *American Idol*: "Not valuable, not important, nope, no, you've got to be joking," until her ACC flagged a subject header she couldn't immediately dismiss because—*oh, shit!*—one of these things was not like the others. It didn't fit the usual, expected pattern. It wasn't corny. It wasn't faking friendship. It wasn't inauthentic or salesy. And anything that doesn't fit the usual, expected pattern is going to cause feelings of uncertainty. Audrey has faith in her team, but this subject header introduced just enough doubt to make her pause. She just couldn't be 100% certain this email was junk, just like Michael Riley couldn't be 100% certain the suspicious blip on his radar screen wasn't just an American

plane, and Ava couldn't be 100% certain that the noise in the woods was harmless. They had to learn more before they could confirm the value of what they were seeing and decide what to do. The only way to achieve certainty is to pay closer attention to the thing causing you uncertainty.

Uncertainty can be uncomfortable. Michael was in a life-or-death situation, and Ava imagined she was, so when they locked in to try to get the information they needed to turn their uncertainty into certainty, they felt concern, dread, and fear. But Audrey felt safe and sound at her desk, even if her office was an icebox, so when her ACC unexpectedly alerted her—HEY! CHECK THIS OUT! THIS MIGHT NOT BE THE GARBAGE YOU THINK IT IS!—she wasn't afraid. She was intrigued.

That was Sam's first sale. Not cyber security services. Intrigue.

Intrigue demands attention. Intrigue makes us stop and look closer. It sparks curiosity and desire by prompting subconscious questions like *What is this? Why does it matter? Why does it matter **to me**?* The only way for Audrey to satisfy her curiosity was to keep reading. That's why she clicked open the email.

Remember Trevor and his gift cards? The people on the street had certain built-in expectations from a random person standing on the sidewalk, trying to hand them something they didn't ask for, and he 100% met them. They noticed him, but he couldn't get their attention because he gave them no reason to stop. He didn't create any intrigue. Their brains glossed right over his gift cards and categorized them as not valuable, even though they were. Your buyers are no different. They're so chronically exposed to terrible, deceptive, low-value, poorly targeted sales and marketing, and so burned by scams, their brains are conditioned to ignore anything that could be more of the same. The only way to pierce the protective veil is to spark intrigue, so they have to pay you at least a split second of attention to determine whether it's safe to dismiss your message, or if it has value and isn't safe to delete.

Here are a few common email subject lines that don't create intrigue. How many have you used?

- **"Quick Question."** This implies a level of familiarity that doesn't exist, even hinting that a conversation has already taken place between the seller and buyer. It's deceptive, not intriguing. In addition, the reader has no context for the quick question or knows whether it's about something at work or at home. So it's annoying and confusing on the surface, and if on the off chance your prospect does bother to open it, off-putting. No one likes to be tricked. In addition, this tactic has been so overused, everyone knows it's just spam.

- **"Not Spam."** When this one pops up, no one says to themselves, "Oh, snap! It's not spam! I should read this." If you're telling me it's not spam, it's definitely spam. Worse, there's a fundamental problem in that it only tells you what it's not. It doesn't tell you what it *is*, nor why you should check out the email's content.

- **"Re: Question about your next project."** Using "Re" the first time you reach out to someone implies that you're following up on a conversation that has already begun. Trying to trick your buyer into thinking they've already corresponded with you will piss them off for sure. It's deceptive and immediately pegs you as a liar. Why would your buyer want to talk to someone who's admitted they're a liar?

- **"We Can Help You [Insert Thing You Do] 10x Faster!!!"** Uh, great! Thanks! Your buyer now knows everything they need to know. However, you've left nothing to the imagination, so they have no reason to read any further.

On the other hand, you can count on any of these techniques to create intrigue.

1. **Offer a Surprise.**
Give your buyers something unexpected and out of place.

For example, not long ago, Will checked his inbox to find an email with a two-word subject line: Greene King.

What the…? It was a blast from the past. Greene King was the name of the very first pub Will had worked at. It wasn't something he talked about much, online or anywhere else. The only way anyone could have learned this factoid about him is if they had gone to his LinkedIn page, clicked on his Experiences, and scrolled all the way to the bottom, where Will had listed his title as *Director of Chief Vice President Head VP of Sales Beverage Revenue.*

That's exactly what the sender, Kevin Chambers of beehiiv, had done. Will's ACC lit up when it saw this piece of his old life staring him in the face. He felt like he had no choice but to open it to see what the email was about.

Of course, that tactic will only work once. We've all heard of the person who, back in the day, mailed in a résumé on bright pink paper so that it would stand out in a sea of white and ecru, or who attached their résumé to the inside of a pizza box and had it delivered to their employer of choice. Imagine the reaction of the first person on the receiving end of those résumés: *Who is this original, creative gem of a human who wants to work for me? I must know!* Then they or their assistant called or emailed the job seeker to set up an interview.

The second time they received a pink or pizza résumé, they thought, *Again?*

Surprises turn into same old, same old really quick.

Surprising Subject Headers:

He failed 7 times. That's exactly why he succeeded.

Most people think sugar causes diabetes...but the truth is way more interesting.

Be careful—trying to surprise can look gimmicky if you don't deliver or aren't as unique as you think you are. Slang, memes, and anything trendy or topical have a short shelf life.

2. **Open a Loop.**
How often has this happened? You're narrating a story from your past, and you blank on someone's name. When you close your eyes, you can see their face floating in your mind, but you just can't find their name anywhere in your mental rolodex. You stammer and try to sound out the first letter of the name—"It's on the tip of my

tongue!"—but no dice. You're forced to tell your story with a substitute name, and the moment passes, but for the rest of the day, it still drives you crazy that you can't remember this lost detail. Then sometime later, maybe while you're trying to fall asleep, the name slams back into your brain—*Kenna! It's Kenna!*—and you blurt it out loud, waking up your husband lying next to you. The relief is instantaneous. *Of course! Whew!* Remembering the name is as physically satisfying as a long-awaited sneeze.

That tension that you experienced between forgetting and remembering is caused by the existence of an open loop—something that's been left unfinished. When we're missing information, leave something undone, or can't have closure, it creates an open loop. Open loops make us uncomfortable and compel us to do what we must to close the loop. So in the case of a TV show cliffhanger, for example, you might count the days until the next episode drops so you can find out what happens next. If you've auditioned for a part in a play, tried out for a team, or applied to a school, and you see an email announcing the results, you'll probably experience big feelings of anticipation until you click open the email to find out if you're in or out. You'll feel something new after that—maybe elation, disappointment, sadness, or even rage—but at least you'll have the answer and information you need to close the loop. Human brains really, really like closed loops.

Salespeople can capitalize on that human desire by purposely creating open loops to spark intrigue. You can do this in one of three ways:

A. **Introduce a Mystery.**
   A mystery is also a surprise, but one that holds your buyer in suspense. Sam's subject header, "Gaps your SIEM isn't catching," would sound super ominous to a CISO like Audrey, who's already hyper-aware that despite her team's best efforts, someone or something might breach the company's security systems. The subject header tapped right into her biggest fear—that she doesn't know what she doesn't know. Her SIEM may be missing something? What could it be?

The only way to appease her uncertainty—to solve the mystery and close the loop—was for her to open the email.

B. **Tell a Partial Story.**
Back in the days when we all still watched network TV, the news would do teasers like "Jetliner goes down in the oddest place; join us at 10 to hear more." (Then as now, newsrooms operated by the rule, "If it bleeds, it leads.") You'd have to watch at 10 p.m. to find out more. You can apply that same technique in your email. Tell a story so compelling, they can't wait to talk to you again to find out how it ended.

C. **Highlight a Knowledge Gap .**
Indicate that you have information that your buyer doesn't about something that promises to affect their industry, field, or product.

Headers That Suggest Knowledge Gaps:

Too many CMOs trust this fake metric

Where L&D programs leak engagement

According to industry research, most forecasts ignore this input

The thing about open loops is that until your brain gets the information it needs to close the loop, it will fixate on the missing pieces or the incomplete activity, a phenomenon called the Ziegarnik effect. The Ziegarnik effect explains why we remember our unfinished tasks better than the ones we complete. It's why we obsess when we can't figure out why someone isn't calling us back, and why it's hard to concentrate on other things when we're struggling with unanswered questions. Knowledge gaps and mysteries compel our brains to return to the unfinished thing, whatever it is, again and again in search of answers and closure. Create an open loop header, and you make yourself almost unforgettable; you'll keep intruding on your buyers' brains until they finally cave and do what they must to get the information necessary to close the loop.

None of this is easy. When prospecting, you're trying to strike a balance between hoarding your candy so no one can see that you've got stuff they want, and spilling all your candy at the front door so they can see everything you've got, thus eliminating any reason they had to keep talking to you. For example, "Product X does the things you need doing 50% faster, with 20% less waste, at half the price of our competitors!" A product-centric line like this is as intriguing as an oven mitt. You've already told your buyer everything they expected to hear. Where's the surprise? Where's the mystery? Where's the thing that's going to trigger the ACC to flag down your buyer and compel them to close the gap between their certainty and uncertainty? It's not there, so unless you happen to land on a buyer who's actively seeking out your product and already plans to buy, there's no reason to read it. Most people's brains will just block it out like it never existed.

SALE #2: INTEREST (MAKES PEOPLE ACT)
Intrigue makes people stop. Interest gets them to respond.

Once Audrey moved past the subject header and clicked open the email, Sam met her with a message that sounded like it was written by a real person who understood, respected, and cared about Audrey's world. She didn't reply to Sam because she felt sold. She replied because she felt seen. It's the same reason why Will replied to Kevin Chambers' email from beehiive. Kevin surprised him with Greene King as a subject header but then held his interest by correctly identifying a problem Will was dealing with—the headaches of signing up for newsletter sponsorships, which take so much negotiating and back-and-forth, it sometimes doesn't even feel worthwhile. On top of that, the email was funny and cheeky—qualities Will appreciates—and dropped hints that Kevin had read a number of Will's posts. Here was someone who had gone above and beyond to learn as much as he could about Will before reaching out, spoke to him like a real person, and had solutions in mind to problems Will hadn't even begun to try to solve. Like Audrey, Will replied, and in time, he became a beehiive client.

Does your outreach make people feel seen? Here are a few common opening lines that are unlikely to work. Are any familiar?

- **"I see you're the [insert your title and the name of the company where you work]."** Why would you tell me something I already know?

- **"I've tried to reach out to you several times, but it seems like you might be away."** This one is guaranteed to provoke an eyeroll. If you've reached out that many times and gotten no answer, doesn't that tell you something? You're just reminding them that they've been ignoring you.

- **"My name is John, Sales Consultant at Acme."** Who cares? Did the buyer ask? This commits the classic sin of offering unnecessary information up front. It's unimportant to almost everyone.

You don't have time to waste. Get to the point fast! That's what Sam did so successfully. The humility he expressed in his first line, "Won't pretend to know everything about your environment," helped disarm Audrey's initial defensiveness, and his next line, "But I'll bet your team's pretty confident in their tooling. And still, there might be things they don't see," spoke confidently to her insecurity.

Then Sam triggered Audrey's ACC repeatedly by leading with problems that Audrey recognized, the kind of stuff that kept her up at night: privilege creep, RDP holes, alert fatigue. Every word in his email was carefully chosen, and every line carried weight. By giving your buyers information that's relevant to their needs, you get a chance to prove that you have a deep understanding of their problems. As they read through your email or listen to you speak, they're always trying to answer one or more of the following questions:

- Could I have this problem?

- Is it a big enough problem that I should solve it?

- Does this person appear trustworthy enough to help me solve it?

If what you tell them in the few seconds of attention they're willing to give causes them to say "Yes" to any of these three questions, they're going to be motivated to keep engaging with you all the way to the end, when you finally give them a reason to respond. Anything to calm that damn ACC down!

REFLECTION

One mega-impactful way to hold your buyer's interest is through the power of reflection. Encourage the buyer to think deeply about their environment and what they think is true by asking a series of open-ended, thought-provoking questions. See, you believe they have a problem that needs to be solved. They may not agree, or they may agree there's a problem but not that it needs to be solved right away, or they may agree there's a problem, and it's no big deal. And they could be right. After all, they're the ones with the front-row seat to their business, not you. But what if they're not? What if you've noticed something they haven't because they've gotten complacent, fallen into poor habits, gotten bad advice, think too small, aren't as up to date on new tech as you are, or haven't recognized the new possibilities available? This is your chance to help them see it for themselves.

Now, people usually respond poorly to being told they're wrong. It makes them defensive, and defensiveness acts like sound-canceling headphones, blocking buyers' ability to hear what you say. Worse, defensiveness also shuts down people's ability to analyze an issue objectively with reason instead of emotion. However, buyers will be more inclined to accept that they may have blind spots, or are even mistaken, if they're allowed to come to that conclusion themselves. In fact, social scientists, psychologists, and others who study how people interpret and respond to their experiences have shown that "reflection yields" what researcher Hannes Gustav Melichar calls "self-distancing."[29] Dr. Melichar studies mental health, but in our work, we see that creating that mental distance can move buyers away from knee-jerk emotion toward reason, which can help bring their guard down so they're more willing to look at their environment objectively. Melichar also writes that "reflection comes with human vulnerability."[30] In other words, when we allow ourselves to be vulnerable, we let our defenses down. When we can use empathy and good questions to help buyers lower their defenses through reflection, we make it feel safe for them to absorb new information, open themselves up to other perspectives and ways of thinking, and overcome the emotions that may be impeding their ability to objectively analyze their environment.

Asking questions that force buyers to pause and think—about how they know what they know, how things might have changed since they first came to that knowledge, and consequences they may not have considered—moves them from a place of certainty to a state of vulnerability, and that's where the productive conversations can happen. Reflection helps people see that there may be a reason for change.[31] Fear of vulnerability and the discomfort it brings can keep buyers from willingly reflecting; in fact, the harder they resist, the more likely it is that there's an issue worth exploring.[32] But if you can get them to reflect…

So don't tell your buyers they're missing the forest for the trees, are stuck in the past, or are thinking about their business all wrong. Don't tell them you know something they don't. Instead, guide them to figuring it out for themselves with a series of open-ended, thought-provoking questions.

We're not going to offer specific examples of what these questions might look like in a business environment because everyone's field is different, and the questions must be nuanced and tailored precisely for the specific individual and company you're talking to and about. But here are some general examples:

- **A therapist working with a couple might ask:** "When you first got married, what did you think it would be like?"

- **You might ask an adult child thinking about quitting their teaching job:** "You chose to teach third-grade math. Why did you think that would be a good fit?"

- **A prospector who sells for a lead generation agency might ask:** "You've built a giant online audience. How many followers are actually paying you?"

You want to push people to think about any information they may have overlooked so they can make sure they understand the real issues and the reality of their present state, and accurately address their problems. The goal here isn't to just get an answer out of your buyer. It's to encourage introspection and prompt them to reflect on their environment and how it's truly affecting them.

Asking these kinds of questions can be tricky, because when they're too intrusive or heavy-handed, they can make people uncomfortable. But if you know your buyer well enough to ask your question the right way, getting them to take a beat and reflect may allow them to see that what they thought was 100% true may only be partially true, or only true in certain situations. They're often surprised: "Oh, you know, I never thought about it like that!" You're not teaching them anything new; you're helping them make new connections and uncover all the implications and unforeseen consequences they haven't yet thought through. Asking questions is asking your buyer to take a journey. It's giving them the chance to slow down enough to see what you see, to confirm (for both of you) that what you see is real, and to consider the repercussions if they choose to leave the issue unaddressed. And no matter what happens next, it builds trust.

Giving people that chance to reflect is one of the major ways gap prospecting is different from how most people do this work. Most sellers don't want their prospects to think! That's the whole point of their high-pressure tactics. But gap prospectors respect their buyers enough to give them a chance to reflect. If you're talking to your buyer and you hear them say, "That's a good question," you're on the right track. We'll show you how letting buyers reflect works in your favor in Chapter 14.

Now back to Audrey. She said, "Yes, this is *intriguing*, I'll open this email." Then she said, "Yes, this is *interesting*, I'll schedule time." How did Sam get her to act? With a well-calibrated offer-ask ratio.

THE OFFER-ASK RATIO

Sparking interest is all about getting your buyer to weigh the cost of action versus the cost of inaction. You want them thinking, *If I don't act on this email or phone call, can I live with the outcome? Will I regret it?* You want to make them afraid (*oh, shit!*) to hit the delete button, or afraid to hang up, because the cost of ignoring you may be higher than the 30 seconds it would take them to give you some more attention. You want their OFC to decide that what you have to offer has value, which, for the OFC, is defined as "anything that will calm the damn ACC down." You do that with an offer that's more valuable than your ask, which is your buyer's time. There's even a formula:

Offer − Ask = Value

You could also think of it like this:

Problem-centric Invitation − Your Buyer's Time = Happy Buyer's Brain

Your buyer is always doing a subconscious cost-benefit analysis: Is this worth my time? It's the same calculation you'd make if you were moving out of your house and debating whether to wrap your glassware in an old shipping box with some leftover newspaper or to purchase a $20 glassware kit that comes with reinforced sides, specially sized dividers, and individual padded sleeves to cushion each packed item. How much would it be worth it to you to make sure that your glassware stays in one piece? If the value of safeguarding your glasses was worth more than $20, it would make sense to buy the more expensive kit. If it were worth much less, an old box and newspaper would suffice.

Or think of it this way. What if you were a strong, healthy person living in Rhode Island, and Keenan offered to give you $100 to travel by foot to visit him in Colorado? You'd blow him off, right? Anyone would. The pain and time, plus the money you'd have to spend on prep and food, wouldn't be worth it. The Offer-Ask ratio in this scenario is way out of whack. But let's say that for funsies he offered you 5 million tax-free dollars to walk to Colorado. Unless you're already really rich, you might start packing your rucksack. The example isn't that far-fetched—reality shows that this kind of Offer-Ask ratio has been successfully drawing contestants for decades.

Examples of Poor Offer-Ask Ratios
"Let's hop on the phone so I can tell you more about what my company has to offer. Do you have 45 minutes on Tuesday?"
No one who's any good at what they do has 45 minutes to spend listening to a product-centric spiel unless you've already proven to them that they have the problem your product can fix. And even then, 45 minutes is probably too long.

"I'd love to send you our survey. It's only 10 pages, and once completed, you'll be eligible for a 5% discount on our premium package."

No one wants to spend their time telling you their life story, especially when they have no idea why they'd want your premium package, even at a measly 5% discount.

"I'd love to talk for 30 minutes to learn more about your business so I can see if we've got solutions that match your problems."

No one wants to spend 30 minutes on the phone with you just to find out in the end you can't help them.

Think about that word, "spend." Ultimately, when closing a sale, we ask people to spend money. When prospecting, we ask them to spend time. Yet many sellers don't see time and money as equally valuable, and customers can feel it. Not only that, but they also resent it. Think about that the next time you ask someone to spend their time on you. You'd never ask anyone to spend hundreds or thousands of dollars on, say, a pen. But it can feel like that to the buyer when they "spend" their time and get a pen's worth of value in return. So when asking someone to spend their time, be very clear about what you're offering in return, and make sure it's worth it.

In sum:

- Your offer needs to be specific, useful, relevant, and tangible.

- It should promise insight, knowledge, data, access, guidance, proof, or clarity.

- In quantitative numbers, think of making an offer that's worth 70% more than your ask.

That's usually enough to make your buyer act.

WHY SAM'S ASK WORKED
First, Sam planted some fruitful seeds in his email before he made his

ask:

- He proved familiarity with Audrey's field and the problems she probably faces.

- He offered a case study of another client who, much like Audrey, thought they had their shit together and were still left vulnerable.

- He briefly explained what his company did—root-cause simulations—so Audrey knew what she'd be signing up for if she decided to work with him.

Then he went in for the ask: **"Would a 20-minute walkthrough of how these issues show up, even in well-tooled orgs, be useful?"**

Here's the formula:

Offer: Evidence of real vulnerabilities that exist in organizations just like Audrey's that she may be unaware of. In the cyber world, that's gold!

Ask: Twenty minutes, which is a pretty low investment, especially for someone like Audrey who is already worried about breaches.

Note, too, the phrasing. You may have learned to write as though *of course* your buyer will want to take the next step. It seems like a display of confidence. But Sam didn't do that. Instead, he prompted Audrey to think harder about the value of what he was offering. How useful would those 20 minutes be? Remember that he's trying to get Audrey to weigh the cost of action—20 minutes of her time—versus the cost of inaction—a cyber threat she's unaware of that could cause her to be breached. He's comfortable doing that because he knows the pressures that someone like Audrey faces every day, and by citing his work with other clients, he shows her that she's right to worry.

Now Audrey's doing the math. For the cost of 20 minutes, she could discover that there's a solution that would help her sleep better at night. If there's a breach (*oh, shit!*), she'll always regret not spending the 20 minutes. If she spends the 20 minutes and finds out that Sam's service isn't useful, she hasn't wasted a lot of time. Sam's offer contains the possibility of high reward combined with low risk. The cost of action is much lower than the cost of inaction. Audrey's OFC decides this offer has value. And that's why Audrey replies and schedules a phone call.

Intrigue opens a loop, and interest gives your buyer a way to close it.

CHAPTER ELEVEN
GET STICKY

We've offered lots of examples of what doesn't spark attention or compel action. But what does? Stickiness. A sticky idea, as explained by Chip and Dan Heath in their 2007 book *Made to Stick*, is one that's so understandable, memorable, and impactful, it can change someone's behavior or thought.[33] And they say that sticky ideas consist of SUCCESs, that is, six principles: Simplicity, Unexpectedness, Concreteness, Credibility, Emotions, and Stories.[34] In our experience, closing the two sales of outreach requires crafting messages that also share these qualities, though for our purposes, it looks more like USCCES.

SALE #1 INTRIGUE
UNEXPECTEDNESS
Unexpectedness sells intrigue because it's a pattern interrupter, but what makes it intriguing isn't shock value. It's proving to your buyer that you know them well, understand their problems, and can draw a straight line between those problems and your solutions. It can also mean sharing information they weren't expecting or were unaware of, such as industry information or new regulations. Not many people can do that. Hence, unexpected.

How Sam's subject header—*Gaps your SIEM isn't catching*—was unexpected:
Audrey always carries a vague sense of unease and worry that she might be missing something that could compromise her company's security. What she doesn't do is worry about any particular aspect of that secu-

rity. When she looks at each layer individually, she sees that everything appears to be locked down tight. But when Sam asks her to think about the security, information, and event management (SIEM), that's a surprise because it's so specific. Only someone with deep knowledge about Audrey's field is going to know what SIEM is. And to a person anxious that she's missing something, the mere suggestion that there could be gaps in the SIEM sends her brain scrambling to think about it. Could their SIEM be overlooking threats?

If you've ever asked yourself while driving somewhere, "Did I turn off the stovetop before I left?" you understand a little of what Audrey is going through. You usually turn off the burner, and there's no reason you wouldn't have this time, but now that you've asked the question, you realize you can't picture yourself turning down the stovetop knob once your food is cooked, so you can't be 100% sure. Now you're filled with doubt, and it makes you uneasy. You're not going to feel better until you close the loop, either by turning around and going home to double check or hoping someone is still home who will answer their phone and check for you. Similarly, Audrey won't know for sure what gaps Sam could be talking about—she can't close the loop—unless she clicks open his email.

Quick checklist for sellers crafting unexpected greetings and subject headers:

☑ Does it break your buyer's common assumption or expectation?

☑ Does it introduce a question your buyer needs answered?

☑ Is it personal? Does it immediately prove your expertise in and familiarity with your prospect's field or job?

Sale #2 Interest
Simplicity

Simplicity is about expressing only the most important elements of your message and the key things you need your buyer to notice. It requires stripping away everything that isn't essential so that the message is easy to absorb and impossible to forget. Simplicity makes it easier for your buyer to see the value of your offer and act on it. Most sellers make their messages too complicated, so simplicity will automatically break through your buyer's autopilot.

As the Heath brothers caution, simplicity isn't the same thing as dumbing things down.[35] It's about highlighting what's *most* important to your buyer in a way that's easy for them to grasp. Just speak to your buyer clearly and concisely, like a person who understands their business and their problems. Say what you mean, and mean what you say.

How Sam's email was simple:
It contained one clear insight for Audrey—the real threat to a company's security isn't usually advanced or complicated; it's often simply overlooked.

Quick checklist for sellers keeping it simple:

- ☑ What's the single most important thing you want your buyer to remember?

- ☑ Can you say it in one short sentence?

- ☑ Did you remove all the jargon and unnecessary layers?

CONCRETENESS
Sellers have an unfortunate tendency to talk in the abstract because they're determined to craft a message that will speak to everyone. But you can't be everything to everyone. Concreteness is the opposite of abstract. It's something your buyer can see, hear, feel, or imagine immediately. The brain can grab onto and hold concrete information, but vague generalities evaporate. When ideas are specific, they stick better because people can literally "picture" them.

They also speak directly to a specific buyer and are utterly irrelevant to anyone else. A concrete idea makes your message relatable, tangible, and vivid.

How Sam's email was concrete:
Real examples—"Dormant accounts with expired passwords still hold-

ing privileges; Two internal servers with RDP exposed over VPN: Alert fatigue that buried a lateral movement signal for 11 days." Specific gaps. No jargon.

Quick checklist to make something concrete:

☑ Can the audience picture it?

☑ Can they feel it happening?

☑ Is there a clear action or real-world example tied to it?

CREDIBILITY

This is what you're building when you get your buyer to answer in the affirmative to those three questions we asked earlier—*Do I have this problem? Is it a big enough problem that I need to solve it? Can I trust this person to help me solve it?* You do this by showing that you know your buyers' problems and business almost as well as they do.

The email that Sam wrote for Audrey was extremely specific and detailed—"SOC," "SIEM," "holding privileges," and "alert fatigue"—without leaning into meaningless jargon. He used these industry terms correctly and powerfully. The only person who could have written that email is someone who understands what Audrey deals with day in and day out, which makes her more likely to trust the sender and want to hear what he has to say.

Talk to your prospects like a peer. Prove that you understand their underlying processes, key metrics, customers, and business model. A good way to do this is by highlighting problems that others have faced, as Sam did when he talked about what another client discovered by using his services. When possible, build your credibility by showing social proof, name-dropping specific individuals or companies who can vouch for you and, most important, who matter to your buyer. There's no point in bragging to a cellular company that you also work closely with a big bank. So what? How does your work with a bank prove that you know a damn thing about your prospect's business? And if you're working with a big bank, don't bother mentioning that you work with a smaller community bank. Their issues are worlds apart. Too many sellers think dropping any big-name brand will have cachet, but unless you're talking about someone who's relevant to your prospect and swims in the same waters, don't bother. Save that information for your website, not your cold call or email.

What made Sam's email credible:
Referenced a peer company's issues—not a big logo, but a realistic situation.

Quick checklist to make something credible:

☑ Does it include specific, vivid details that are hard to fake?

☑ Does it leverage an authority or a relatable example that your audience trusts?

☑ Is there a way for your audience to test or verify your claim?

☑ Does it convey a solid knowledge and understanding of the buyer's world and their challenges?

EMOTION

We've talked about how people are more motivated by loss than gain. Why? Because as good as it feels to gain, it feels worse to lose. Is that rational? Not really. But this is why when you're prospecting, you want to make your buyers **feel** something, not just think something. People act because they care, not just because they understand. Logic informs, but emotion moves. A well-crafted, problem-centric message will stir up emotions your prospect is already having—frustration, annoyance, anxiety, or doubt, for example. If you make them believe that buying from you will make those unpleasant feelings go away, and that by not buying from you, they'll continue to lose, *and* you tap into feelings they want to have, like hope or pride, and ease feelings they want to get rid of, like frustration, fear, anger, or loss, they'll take the next step with you.

What made Sam's email emotional:
He didn't fearmonger, but rather reminded Audrey that even good

teams can miss critical things.

Quick checklist to trigger emotion:

- ☑ Does your message evoke feeling—pride, fear, hope, anger, joy, belonging?

- ☑ Are you speaking to the pain of the problem or the relief of the solution?

- ☑ Would a reader feel something instantly after hearing your message?

STORY

People remember in pictures, not data, so when you're sharing information, show, don't tell. When you tell stories, you tap into emotion, concreteness, and simplicity all at once. Stories let your buyers see your product or service in action, making it feel real and proving that it matters. Show them how other buyers have been positively affected by their choice to purchase from you. Help prospects picture themselves in a better future state that your product or service made possible.

How Sam folded a story into his email:
He included a brief before/after narrative inside a short email, enough for Audrey to be able to imagine her team in the same position.

Quick checklist for a sticky story:

- ☑ Does it feature a real person or company?

- ☑ Is there a clear conflict or problem?

- ☑ Is the outcome surprising or emotionally satisfying?

CREATING INTRIGUE AND INTEREST AT SCALE

Everything we've talked about in this chapter takes massive amounts of creativity to pull off. And it requires applying your creativity differently, depending on your medium; building intrigue and getting interest via email will be different from how you would do it on a cold call or through LinkedIn. Unfortunately, we're not prepared to try to teach you how to be creative. We can't tell you, "Do this," or "Do that," because it would undoubtedly end up being a gimmick. Instead, we're going to teach you to use AI to help you craft better outreach at scale. When you know what you want done, and you learn how to phrase and draft the right prompts, you'll have an endless supply of ACC-triggering, intriguing openers and interest-grabbing messages that compel your buyers to respond to you to get more information. We'll get to the specifics on how to do this—including what prompts to use—in chapters 13 and 16.

CHAPTER TWELVE
GET YOUR MIND RIGHT

In the early 1980s, Metropolitan Life had a painful, pricey problem. Every year, out of a pool of about 60,000 hopefuls, they hired 5,000 new insurance sales agents. The company actually needed to fill many more jobs than that, but their screening process was so tough, it was like trying to enlist as a Marine—very few made it through. First, applicants had to complete something called the Career Profile, a mandatory industry test designed to measure a person's sales career potential. Not many people passed, and of those who did, only the handful who scored in the top bracket were granted interviews. The few who got hired were then put through a super-intense training process. With MetLife being so selective about their new hires' temperament and skill, and investing so much in their training, every new sales agent should have been set up to succeed. Yet according to John Creedon, MetLife's former president and CEO, by the end of every year, half of them had quit, and by the end of the fourth year, worn down by the constant rejection, 80% had walked away. To regularly lose that many new employees represented a staggering waste of talent and capital. How much? The high rate of sales-agent churn was costing the company over 75 million dollars per year. Creedon needed to stop the hemorrhage.

Clearly, the industry Career Profile test did a crap job of predicting sales agent success—high scores didn't correlate with high sales stamina. So Creedon wanted to know, was there a way to tell if people who scored less well on the test still had the potential to be great agents?

Enter Dr. Martin Seligman, a clinical psychologist at the University of Pennsylvania. He'd spent his career exploring how we explain the positive and negative events in our lives to ourselves—our explanatory styles. These determine our expectations and how quickly we give up or persist in the face of challenges. Until then, Seligman's research had mostly focused on the study of pessimism. Pessimists have negative explanatory styles that tend to make them give up easily. But that means that optimists, with their positive explanatory styles, should be more persistent. Creedon already knew that optimism was an essential quality for sales and was thinking that maybe MetLife should start screening for optimism in its new hires, not just sales skills. But to do that, you would need to be able to measure optimism. Could Dr. Seligman figure out a way?

Seligman was game to try. He developed an Attributional Style Questionnaire (ASQ) to measure rates of optimism and pessimism and gave it to MetLife's top-performing and lowest-performing sales agents to complete. Not only did the top performers score higher on optimism, but the performers who scored most optimistically had also sold 37% more insurance within their first two years at the company than the agents who scored with high rates of pessimism. The question was, did pessimism cause the lower-performing agents to sell less than the optimists, or did lousy sales streaks turn sellers into pessimists? The only way to find out was to test sellers who hadn't actually tried to sell anything yet

So Dr. Seligman tested the optimism and pessimism of newly hired MetLife sales agents. Their optimism tested through the roof, higher than any other group of professionals he'd ever tested. And yet, one year later, more than half had quit. Who was left? Agents who scored in the top half of the testing range. They were twice as likely to stay and sold 20% more insurance than agents who scored in the lower half. Interestingly, the scores on the Career Profile test didn't predict anyone's quit rate, only how much they sold. As you might expect, agents who scored in the top half sold more than agents who sold in the bottom half.

Finally, MetLife agreed to apply the ASQ to the hiring process itself. Fifteen thousand applicants across the country took both the industry Career Profile test and the optimism-pessimism ASQ test. One thousand agents were hired strictly based on their Career Profile test scores; their ASQ scores would only be examined to compare how the optimists and pessimists performed. MetLife also hired 129 agents who missed a passing score on the Career Profile test but scored in the top half of the ASQ. Dr. Seligman named this group the special force.

What happened?

Optimists in the regular force sold more than the pessimists in their cohort—31% by the second year. But get this—the special force outsold the pessimists on the regular force by 57% the second year and kept pace with the regular force optimists as well.

Ultimately, MetLife began administering both the Career Profile and the ASQ to all its sales applicants. Applicants who passed the Career Profile and scored in the top half of the ASQ were hired. Anyone who scored just under the passing cut-off of the Career Profile but within the top half of the ASQ was also hired. But candidates who passed the Career Profile, yet scored in the lower half of the ASQ, were not hired. In effect, MetLife eliminated from consideration the group of employees with more negative explanatory styles, because even if they had solid sales skills, they were also the most likely to quit. This change in hiring strategy led MetLife to develop a larger, more skillful, and more resilient sales force. The result? In less than two years, MetLife saw a nearly 50% boost in personal-insurance market share.[36]

You can read more about this cool study and all of Dr. Seligman's early work in his book *Learned Optimism*. In fact, you should read that book once you're done with this one so you can test your levels of optimism and learn how to strengthen them. Because as the study showed, talent and skill can predict initial success, but optimism predicts persistence. That's why, for outbound sellers who live in the world of constant rejection, an optimistic mindset is critical.

But it can't work alone. There are actually five mindsets that every power seller brings to their work, perspectives that shape the way sellers think about how and why they do what they do and set them up for success. You can know everything there is to know about root causes and problem-centricity, the OFC and the ACC, and the principles of stickiness, but if you sit down to make a call or type an email without being in the right mindset, you'll screw everything up.

THE FIVE MINDSETS OF POWER SELLERS

Adopting and leading with these five mindsets is the key to making everything you learn in this book work for you. Not just one or two—all of them. You don't get to pick and choose which ones you're feeling on any given day. Without all five, you're like an artist without inspiration or a chef without taste buds. There's no faking it. Your skills won't be enough to help you succeed. Your knowledge won't be enough either. Your head has to be in the right place each and every time you sell, but especially in prospecting and cold outreach. Why this is true, and how you can adopt these mindsets so they're as natural to you as breathing, is the subject of the rest of this chapter.

OPTIMISM

So we know that having an optimistic mindset is fundamental to successful prospecting, but why? Key is your explanatory style, or how you explain your world to yourself. As Dr. Seligman wrote in *Learned Optimism*, there are three "dimensions" to an explanatory style: permanence, pervasiveness, and personalization.

- **Permanence.** The pessimist sees everything bad that happens to them as permanent—everything is as it will always be. On a bad prospecting day, they'll tell themselves, "I'll never figure it out." Their belief that there's little they can do to change their circumstances erodes their sense of resilience. But people with an optimistic mindset see negative events and outcomes as temporary. They might think *Calls didn't go great today. Tomorrow will be better.* They believe they have some control over what happens to them. On the other hand, optimists attribute the good things that happen to permanent causes: *I always find a way.* They believe their success isn't temporary or lucky but rather the expected result of their capabilities and hard work.

- **Pervasiveness.** The pessimist allows their failure at one thing to color their perspective on everything else. So after a few rough days of prospecting, the pessimistic seller might think to themselves, *I don't know why I bother; I'm obviously not good at selling.* The optimist, however, thinks, *I'm doing something wrong here. Better go back to* Gap Prospecting *and review.* They understand that failing at one thing doesn't mean they're doomed to fail at other things; the failure or weakness is specific and isolated. The reverse is true with regard to success. After a good day of prospecting, a pessimist will think, *It's the holidays; people are in a generous mood.* The implication is that if it weren't the holidays, the day would have been a bust. But the optimist will take the credit:

Skills and rizz, baby; that's what it takes! They attribute their success to factors and qualities they carry with them at all times.

• **Personalization.** Who do you blame when things go wrong? Pessimists internalize their failures. *I suck at prospecting. Why did I think I should try this?* That's not taking accountability, that's punching themselves in the face and tying their failure to their overall self-worth. Optimists take responsibility when they make mistakes, but they also know they can improve. They may feel crappy when bad things happen, but it doesn't shake their overall belief in themselves.[37]

The most productive, successful sellers have positive explanatory styles, which leads to an overall optimistic mindset. If you don't think you have one now, start cultivating one (*Learned Optimism* will show you how). You won't survive prospecting or sales otherwise. Prospecting is hard. It takes a long time to get good at it. There will be days when you feel like the world hates you. And that's when you're doing everything right! No matter how much you excel, you're still going to get turned down or ignored more often than you connect and close. It's part of the game. So you have to start out every day believing that you're going to be successful and people are going to want to hear what you have to say. You'll practice this hundreds of times, and if you've got that optimistic mindset, with each rejection, you'll only get better. It's not about wearing rose-colored glasses to hide from reality; it's about staying open to learning, adapting, and growing.

TIP

If your inner Eeyore (the donkey from *Winnie the Pooh*, and a quintessential pessimist) comes out when you talk about your prospecting, don't sweat it; it happens to everyone.

Fortunately, there's a quick way to shift your explanatory style from permanent to temporary and nudge your way a little closer to optimism. Simply add the word **"yet."**

"I can't do this...yet."

"This isn't working...yet."

"I can't get buyers to listen...yet."

Psychologist Carol Dweck explains that by repeatedly adding the single, powerful word "yet" when you're judging your skills or abilities, you remind yourself that you're on a "learning curve." And if you're on a learning curve, that means you still have room to develop and acquire the skills you need to succeed.[38] Dweck says that this belief in your ability to learn and improve represents a growth mindset, and her research, outlined in her book *Mindset*, established that people who have one are more open to change, growth, and confidence, and take rejection better because they see it as an opportunity to improve. A growth mindset is inherently optimistic—it looks to the future, enjoys the learning process, and has faith in the value of its own hard work. It might be disappointed, but it's never defeated. Sounds like every successful seller we've ever known.

HELPFULNESS

Malik, looking forward to grabbing some lunch from the Korean place he likes a few blocks from his office, bounces on his toes, waiting impatiently for the Walk sign to turn so he and the crowd around him can cross the street. Directly in front of him, a young woman is also bouncing in her athletic wear, probably to keep moving but maybe also to the rhythm of whatever's playing through her earbuds. The sign turns to "Walk," and without looking, the young woman moves forward. Malik hears a horn beep from his left, but the woman doesn't respond—she likely can't hear the noise over her music. Malik grabs the woman's shoulders and yanks her backward just as a delivery bike whizzes by. The woman jerks her body out of Malik's hands and whirls around, her face quickly shifting from surprise to fear, and then, as her eyes dart from the road to Malik and what just happened sinks in, to relief. She smiles sheepishly and says, "Oh, my God, thank you so much. I'm an idiot."

Malik waves her off and calls out as he starts to cross the street, "Don't worry about it; it could happen to anyone. Just glad you're okay!"

The woman was rightfully alarmed when she felt a stranger grab her from behind. It's never okay for someone you don't know to touch you without permission. But Malik wasn't grabbing the woman because he was a creep; he grabbed her because he was trying to keep her from getting knocked over by a speeding bike. And the second the woman understood that his intent was to help, not hurt, her defensiveness and fear fell away. In this instance, Malik was met with gratitude, not fear or anger, for daring to break social norms.

We've talked about why humans treat strangers with skepticism, how much people today hate to be interrupted, and how generations of exploitative and manipulative sellers turned buyers against us altogether. But all that can change when buyers understand your intentions. When it's clear that your intent is to give, not to take, and to help, not harm, interruptions and broken social norms become not just acceptable but welcome. You'll be a lot more likely to earn your buyer's trust if you're in a truly helpful mindset, not a selling mindset.

The way to keep yourself in that helpful mindset is to stay problem-focused. Say you're selling skin care, and a big problem for the people who can benefit from your product is dark undereye circles. First, it's important to know why your buyer is bothered by dark circles. Is it that they're recently single and are concerned it's affecting their dating prospects? Is it that the discoloration has gotten worse over the years, and they're losing confidence in their physical appearance? You can't help if you don't know why someone wants to change, and to what. Second, yet equally important, you need to know the root cause. Is it age, illness, or insomnia? You know that your product has properties that can help with the first issue, but it's not going to do much for buyers struggling with either of the other two. The thing is, to get to the root cause, you don't even need to talk about your product. Try it. You'll see that your tone and approach will sound completely different if you're just trying to confirm whether this thing you think could be at the root of a problem is actually causing the problem, rather than convincing your buyers they have a problem. See the difference?

If your buyers agree that they have the problem and it bothers them, great. Now you can suggest a chat to talk about how you've helped other people with this problem solve it. But if they say it's not a problem, or it's not a problem they care about, that's great too! Now you're free to move on. You'll feel good about it if your goal isn't to book a meeting but to find the truth.

Prospecting with a helpful mindset can also help you get over any of the natural discomfort that comes with knowing that you're breaking all the social norms, like interrupting people and talking to strangers. You might have been told that your motivation should stem from your belief in the value of what you're selling. That's dead wrong. You want to believe in your power to spare buyers from the potential impacts of the problems you could solve. Lost money, time, resources, employees, reputation—saving buyers from those consequences is your motivation. In fact, that's what we're always doing when we're in a helping mindset—we're trying to save people. When you've done your PIC, and you can see the damage these problems can cause, it becomes your ethical responsibility to talk to people and help them. You're interrupting them the same way throwing a life preserver into the ocean interrupts a potential drowning. If it turns out your buyer's not drowning, well, cool then. Better safe than sorry.

RESILIENCE

A helpful mindset requires reaching deep into your humanity; a resilient mindset balances it out by demanding you stay detached. When you're unfazed by rejection, you can see it as a math problem—every person who tells you "No" statistically gets you closer to the person who's going to say "Yes." It's like playing pool—it's technically possible to sink the 8-ball on the break and win, but even good players usually have to take several shots first. That's not something to get you down; that's how the game is played.

Staying problem-focused and helpful also makes it easy to brush off rejection. Because when you're having a problem-focused conversation, it has nothing to do with you. It's much easier to bounce back and try again when you understand that it was your effort to help that was rejected, not you. If a buyer can't or won't admit to a problem they obviously have, or they're too short-sighted to see that they're hurting themselves in the long run by letting a problem fester, a resilient seller takes solace in knowing that they did what they could. When you carry a resilient mindset, you know that rejection is information and gets you one person closer to yes.

Take a good look at what's really happening when you're getting rejected, though. Are your buyers really saying that they don't have a problem or don't want your solutions, or is something else going on? You might take an unanswered email or unreturned call as evidence that the buyer isn't interested in your product. But how would you know? If your buyer didn't even read the email or listen to the voicemail or call, they don't know what you had to say. They're not rejecting the problem or even the product; they're rejecting the interruption. They're saying no out of reflex. You're Trevor when he was trying to give away the free gift cards. The passersby weren't rejecting free money; they were reacting to a stranger trying to hand them things they didn't ask for, because the pattern they'd learned is that to engage with strangers trying to hand you things you didn't ask for is generally a bad idea. You can fix that by selling intrigue and follow up by selling interest.

> **TIP**
>
> If you find it hard to recoup after rejection, try brainstorming ways in which rejection can be beneficial to you. A small study at UC San Diego suggested that reframing rejection as a positive experience might be helpful in improving our perception of our performance and persistence.[39] It certainly can't hurt to try.

ACCEPTANCE

Neither of us are patient people by nature. We're *get things done, solve problems now, live like there's no tomorrow* types. We're happiest in a world of variety and action. Meanwhile, prospecting is a damn slog. It's slow, boring, and monotonous and offers zero instant gratification. That's what makes it so hard. It requires patience, which is doubly hard for people like us. That's why we're not going to advise anyone to come to prospecting with a patient mindset, even though that would be ideal. The mindset that will get you to be patient, however, is one of acceptance. If you start out by accepting that prospecting is hard, that no silver bullet exists, and that you're not the super special person who's going to revolutionize it, you'll find it easier to take ownership of the process.

Acceptance gives you a competitive advantage. As Eckhart Tolle wrote in *The Power of Now*, "To complain is always nonacceptance of what is."[40] The person who's bitching and moaning about what a drag it is to make cold calls, even if just to themselves, won't be making cold calls much longer. They're expending too much energy on the whining instead of the work. If you're complaining, you haven't taken ownership of the process, because ownership is a matter of choice. Victims don't own shit except their victimhood. Owners embrace the process, which is why they're willing to do what other people don't have the patience, stamina, or emotional steel to do.

Don't get us wrong: Acceptance isn't passive. Acceptance gives you the wherewithal to make the intolerable, tolerable. Pool isn't much fun when it's easy—the challenge, competition, and satisfaction of making a tough-angle shot is the point. The same can be true of prospecting. So to turn tedium into something you look forward to tackling, gamify it. Lean into your competitive streak.

Both of us like to win. Like, a lot. We perform at our best in environments where we can pit ourselves against other sellers for the time we're on the clock. A leaderboard, a prize, or even just recognition is our rocket fuel. It isn't about the money, although that's not nothing; it's more about the bragging rights. We take pride in going all out, and it pays off. The side benefit is that when you can focus on the game of winning, the routine doesn't feel so boring. And the winning doesn't even have to be about who books the greatest number of meetings. Fight to see who can rack up the most rejections. That way, you lessen the pain while helping everyone get closer to the next yes. If you work alone, find some other way to challenge yourself, like trying to best your total calls made from day to day, seeing how many people you can make laugh, or doing push-ups every time you're rejected.

TIP

If you get rattled by rejection or have trouble tolerating what feels intolerable, you need to develop your grit. Grit is your way out of boredom and monotony. Earlier we said that an accepting mindset is a competitive advantage. So is grit. Grit has nothing to do with how skilled you are or how naturally talented. It's all about how hard you're willing to work, and specifically, how hard you're willing to work on the things no one else wants to do. Psychologist Angela Duckworth, who popularized the concept with her book *Grit*, says that being gritty isn't just about being stubborn. In fact, sheer stubbornness can be a trap that keeps you from making rational decisions to change course when necessary. According to Duckworth, grit is embodied by interest, practice, and hope tied to a sense of purpose, to a belief that what you're doing will have some meaning beyond yourself.[41] It's just more evidence of the power and benefits of having an optimistic and helpful mindset.

MASTERY-FOCUSED

We're often advised that the way to achieve our goals is to keep our eyes firmly on them. Not when it comes to prospecting (and maybe not when it comes to life in general, but that's another book). If instead of focusing on the endgame, you focus on your process and on the work you're putting in, and you do it well and consistently, the outcome will follow. The difference between a goal-oriented and mastery-focused mindset, though, is in what can happen if, for some reason, the outcome doesn't follow. If you're goal-oriented and you miss, there's nowhere to go, and it's easy to internalize it as a failure. You can see how that would sap someone's energy after a while and eventually cause them to quit. But when you're mastery-focused, there's no failure. Not only that, it makes you lose your fear of failure. You know that failing is good because it's an opportunity to learn and get better.

The mastery-focused mindset keeps you in the growth mindset, which is inherent in an optimistic mindset, which helps us stay in a helpful mindset, which makes it easier to be resilient in the face of rejection, which enables us to adopt an accepting mindset and find the grit to power through. All the power prospecting mindsets feed into each other. Make them yours, so that they're setting you up for success every time you start to craft an outbound message. If you commit to these mindsets, everything else will fall into place, and you'll have a lot of fun too.

In the next part of the book, you're going to learn how to take everything you've learned and apply it to individual channels. We'll do our best to give you timeless advice that won't become outdated, but the truth is, the world moves fast. Regardless, remember that no matter how AI turns everything upside down in ways we can't predict, and no matter how the best tactics change over time, the five mindsets are forever.

There is nothing so useless as doing efficiently that which should not be done at all. —Peter Drucker

PART IV

DOING THE WORK

PART IV · DOING THE WORK

You've come to the nuts-and-bolts part of the book, where we teach you to construct the most effective, intriguing messages that will grab your buyers' interest and launch you into the discovery and sale. We're not going to give you the perfect formulas to follow because what works today won't work as well or maybe even at all in five years. But we will explain the key elements for success in every currently popular channel and source for leads, such as referrals, because they won't change.

You probably have your favorite methods of outreach, but you need to use as many as possible. Better yet, use all of them. Every buyer and industry is different, of course. Most people ignore any phone call from a number they don't recognize, whereas Will picks up the phone every time it rings,* and he'll even respond to texts if they're interesting enough. Most of the emails in his inbox, however, remain unopened. Meanwhile, Keenan opens every email he gets.** To have the highest chance of connecting with people, you need to go where they live. If your research told you that a high concentration of your buyers love beignets, you would naturally start metaphorically (or not—face-to-face can work beautifully sometimes, as we'll see) knocking on doors in Louisiana, not Idaho. But you know there have to be plenty of people in Idaho who love beignets too, and probably even more who don't know they love beignets but would if given the chance to try them. Leave no beignet lovers behind! So, if you write perfect emails but suck on the phone, or vice versa, we've got some ideas to help you lean into your

---

* And usually hangs up just as fast, because most of what he hears are pitches, and most are, in his words, shite.
** And reads the first line or two before dumping them, because most are, in his words, shit.

strengths and to develop your skill set so you can reach your customers wherever they are. We'll also talk about when it's worth experimenting with niche or new channels, how to establish the right sequencing and cadence, and what you can do to create personal content that expands your ability to connect with people, in essence, using inbound to drive outbound conversations. Oh, and AI. You want to learn how to use AI correctly, right? We got you.

Ultimately, your success will depend on stuff we've already discussed, like your levels of optimism, dedication, and consistency. But above all, it will rely on your creativity. You can't win without it. Don't be intimidated. If you communicate from a place of caring and problem-solving, and commit to being yourself, you'll automatically come up with your own unique, credible, creative messaging.

The sales world sends too many emails. It builds campaigns at scale. Sellers are told to chase engagement from as many people as possible—even when most of them will never buy—and to call that progress.

You see it every day. You're expected to push volume, hit activity targets, and "scale" outreach, even though you know most of it is wasted effort. More touches. More sequences. More noise.

Prospecting may be a numbers game, but it is not a volume game. It's about reaching the right people, with the right message, at the right time, for the right reason.

Everything else is noise.

Everything else is wasted effort.

It's time to use more brain—and far less brawn.

CHAPTER THIRTEEN
IT'S ALL ABOUT THE LIST

Efraim lay on the couch, his head propped by a throw pillow. He was a classic portrait of modern-day relaxation. On his chest, a bowl of microwave popcorn. On his thighs, a laptop, playing his favorite YouTuber's channel. One hand carried popcorn from bowl to mouth with the regular rhythm of a metronome; the other, he used to scroll through his socials. His thumb pushed past one post after another—photos of Larissa's trip to Patagonia, Dante's latest bowl of ramen, and Mark complaining that his weekend plans had fallen through—and did anyone know of anything cool going on? His watch pinged him the first three notes of a lullaby, telling him it was time to go to bed. Eyes still glued to his phone, he was placing the popcorn bowl on the coffee table and starting to sit up when his thumb froze.

There she was with that familiar grin. Amy had hardly changed since they'd been in school together. In the picture, she and her son stood on the deck of a boat, smiling over a shiny, freshly caught fish. While her son beamed straight at the camera, Amy's face was turned toward the boy. The caption read *#mybestcatch*. *Sweet*, thought Efraim. He clicked to scroll through the rest of her feed to see what she'd been up to. They'd talked and had coffee when he first moved to the area but had lost touch, so much so that his algorithm hadn't shown him any of her content in what felt like forever. It looked like she was still living a nice life not too far from his. Lots of friends, lots of outdoor activity, lots of pictures of her son, or of her with her son, or of her son with friends. Efraim kept scrolling backward. Now he was looking for something. There. He was right—Amy's husband used to show up in her photos, yet there was no sign of him anywhere in the last two years' worth of posts. As Efraim headed to get ready for bed, he was testing out openers in his head for the text he'd send the next day: *Hey, Amy, it's been too long! Want to catch up?* In school he'd been too shy to ask her out. Maybe he was being given a second chance.

In another era, Efraim and Amy would have dropped out of each other's lives and probably never spoken again unless a random encounter at a concert or the airport had thrown them back into each other's orbits. But today, unless someone is actively keeping their online presence as incognito as possible, we're always just a few clicks away from anyone we want to talk to. Efraim wasn't stalking; he was doing his research the 21st-century way. Which is what sellers need to do before even thinking about making a cold call or writing an email. And maybe you are. But in our experience, many sellers are still using tools and methods developed a decade ago. As we've often told friends mourning breakups, you can do better.

Some people object to making comparisons between selling and dating, believing it trivializes relationships and flattens an emotionally complex process. We're not those people. Dating isn't that deep—it's about making a connection. To get there, you have to ask the correct questions. Are we right for each other? Do we complement each other? Do we want the same things? Is all that true at this particular place and time? And someone has to make the first move, especially when the person of interest has no idea the first mover exists. Using online recon and social media sleuthing to learn about people, the way Efraim did, is just a natural part of the process unless you're going on a true blind date. The parallel to the seller-prospect relationship is simply impossible to ignore. In outreach, there are no blind dates, but you can flirt with the right prospects. While you can't learn *everything* you need ahead of time to know whether you and a prospect will be a perfect match, in the history of selling, it's never been easier to make an astute, educated guess.

That's what Hansel Alvarez of Halva Editing did when he reached out to Will to talk about improving the quality and frequency of his YouTube videos. We introduced Hansel in Chapter 9 when we first talked about targeting buyers. He'd looked at Will's channel and seen great content and a few very successful videos. He'd also noted that the number of posts had recently decreased. Aha! A symptom. And like an experienced doctor, he knew that that particular symptom was generally caused by a certain big problem: a creator growing a successful business, too overwhelmed to be able to take the time to make, edit, and post videos regularly. Which, as it turned out, is exactly what Will was. Will was well aware that without a steady stream of new videos, his channel's growth was going to slow down. So when Hansel's email landed in his inbox and made Will feel seen and announced that Halva helped creators ideate and produce videos at a rate that encouraged their channel's growth while leaving them more time to tend to other parts of their business, and asked if Will wanted to have a conversation about that—well, yeah, Will was hella interested.

We already know how sellers like Hansel find buyers like Will—by scanning their publicly available information for symptoms and catalysts indicating the presence of particular problems. But the issue for sellers isn't just about finding people like Will, is it? It's about quickly and reliably finding enough people like Will to fill a whole sales pipeline. That's where a lot of sellers get stuck. Because even when they know their customers' problems through and through, and even when they've accurately identified the symptoms and catalysts that would indicate customers are suffering from those problems, most sellers do one of three things: 1) Randomly call or email companies, any companies, and send them all the same message, 2) Use prospecting platforms and outreach tools to identify large numbers of customers who might fit within a select parameter—say, medium-size software companies who've recently grown their HR department from 10-50%—and send them all the same message, or 3) search through each individual prospect's website, LinkedIn, and social media accounts to find specific symptoms or catalysts and customize each email or call script accordingly.

The first is like DMing everyone in your contact list and crossing your fingers that the single ones reply, guaranteeing a crap return rate, and contributing to the spam issues and distrust we talked about earlier in the book. The second is more targeted but still has a crap return rate. The third has a high return rate but takes eons and is impossible to scale. Regardless, any of these three tactics is like using printed maps in the age of GPS. There is another, better way.

We're going to show you how to bring your targeting strategies up to date with a method that allows you to compile a bigger list but still customize and personalize your outbound so you can connect with the right people efficiently, effectively, and successfully. If you're already using these tools, we'll make sure you get the most out of them. In the end, you won't just have a list; you'll have a list filled with the prospects most likely to be facing the problems you can solve.

Start Your Search

You know your product or service inside and out. You created a PIC (see Chapter 8) so you know what problems you can help solve, the impact they have, and their root causes. If you've followed the advice from Chapter 9, you've brainstormed all the external signs—the symptoms and catalysts in your CRM, and the ones AI may have provided. You could get good, specific information by scouring individual websites and LinkedIn pages, but the clock is ticking, and you have a quota to meet. This is why LinkedIn Sales Navigator has become many salespeople's best friend.

For any newcomers, this is how it works: Let's say were tracking a company called Clockworth, for which we identified ten viable symptoms and catalysts:

Pain Signals

1. Job listings with "track time," "billable hours," or "time reporting"

2. Mentions Clockworth or competitors in job listings or LinkedIn profiles

3. Company website offering an hourly paid service

4-9. Etc., etc.

10. Social posts complaining about time tracking, burnout, or scope creep

To find companies coping with Clockworth's #1 time-tracking symptom, you'd choose the geographic area on which you want to focus, and in the search bar, type "track time." LinkedIn can now present you with a list of all the job postings in your select area that mention the term—a flashing sign that a company is struggling with inaccurate time data, the most severe and common problem your company solves.

When you've exhausted your search, you'd go back to your AI suggestions and choose another symptom, such as #2, "Mentions Clockworth or competitors in job listings or LinkedIn profiles," or #3, "Company website offers an hourly paid service."

The process is time-consuming, but not as much as scouring hundreds of randomly chosen company websites, hoping to find a good reason to reach out. It's also super high-quality, promising a far better ROI than blindly sending out millions of emails or calling random numbers with a generic message. When you're done searching for all the symptoms and catalysts pointing to the biggest problems your product or service solves, you end up with a solid list of companies you have good reason to believe need your help. Not only does doing things this way make it easy for you to draft a personal and relevant message-opener, but it also allows you to prioritize these buyers ahead of hundreds or even thousands of other prospects about which you know absolutely nothing, and increases your chances of making a connection.

SCALE IT UP

Many salespeople use the strategy above successfully. The primary drawback, however, is scale. LinkedIn Sales Navigator is a great resource, but it still takes time to hunt all over each site to find the information you need. Nor are you going to be able to find all the symptoms and catalysts there. For example, a company's LinkedIn Page won't tell you that its employees are complaining about burnout or scope creep (public time-tracking symptom #10). You'd have to do a lot more poking around on social media sites or job-hunting platforms like Glassdoor. Unless for some reason you have a very short list of customers you want to focus on, you don't have time for that. Fortunately, there are tools you can use to quickly and efficiently search the internet for symptoms, catalysts, intent signals, and familiarity—in about the same time as it would take you to shower and brush your teeth.

The tools are called web scrapers. Some of the more popular ones at the moment are Clay, People Data Labs, and Ziggy AI. We have our favorites, but we're not going to make any specific recommendations.

Things move and change quickly; by the time this book goes to press, there could be another tool on the market that we like even better. So take what we offer here as a general guide to using this type of tool, not any one in particular, and keep an eye out for new products that will surely become available in the near future. Once you understand the possibilities, you'll be better able to experiment and find the one that works best for you. The process might look like this:

1. Use **LinkedIn Sales Navigator** to search for companies using the firmographic data you compiled about your ideal prospect, such as headcount, industry, and growth rates (see Chapter 9). Alternatively, if you already have an assigned account list, you would start with that.

2. **Transfer the list** of company names you got from LinkedIn or your account list to the web-scraping tool of your choice. Now, ask it to search for the symptoms or catalysts you've identified. All of them. Be specific with your prompts. The tool will scour the entire internet—LinkedIn, social media, Reddit, company blogs, you name it—and in seconds, identify which companies are flashing those signals. It can also show you which companies are showing one, two, or more of those signals. The companies ticking off the most boxes at once are the ones you should prioritize, as they're showing the most signs that they need your help right away.

Start Connecting!

What you have now is the material to ensure that you're talking about the right things to the right people. Using what you've learned, you can place your prospects into prioritized categories. For example, your first group shares four of the same symptoms, the next group shares three symptoms, and so on and so forth. Now you can rapidly draft a single message that's personalized enough to make all the prospects within each category feel special and chosen and specific enough to spark intrigue (cue the dating parallel again).

We'll talk about how to craft those messages in the next chapters. Starting off with a robust, trustworthy list sets a solid foundation that will make everything you do next easier and ratchet up your chances of sales success. You'll see—prospecting doesn't have to break your heart. Just ask Efraim. His hunch was correct, and Amy was divorced. When she agreed to meet him to catch up, it was just the first "yes" of many that led to a long, happy relationship.

CHAPTER FOURTEEN
HOW TO WIN AT COLD CALLING
WITHOUT BEING A PUSHY WANKER
(AS WILL WOULD SAY)

We're not ones to sugarcoat, so here's the truth: Cold calling's a bitch. We shared the bonkers-bad cold-calling numbers and technology-driven trends in Chapter 1—a 3.9% connection rate, with fewer than 40% of people who pick up staying on the phone for more than 30 seconds;[42] the vast majority of Americans admitting they don't answer phone calls if they don't recognize the number;[43] and the young generations just now entering the workforce at best treating live phone calls with suspicion and, at worst, as useless relics from the dark ages.[44] We've also talked about how actions and behaviors inherent in cold calling, like interrupting strangers and making ourselves vulnerable, force us to go against every evolution-designed socialization rule meant to keep us safe and "in" with the group to ensure our survival. And here's something we haven't yet talked about—today, most cold calls are recorded. So if the call goes pear-shaped, as they say in the UK, you don't always get to hang up, shake it off, and move on. Rather, there's a good chance you'll get to relive your misery over and over while your manager dissects your performance and tells you why you suck. Together, that makes for a list that could cause anyone to crash out. So we truly, deeply get why so many people would almost rather get a chili-powder enema than make cold calls.

However, while the above is true, so is this:

- "Top-performing reps are **2.5x more likely** to use the phone than their lower-performing peers."[45]

- In 2023, **69% of buyers** had accepted a cold call from sales representatives within the last 12 months.

- **More than 50% of C-level and VPs** prefer to be contacted by phone than other channels. Almost half of managers prefer it.[46]

So the truth is actually two-fold: Cold calling's a bitch, and it still works. That may be hard for you to swallow. We suspect a lot of people embrace the myth that cold calling is dead because it lets them off the hook. After all, if it's dead, why bother trying? The myth gives them permission to tell themselves it's okay to send out a bunch of emails, and then a bunch more, and then more and more and more, and not make any calls. But it's not as if cold email-open rates are dramatically better than cold-call connection rates. Moaning about a light pipeline but refusing to cold call because people might not pick up, or might be mean if they do, is like complaining that you can't find a romantic partner but refusing to date because you run the risk of getting ghosted or rejected. You need to use every means possible to reach buyers, because they need to hear from you, even if they don't realize it yet.

Consider what happened to Michele Ferri. In 2013, the Italian received two phone calls from an unknown number. Obviously, he ignored it, as most people do when they don't recognize a phone number. The next day, the phone rang again.[47] Same number. Who the heck was this? This time, his curiosity piqued, he picked up. The voice on the other end said: "Hello, Michele, it's Pope Francis." At first he thought it was a prank. But then the caller mentioned the contents of a letter Ferri had written to the pontiff in a moment of deep grief following the murder of his brother in a gas station robbery earlier that year.[48] Ferri couldn't believe it. The head of the Roman Catholic Church was calling *him*? Direct? "I was speechless," Ferri told *GQ*.[49] In the end, he said that the call gave him "comfort and hope."[50]

You don't have to tell us that there would be a big difference between how people would react to getting a cold call from the pope—certainly if they were devout Catholics—or a well-loved celebrity like Harrison Ford or Beyoncé, and how they'd react to receiving a cold call from, like, Frank the insurance broker. We know that. But the fact that people would be surprised and delighted if someone important, famous, or popular called out of the blue just to be nice means that cold calling in and of itself isn't something people object to. What people object to are cold calls that lack relevance to their lives, serve no purpose, or are obvious money grabs or scams. In fact, your initial excitement over hearing from Beyoncé or Harrison Ford would wear off in a millisecond if you realized the only reason they were calling was to pitch you life insurance or a banking app—that they were selling for themselves, not for you. Cold calling does work—*so long as you're doing it right.* And if you're doing it right, your cold calls aren't that different from those made by Pope Francis (who made so many, Italians nicknamed him the "Cold Call Pope"[51])—they're a form of service, a way to be helpful and offer value through something you believe will make people's lives better. They're also the quickest way to get the information that will tell you if your buyer needs what you're offering. So it's a fundamental part of sales, and unless you have a team of SDRs doing this work for you, there's no getting around it. And since you have to do it, you also have to get good at it. This chapter is going to show you how, step by step.

SUCCESSFUL CALLS DEPEND ON GOOD PREP

There are several preparatory steps you must take before you start to make calls. Skip any one of them, and you'll set yourself up for failure.

- **Build a strong, personalized list.** You just read about how to do this in the last chapter. It ensures that while your prospects may not be expecting your call, they might at least be receptive to hearing you out.

- **Remember the purpose of the call.** It's not to book a meeting. It's not to get information that you can use. It's to get to the truth. Does the person you're calling have a problem you can solve or not? The end. The purpose of the call shifts once you get your answer. If they don't have a problem, or one you can solve, your purpose then becomes to quickly move on so you can get to the next prospect. If they do have a problem that you can solve, the purpose of the call now is to build trust and help them see the value in letting you help them. Only when you've achieved that milestone should your thoughts turn to booking a meeting.

SET YOUR GOALS

Not your sales goals. Your call goals. First, decide how long you're going to spend making calls without stopping, and block that chunk of time out on your calendar. Coming to the calls with a solid list will help keep you focused and moving quickly, because you won't need to stop after every call and figure out who you're going to call next. You'll simply move down the list from name to name, leaving no room for wasted time or distraction. Second, remove all temptation to do anything other than make those calls. Getting rid of distractions is important, because if you hate cold calling as much as most people, anything—answering a Slack message, writing an email, cleaning up your desk, scrolling on social media—sounds better than making cold calls, and if you allow it, you'll wind up doing those immediately gratifying things and not the hard but productive thing. Some people even turn off emails and put their cell phones on silent or Do Not Disturb to make sure no distractions can pull their attention away. Whatever it takes to keep you focused on your calls, do it.

Technology will help you speed through your block of time too. We're going to assume that you're using some kind of online platform. If you're still using an office or mobile phone, stop. It's just too inefficient to tap out the numbers one by one, and the lag between calls makes it super tempting to allow yourself to be distracted. Our first picks at this moment are Orum, PhoneBurner, or Salesfinity, but use the platform of your choice. There are a few types:

- **Click-to-Dial.** This allows you to manually work through your CRM by individually clicking on each number. You initiate the call, and the platform does the dialing. It's up to you to decide to move on to the next number, so you're essentially recommitting to your goal every time you choose to make a call. It's effective, but it requires a lot of willpower, and it's not the speediest option.

- **Power Dialer.** This system automatically moves you down your list from one number to the next, speeding up the process and putting you on autopilot until you decide you want to take control back. The moment you end one call, the next begins, so there's little time between each call. You don't lose momentum, and there's no room to get nervous while you're waiting for someone to pick up.

- **Parallel Dialer.** This is like a premium version of the power dialer. Instead of calling one person at a time, it automatically calls multiple people at once. The second someone picks up, it drops all the other calls. If two people pick up at once, it prioritizes the person who answered first. You do run the risk of missing an opportunity should two people pick up at the same time, but with pickup rates so low, that scenario is pretty unlikely. This tool is especially useful if you have a big market and a long list. It's also the most expensive of the three options we've listed here.

Decide how many calls you'll make within your dedicated block of call time and how many connections you want to make. A call doesn't count as a connection unless it lasts 30 seconds or more. Thirty seconds will give you enough time to say more than a cursory hello and allow you to confirm you're talking to the right person for the topic of your call. After that, the length of your call will depend on your prowess in showcasing problems and handling objections and excuses (more on that later).

PROTECT YOUR PHONE NUMBER

You'll want to take steps to prevent your phone number from getting flagged as "Scam Likely," or "Spam Risk," which is a sure-fire way to keep you from reaching your intended prospects. It happens when carriers detect high call volume with low answer rates, frequent calls that disconnect quickly, or your number is reported by a recipient. Use multiple phone numbers and rotate them regularly to reduce the risk of any one line getting flagged. We don't recommend that you alter your zip code to match every prospect's, but do call from a mobile number and make your area code reflect the country you're calling from (for example, New York if you're in the U.S., or Toronto if you're in Canada) so it feels familiar to your buyer and eases any concerns about getting hit with long-distance calling fees. Finally, test each number you use by calling yourself to confirm it doesn't appear as possible spam.

Track Everything

Don't just trust that you'll stick to your goals or measure progress by vibes and feels. Create a dashboard to track and analyze all your data. You do this for two reasons. First, so you can hold yourself accountable for your effort, interactions, and results. Second, to keep yourself motivated. Once you see your numbers start to sing, you'll be encouraged to keep doing what's working and do more of it. If you don't like what you see, that's good information too. Now you won't get stuck flailing around in a hopeless vacuum, wondering what's gone wrong. Instead, you'll have access to high-quality data that shows where you're falling short so you can start figuring out how to do better in the areas where you have the most control.

Check your progress at the end of each week to see where you're making progress or even nailing it—or not. You can use the dialer, sales engagement platform, or CRM of your choice, or even create an Excel sheet or Google sheet.

Your dashboard should include:

- Your call goals

- The number of calls made

- The number and duration of your connections

It might seem like these data points are out of your control. You can't force someone to be at their desk at the right time, pull their attention away from what they're doing just because their phone rang, or pick up at all. What you can do, however, is optimize your chances of making that connection. It may take double-checking your contact data and some time and experimentation, but since you're tracking, you'll be able to see inflections where you reached more people and were able to book more meetings. You'll learn what times of day your buyers are at their desks, which companies shut down for lunch, and which have an owner who's frequently on-site. If you find that you're frequently not reaching the right person, that's a sign that you're calling too late, too early, or on the wrong day. One of our clients sells to dentists. He learned that if he called at normal business hours, he connected with receptionists who usually kept him away from their bosses and had no decision-making power. When he switched things up and started calling a little before 8 a.m., the office manager or even the owner of the practice was usually already in the office alone and would often pick up the phone. You'll learn how to adjust for different time zones if you're covering a broad or even international market.

Your Meeting Goals

Though the purpose of these calls won't be to set meetings, you'll want to keep in mind how many meetings you ultimately want to make. Whether you reach that goal will be contingent on your problem proposition, your skill in handling objections, whether you ask the right questions, and your method and timing when setting up the meeting.

Meetings Held

How many of the meetings that you set actually happened? Keep track of the reasons people offer for canceling. Follow up to see if you can find out why someone is a no-show.

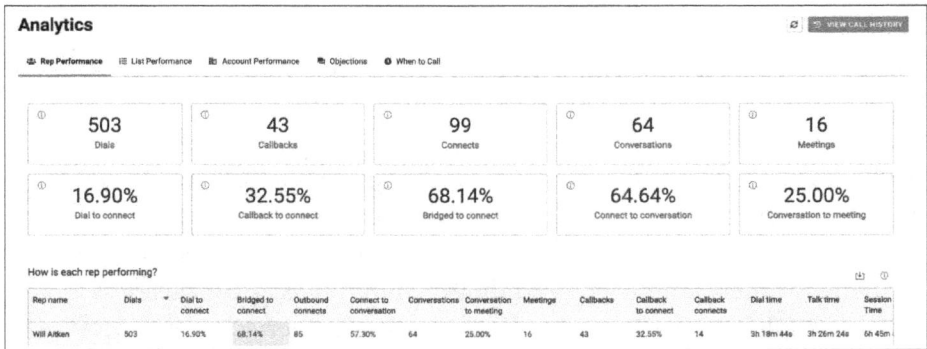

Analytics

VIEW CALL HISTORY

Rep Performance | List Performance | Account Performance | Objections | When to Call

503	43	99	64	16
Dials	Callbacks	Connects	Conversations	Meetings

16.90%	32.55%	68.14%	64.64%	25.00%
Dial to connect	Callback to connect	Bridged to connect	Connect to conversation	Conversation to meeting

How is each rep performing?

Rep name	Dials	Dial to connect	Bridged to connect	Outbound connects	Connect to conversation	Conversations	Conversation to meeting	Meetings	Callbacks	Callback to connect	Callback connects	Dial time	Talk time	Session Time
Will Aitken	503	16.90%	68.14%	85	57.30%	64	25.00%	16	43	32.55%	14	3h 18m 44s	3h 26m 24s	6h 45m

Buyer Responses and Objections

If you consistently get pushback after your opener, the problem is probably your opener. (Instructions for great openers are coming later in this chapter.) Is there a particular moment in the conversations where you often get stumped and lose the prospect? This is the kind of information you want to have so you can fine-tune your approach. Practice doesn't make perfect simply because of repetition. Practice makes perfect because you pay attention to what does and doesn't work and adjust accordingly. If you regularly try to bake your favorite chocolate-chip cookie recipe but substitute carob every time, they will never, ever taste right until you make the correct adjustment, which is to use real chocolate chips.

CHECK YOUR MINDSET

We covered the five mindsets of prospecting in Chapter 12, but there is one—Helpfulness—that deserves to be mentioned again because it's the main bulwark against fear, which is most responsible for keeping people from cold-calling success or cold calling at all.

If you saw someone drop their credit card and not notice, what would you do? If you're a loser, you'd say nothing. But you're not a loser. You're helpful, so you'd pick up the credit card and hand it back to its owner, because you wouldn't want a thief to get their hands on the card, and you'd want to spare the card owner the headache of canceling the card once they realized it was missing.

If you met someone at a party who mentioned their special-needs kid would benefit from a specific program at a private school, but they hadn't yet found a better-paying job that would allow them to afford tuition, and you knew about a good-paying job opening that was a perfect fit, what would you do? You like to be helpful, and you want what's best for your new acquaintance and their child, so you'd tell them about the job.

When you have a helpful mindset, you do what you do because it's right. Keeping that mindset while cold calling makes prospects' behavior when answering the phone irrelevant, at least in the short term. You're there to save people money and put more in their pockets, help bosses provide for their employees and their own families, grow businesses, and make people's lives easier. That's the case whether someone decides to talk to you or not, which means if they don't engage, it's really their loss, not yours. Keeping that mindset will help you go into every call with more confidence, because when someone picks up the phone, you'll know you're not being a pest; you're doing them a favor.

WELCOME THE CHANCE TO PRACTICE

Don't think of cold calling as something you have to do; think of it as something you get to do. You get to talk to new people. You get to share your knowledge. You get to improve. Go in knowing that the more you're exposed to rejection, the less it will bother you. So get it over with! You'll see how resilient you are. You'll see that with repetition comes inoculation. You'll build a resistance to negativity. Your skin will get tougher. And one day, you won't be afraid of cold calling anymore. To get to that state faster, you need to get busy doing it...over and over and over, until you no longer feel fear, and all the world sees is an effective, confident, and smooth operator

Confidence is key, and yours will grow when you realize that even if the call goes badly, the world isn't going to end. The buyer can't find you. They can't hurt you. You'll still be the same person, even if someone decides to call you a name or treat you like dirt (hey, it happens). Remember that when people are rude or abusive, it says more about their state of mind than your character or worth. As Keenan likes to say, no one can make you feel anything you don't allow them to. When it comes to cold calling, the only real thing you have to fear is losing your job, or a chance at an awesome career, if you don't do it. As Zig Ziglar supposedly said: "You don't have to be great to start, but you have to start to be great."

FOLLOW THE 5 RULES OF COLD CALLING
Ignore this advice at your peril:

1. **Be yourself.** This isn't a performance. You have to believe in what you're saying and feel good saying it. There's no faster way to make someone hang up on you than to put on a fake "best friend" voice—"Hey, Beth! How ARE you on this beautiful day?" Similarly, if you sound bored or tired, or like you're reading from a script, don't bother. You want to project friendliness, helpfulness, and confidence.

2. **Control your tone.** Some sellers believe that cold calls are superior to written communication because when we call, we have the ability to control our tone. Chris Ritson, co-founder of The SDR Leader, goes so far as to claim that vocal tone is 4.5x more powerful than our actual words.[52] Regardless, there's no dispute that the tone of your voice matters when you're try-

ing to engage with people, and matters a lot (just ask those of us who tried challenging our parents with a dramatic sigh and seemingly innocuous, "What?" only to be met with a threatening "Watch. Your. Tone." that sent us racing to our room). You want your tone to sound strong and steady, so take deep breaths through the diaphragm, which will support your voice. And smile, especially at the beginning of the call. Research from the University of Portsmouth revealed that even when they can't see the person speaking, listeners can not only determine when speakers are smiling, but they can also tell what kind of smile is on the speaker's face (full-blown showing teeth, for example, or a smaller half-smile).[53] And there's evidence that even "auditory smiles" compel listeners to smile back, even when they can't see the speaker.[54] To make sure your face and voice reflect the enthusiasm and positivity you're feeling inside, and encourage that same feeling in others, try propping up a mirror and watch yourself as you make calls.

Now, you'll probably have to adjust your tone as the conversation progresses. That's where your empathy will come into play. If your buyer gets real with you and admits they're struggling with a big problem, or expresses anxiety, don't respond with sunshine and pep—that would be tone-deaf. Listen closely to your buyer and use your voice to reflect back the emotional support they need. Your tone will be a key tool for building trust.

3. **Keep it short.** Get to the point fast. Make every word count. That said, you'll see later in this chapter that we disagree a little on what words count—some things have to be left to personal taste. But the general rule will still be to select your words carefully and keep your sentences and message very short and simple, so they're easily heard and absorbed.

4. **Pace yourself.** Don't talk too fast. Slower speech sounds clearer and more confident, which leads people to pay closer attention. You don't want buyers straining to understand you or asking you to repeat yourself. Most won't bother anyway. They'll just hang up or make up an excuse to get off the phone.

5. **Practice outside work time.** You'll never get enough practice if you plan on using your cold calls as actual practice time. With the rate of connections what they are, you'll only get a few chances to speak with actual prospects; you don't want to waste a real opportunity as a practice round. Treat cold calling as a competitive sport. That means practicing on your own time and showing up for the main event warmed up and ready to do your best.

   Rehearse your script with a teammate, friend, or family member. If you're not comfortable doing that, use AI to role-play. (Keenan's company, ASG, offers a powerful roleplay and AI-coaching tool that can make a huge difference here. We'll put more information about it in the back of the book.) The ChatGPT and Claude mobile apps currently have voice modes that support a two-way conversation, and most other AI systems are in the process of developing voice mode. Ask your system to play the role of CEO, or whatever title is most appropriate for your purposes, and make it challenge you so you can practice working through a variety of types of calls. Do it enough, and you'll prime your brain so that it knows what to say in all circumstances.

6. **Don't give up too soon.** You might decide you like some of our ideas, try them twice, and then decide they don't work and go back to your old way of doing things. You have to give new techniques time. It takes a lot of repetition to get good at this.

How to Write a Call Script

So what do you actually say to increase the chances of you having an actual conversation when someone picks up the phone? Depends on who you ask. Like most experts in their field, we agree on the big picture of what a great sales call should sound like, but our approaches subtly differ. We're going to present both options to you, along with our thinking on why they work, and you can pick the version that makes the most sense to you. Or try them both (for at least a few hundred calls—see Rule #6 above) and see what feels most natural. Neither strategy is better or worse. The one you're most comfortable with is the one that will work best for you.

For the sake of this exercise, the product we're selling is a global online payment platform to e-commerce businesses—the system that allows you to securely make online purchases by plugging in your credit card number. We've named our fictional company Solvis.

COLD CALL OPENER

We're going to assume that you followed our advice from the last chapter and put together a killer list that ensures you're reaching out to the right people about relevant problems, which will allow you to use the same personalized opener for every call. As you can see, Will tends to warm up his prospects a little more, and Keenan prefers to be more direct.

> **Will:** Sophia, I was just on your payments page and saw that you're using Slo-Mo online payment provider. I have a weird question for you. It's Will Aitken from Solvis. Got a moment to help me out?

> **Keenan:** Hi, this is Keenan from Solvis online payment company. I know I'm interrupting you. Can I take 30 seconds to tell you why I called?

There are two parts to these openers: a greeting and a call to action.

GREETING

Pop quiz: What's the first sale you make in any greeting, in any format, from calls, to email, to DMs?

Answer: Intrigue. (For a refresher, go back to Chapter 11.)

Our cold call greetings create intrigue in ways that reflect our distinct philosophies and preferences. Let's break them down:

> **Keenan:** "Hi, this is Keenan from Solvis online payment company. I know I'm interrupting you. Can I take 30 seconds to tell you why I called?"

Keenan believes in acknowledging the interruption right up front. People generally appreciate it when you make it clear you know they're working hard, and that they just intruded. *Hey, someone who gets that my life is super busy. I like that.* Not many sellers do it, so it will be a nice surprise.

What does surprise do? It creates intrigue.

> **Will:** "Sophia, I was just on your payments page and saw that you're using Slo-Mo. I have a weird question for you. It's Will Aitken from Solvis. Got a moment to help me out?"

Will finds that making observations builds familiarity. That's why he doesn't start out by saying his name but by making a statement about something he knows to be true about the buyer. By showing he's done his research, he's announcing that he's not some generic telemarketer calling at random but a seller who has targeted his buyer for a specific reason. Most people find it unexpected to meet a seller who's done so much homework already, and unexpectedness sparks intrigue.

He continues with: "I have a weird question for you."

Will likes to use the adjective "weird" because it creates curiosity and more intrigue. It's not what the buyer is expecting to hear, which leads them to think *Weird? What kind of question could this be?*

"It's Will Aitken from Solvis."

Only now does Will say his name, almost as an afterthought. You want to identify yourself to keep people's natural defensiveness and suspicions in check, but only after you've piqued their attention with intrigue.

CALL TO ACTION

Keenan: "Hi, this is Keenan from Solvis online payment company. I know I'm interrupting you. Can I take 30 seconds to tell you why I called?"

This call to action is for time.

You're telling your buyer what you're asking for and presenting them with the cost of action versus inaction. *Thirty seconds? That's nothing! I can take 30 seconds to make sure I know what I'm turning down.* Now you've sparked interest and primed the prospect to listen closely.

Now let's see Will's call to action.

Will: "Sophia, I was just on your payments page and saw that you're using Slo-Mo. I have a weird question for you. It's Will Aitken from Solvis. Got a moment to help me out?"

This call to action is for help.

Again, it's a surprise, so more intrigue. Usually, when you ask someone for help, they're inclined to say, "Yes." Most of us have been taught that we're supposed to help people when they ask for it, so for most people, it feels weird to refuse.

Both of these calls to action are permission-based. That is, they explicitly allow the buyer a chance to opt out of the conversation. Critics will say you should never give a prospect the option to say, "No." We disagree. Give people a choice. Without choice, they feel trapped or like you're bulldozing them into submission. That doesn't spark their intrigue; it sparks their fight-or-flight instinct. Now instead of a willing participant in the conversation, you're dealing with a wild animal looking for a way out, one that's more likely to shout at you, or even curse and insult you, and then hang up. In our experience, staying humble and giving people the choice of whether to talk to you diminishes the chances they'll react in a volatile way and increases the chance they'll a) want to hear why you called, or b) help you out.

The other commonality in these two greetings? Nowhere do we mention our product or what it does.

Pop quiz: What's the #1 rule of prospecting?

Answer: No one gives a shit about your product or service.

The only way to earn a buyer's time is to talk about the buyer and prove you understand their world.

You can tweak your opener any way you choose to fit your style and personality, as long as it's crafted to send the greeting and call to action in a quick, easy-to-absorb way.

ICEBERG CALL OPENER

If you've built a good list, you'll always be able to find a reason to connect with a prospect. But let's say you're new at this, or you inherited a weak list, and you really are just randomly calling a number, making it an iceberg-cold call. You can try this:

"Hi, Jerome. You weren't expecting my call; however, if you have a moment to chat, I promise I'll be brief."

Honesty can be disarming and refreshing, which is intriguing.

WARM CALL OPENER

The highest-quality prospect, the crème de la crème, is one who has already expressed some level of interest in, or had a positive interaction with, your service or product. For example, you can see that they downloaded something from your website, or they attended one of your webinars. This is when you can make a familiarity play, as discussed in Chapter 9. From that information, you should be able to infer what problems they might be dealing with. So your greeting should lead with that.

"Hi, Sophia, it's Will from Solvis. I saw that you downloaded our failed-payment benchmarking guide. Typically, when people do that, they're unable to accept certain credit card types, or they're dealing with chronic transaction failures."

Remember, when familiarity exists, intrigue is less important. So in a warm call, once you announce why you reached out, you can jump straight to the next phase, Probe for Problems.

PROBE FOR PROBLEMS

Back to our original cold call. We've requested a call to action—give us time or help. Let's assume the buyer agrees to one or the other. That's our cue to move on to the next part of the call, the problem proposition.

Will: "I can't be sure if it's the same for you, but when I work with people who are also using Slo-Mo, I've found that they're usually running into one of two *really* big challenges. Do you mind if I briefly share those with you?"

Wait a minute, Will's asking permission *again*? Yes, and here's why: If you can get your prospect double opted-in with another "Yes," it ensures they understand what you're doing, and that they're actually going to listen to the next thing you say. If they've said "Yes" twice, they're much more likely to say "Yes" again, which, as you'll see, will be important when we get to the next phase of the call.

Note that Will emphasizes the word "really," as in "one of two *really* big challenges." That's intentional. Modulating your voice, making it a little louder and giving the word some oomph, offers up another surprise and helps enhance that sense of intrigue. (If it feels more natural to emphasize the word "two," or "big," that's fine. The point is to avoid losing your buyer's attention as they get used to your voice.)

The prospect says, "Yes," so Will continues:

Will: "The first big challenge for Slo-Mo users is that they aren't always able to accept certain credit card types, and the second is transaction failures. Can you relate to either of these? Or are you going to tell me I'm off base, and your transaction success is so high, this isn't even on your radar?'

A few things to note here. First, the questions are specific. Will isn't mentioning problems that anyone with a good AI prompt could come up with. These problems should be born from long-term experience with your customers and a deep understanding of the issues that plague them most.

Second, it's useful to ask a two-part question. Like a lawyer who never asks a question to which they don't know the answer, you'll ask the first one—"Can you relate?"—because you'll know that most of your competitors' customers have these problems. That's where the second question comes in—"Or am I off base?" Will says it playfully because he finds it's a good way to take accountability, to not come across as accusatory, and to mitigate against the common knee-jerk response, which is usually that everything's fine. Asking the question like this challenges the buyer's thinking in a non-combative way: *Like, are you sure?* When they stop and reflect about what they've been asked (remember how important that is), they usually realize that actually, everything isn't fine. If they're lying just to get you off the phone, you've given them a way to save face and end the conversation if they choose. And if they're not, you just solidified your connection, and the chances of you both getting something out of this conversation just went up tenfold.

Keenan, however, has a different method. He doesn't want to utter a single syllable that he doesn't have to, so he'd ask the question like this:

> **Keenan:** "The reason I called is that we've found that compa-
> nies suffer with walk-away customers, or lost sales (problem), when
> they're not able to accept certain credit card types or when there
> are transaction failures (root causes). Do either of these issues sound
> familiar?"

Keenan *wants* their knee-jerk reaction, because if they say, "No,
we're fine," that gives him an opening to keep talking.

> **Keenan:** "Really? That's surprising. Can I ask you one question?
> When you don't accept the payment type the customer has, what
> happens to the sale? Do you ever lose the sale, or do they always
> have cash?"

This allows Keenan to challenge the prospect to reflect on the situation. Keenan knows that when a vendor doesn't carry a certain payment
type, it's common for them to lose the sale. The vendor knows this too,
but they're operating from their flight-or-fight response. By posing the
question as Keenan does, he's forcing the buyer to confront their reality
and ask themselves, *If this is true, and I know we lose sales because we don't
have a certain payment type, am I willing to continue to live with it, or is it in my best
interest to give this caller a few minutes to see if they can address it?*

ASK QUESTIONS

In Will's scenario, our prospect admits that they've experienced transaction failures. Now it's time to drill down to the specifics.

> **Will:** "How long has this been happening? When did you notice?
> It sounds like this is actually costing you some opportunities. Am I
> getting that right?"

In Keenan's scenario, the prospect denies that their business has experienced either problem, but because Keenan knows his customers,
and he knows his competitors' strengths and weaknesses, he suspects
that's not true. Because his question put the buyer in a place to reflect

and choose between addressing a known issue by giving this caller time, or denying the truth and letting it fester, more times than not, the buyer will give Keenan the few minutes he's asking for.

> **Keenan:** "I understand you lose sales because you don't offer certain payment types. How often does this happen, and what is your average transaction size?"
>
> **Prospect:** "About 5-15% of the time, or about 20 times a day, and our average transaction is $100."
>
> **Keenan:** "So what I'm hearing is you're losing about $2,000 a day because you don't offer other types of payment options. Am I understanding you correctly?"
>
> **Prospect:** "I've never thought about it that way, but yes, I guess that would be close."

For those not doing the math, that's $700,000 a year in lost transactions because the prospect doesn't take certain payment types. By forcing the buyer to reflect, the buyer is confronted with a problem they may have felt but not truly understood or quantified. Now that Keenan has helped them see it, they can't unsee it and are almost certain to engage in solving it.

ASK FOR THE MEETING

We agree on how to ask for the meeting.

> **Seller:** "Understanding that you're losing customers and potentially up to $700k a year because you don't take other payment methods, does it make sense to schedule a meeting to discuss how we can help address that?"
>
> **Answer:** "If you show me how to get the leads back, yes, I'd be interested."
>
> **Seller:** "What works for you? I have time on Friday at 2 p.m."
>
> **Answer:** "Friday, 2 p.m. works."
>
> **Seller:** "All right, for your email, I've got name@email.com. Is that the best address for me to send you an invite? Great. Talk to you then!"

If someone seems chatty and interested in giving you more time, you can match their mood and energy and extend this phase. Will would use it to grab any qualifying information he hadn't yet been able to get, like transactions numbers per month, how long they'd been using their current payment system, and what other systems they'd tried.

But your #1 goal should be to move as fast as you can to getting them to admit that yes, they have a problem that they need to fix, and yes, they'll give you a chunk of time later in the week to talk more in depth about the options and how you, the seller, can help. The faster the better.

OBJECTIONS

If you craft your script by following the rules as outlined above, you won't hear as many objections as you might expect. If you do, it's probably because, though you don't realize it, you're still talking about your product or service and how and why it works. Notice that in our example, by the time we get to the end of the conversation, we *still* haven't once told our buyer anything about our product or service. We've suggested that we can help, but we haven't yet explained *how* we can help. We know as much as possible about the buyer's world and the buyer's problems, but they don't know a thing about us. That's the secret. Do not pitch! No one can object to your product if the conversation has solely revolved around their problem. All they can do is object to the call itself.

Here's how to handle those types of knee-jerk responses:

YOU ASK THE PROSPECT IF THEY CAN HELP YOU OUT OR SPEND 30 SECONDS ANSWERING A QUESTION, AND THEY SAY, "NO, I'M HEADING INTO A MEETING."

Might be a lie. If you hear this one a lot, you should probably analyze your tone and opener and see if you could be coming across as off-putting or salesy. But maybe it's true. Which is why if you hear that objection, you could respond with:

> "I understand. I don't want to keep you from the meeting. While I've got you, though, could I take just 30 seconds to explain what I saw on your website that prompted me to call? That way I won't interrupt you again if I call back later."

By agreeing with them that they should absolutely prioritize their meeting, you're respecting their busy schedule and making sure they understand that this isn't a random sales call but a targeted outreach to discuss a real issue, which they might find intriguing enough to warrant telling you a better day or time to try again.

You Announce the Two Common Problems You See People Dealing With, and They Say, "We've Already Got a Solution In Place for That."

If you're getting this objection, it's the first sign that even if you think you did what we told you to do, you didn't. This objection only arises if you come out the gate sounding like a telemarketing game show host, which will send your prospect's lizard brain scrambling for the first excuse they can come up with to make their escape. The other possibility is that you think you talked about your prospect's problems, but in reality, your opener was product-focused. Go back and analyze your script.

However, your goal is to get to the truth, right? And you might still be able to with the following reply:

> "I'm not surprised to hear you're doing something for this already; most folks are. Many still run into [problem], though, so is it that this just isn't an issue, or did I call at a bad time, and you actually just hate getting these calls?"

You might as well learn if they really don't need you or if they think you're a pain in the ass. If it's the latter, you might be able to redeem yourself.

"We Don't Have Either of Those Problems"

Hooray for them, but if you've done your research and they still wound up on your list, it's probably not true. Try to establish their success metrics.

> "You're not seeing failed payments? Terrific! One hundred percent across the board? Oh, not quite? I see. So there's still a percentage of your payments that fail."

This is where the knowledge and expertise you've worked so hard to gain are going to serve you well. Don't challenge; do be curious enough to question the buyer's definitions and vague statements. If you drill down to the specifics, you can often discover inaccuracies and introduce a level of doubt, leading them to realize that what they thought was "great" could be measurably greater.

"Send Me an email"

Too many sellers agree to this and never make contact again. Don't waste this opportunity, and don't waste your time sending a generic email this buyer will never open. Here's what you say:

> "I'd be happy to send you an email, but the last thing I'd want to do is clutter your inbox with irrelevant information that's not valuable to you. If I could just ask a few questions to get a feel for what's going on in your organization and what problems you're dealing with, I can then send you some specific information that targets those issues specifically."

"Not Interested/No Thanks"

Not interested in what? No thanks to what? If you properly led with a problem, those responses don't make sense. They're not natural. More likely, what you're hearing is a reflexive response, and the buyer's not really thinking about what you've said. So get them to clarify:

> "I'm a little confused. Can you help me understand? I asked about your problems. Are you telling me you don't have any?"

If you get this objection, it doesn't mean the buyer isn't interested in your product. It means the buyer isn't interested in your call. Hang up, rework, practice your opener, and try again another time.

"Call Me Back Later"

This is similar to the "send me an email" objection, but you don't have to draw more information out of them. They're not dismissing you or saying they're not interested in learning more; they just need to know that you respect their time. So the answer here is simply:

> "Absolutely. When's a good time for you? What day and time works

best?"

You'll piss them off with any other answer. Keep it short and sweet.

THREE REAL OBJECTIONS
All the responses we just discussed are actually excuses and knee-jerk reactions. There are, however, three legitimate objections you need to prepare for:

THE PROSPECT ASKS, "WHAT DO YOU DO?"
Don't answer that. The minute you start pitching yourself, you'll lose them. Turn the conversation back around on the buyer, because if they're asking you what you do, it's probably because one of the problems you listed resonates. So respond with:

"It sounds like those problems I mentioned rang a bell. Which one?"

Hopefully they'll answer, and you'll be able to continue with your script:

"Ah, yes, that is a common problem; we see it a lot. Here at [insert company], we offer a unique/powerful/new approach to prevent [insert root cause] and limits/solves/address that [insert problem again]. Understanding this, does it make sense to schedule some time to talk about how we do that and the impact it could have on your business?"

If they don't answer and say instead, "Just tell me what you do," you can respectfully respond with:

"We provide a unique [approach, software, product] that [limits/ addresses/fixes] the [insert problems you opened with] that many organizations tend to struggle with that tend to [affect/cause] [insert impacts]. Would it make sense to dig a little deeper?"

"WE USE YOUR COMPETITOR FOR THAT"
If you hear this objection, you're doing something wrong. It means you've been product-centric, and you need to go back to focusing on the

problems. Say,:

> "That's not uncommon—we see that often. I understand you're using [competitor]. Are you suggesting that you rarely experience [insert problem or root cause]?"

Again, you're guiding them to reflect. Yes, they use someone else, but just because they use someone else doesn't mean those problems don't exist. You want them to realize that by encouraging them to think about their current environment.

"WE AREN'T SPENDING MONEY RIGHT NOW"

> "I understand. It's a tough time right now, and a lot of people are cutting back their budgets, dropping some tools, and even getting rid of vendors. Help me understand. Is it that you're not seeing all these errors in your time tracking, and you feel like you're completing it in a short amount of time? Or is it that you do see the errors, but your CFO would rip your head off for even suggesting that you spend money right now?"

The buyer would then answer A) No, they're not problems, or B) Yes, I see the errors, and my budget is tight.

If A, you'd reply:

> "Great, glad to hear it. You wouldn't happen to know anyone else who might have that problem?"

If B, you'd say:

> "Understood. I'm not asking for your credit card, but given that budgets frequently change, and that some companies we've worked with have found that leaving the problem alone actually costs them a lot more money than if they'd invested in fixing it, would this be worth exploring further? That way, even if it's not a fit now, you'd be more informed about your potential options in the future if you do decide to move forward."

It's totally okay to be casual and inject some humor into your dialogue. The point is, you're trying to get to the truth—is the budget *really* frozen, no matter what, or is there some wiggle room if you can get your buyer to see the loss of not making an investment?

In all three cases, the way to overcome the objection is to increase the offer-ask ratio. Get your buyer to really think about what they're letting slide and their exposure if they decide not to talk to you. If they ask themselves, "Can I afford not to talk to this person?" make sure the answer is an obvious no.

VOICEMAILS

Does anyone really listen to their voicemails anymore? Is it worth the bother to leave a message?

It is. Because if you don't leave a message, you've missed out on your first opportunity to set the tone of your relationship. You're on the phone anyway; why would you waste the chance to leave your name and build some familiarity and rapport? You can say something like this:

"Hey, I was taking a look at your website and wanted to talk to you about what I found. Don't worry about calling me back. I'm going to pop you an email. It'll have the subject line: 'Threats to your business.' Let me know if you find it interesting. This is [insert your name] over at [company name]."

Now when they see your email, they may not delete it right away. "Oh, hey, there's that person who left me the voicemail. Hm. They must be for real if they're trying this hard to get a hold of me."

Don't call back five times and leave five voicemails unless you enjoy making people hate you. (Remember Michael in the movie *Swingers* for an example of what happens when you make this bad decision; yeah, don't be him. If you haven't seen it, watch the film. It's low-key hilarious.) Say what you need to say, say it fast, and don't elaborate.

COLD CALLING IS DEAD. LONG LIVE COLD CALLING!

The death of cold calling has been predicted for decades. Technologies like Caller ID, email, Do Not Call registries, and smartphones were all supposed to make cold calls obsolete. Today there's a new one. Apple's newest iOS upgrade will make it even harder to get through to prospects. When a number comes up that isn't in your contacts, the phone is going to answer and ask the caller what they're calling about. All you'll see is the text of their reply scrolling up like the *Star Wars* intro, which you can then choose to ignore or answer. Maybe to some people it's a cold-calling death knell, but we think it's the opposite. It just means that sellers will have to pull out every creative, humorous, and intriguing stop they can. The pressure will be on to say something so intriguing, your prospect won't be able to stop themselves from giving you a chance to say more. In the past, people had to pick up to find out who was calling. Now you get more chances to get your message across. That means there will be MORE opportunities to connect. Because it's served up when they don't know who's calling, they will read your message to decide if they want to answer. That's more eyeballs you weren't getting before. We see that as a benefit of the new feature, not a negative.

Hopefully, cold calling now seems a little less daunting. What's great is that the same mindset and preparation that raises the odds for a successful cold call are also applicable toward other channels you can and should use to spark intrigue and grab attention.

CHAPTER FIFTEEN
ANATOMY OF A PERFECT COLD EMAIL

C old emails are a bit like karaoke—lots of people do it, most suck at it, and every now and then, someone surprises you and knocks your socks off.

At least, that's Will's experience.

Keenan swears he's never received a good cold email. Like, ever.

In any event, the fact is that sellers are sending out too many cringey, shitty emails destined to be deleted without a second thought once they land in buyers' inboxes, assuming they even make it that far instead of getting caught in a spam folder.

It's our own fault. When platforms like Outreach and Salesloft were developed to help us increase our ability to reach more buyers on more channels, sellers jumped on board. But in our desire to scale, we traded sincerity and thoughtfulness for speed and volume. The whole point of an email is to entice buyers to engage with us, yet for five to ten years now, we've sent out billions of bullshit emails that not only don't engage but are also so dull, deceptive, or manipulative, they can prompt actual hostility when buyers do bother to pay attention. And can you blame them?

Here are some samples of **REAL-LIFE** garbage that sellers have asked Keenan to read:

Let the journey begin

New Message — ⤢ ✕

To   keenan   Cc Bcc

Subject   Quick not on AI and data engineering services

Hi Nathan, just kidding—good morning Keenan,

Wondering if A Sales Growth Company is exploring AI/ML models, predictive analytics, or data-pipeline modernization?

Alongside our web/mobile builds (.NET, Java, Python, Rails, iOS, Android), we deliver advanced data engineering and AI integration.

Choose one letter to guide me:

A) Yes—call Thursday 10 a.m. ET

B) Later—ping me in a few weeks

C) Redirect to _____

D) Not a fit—remove me

Happy to share client stories from NBC Universal and Groupon.

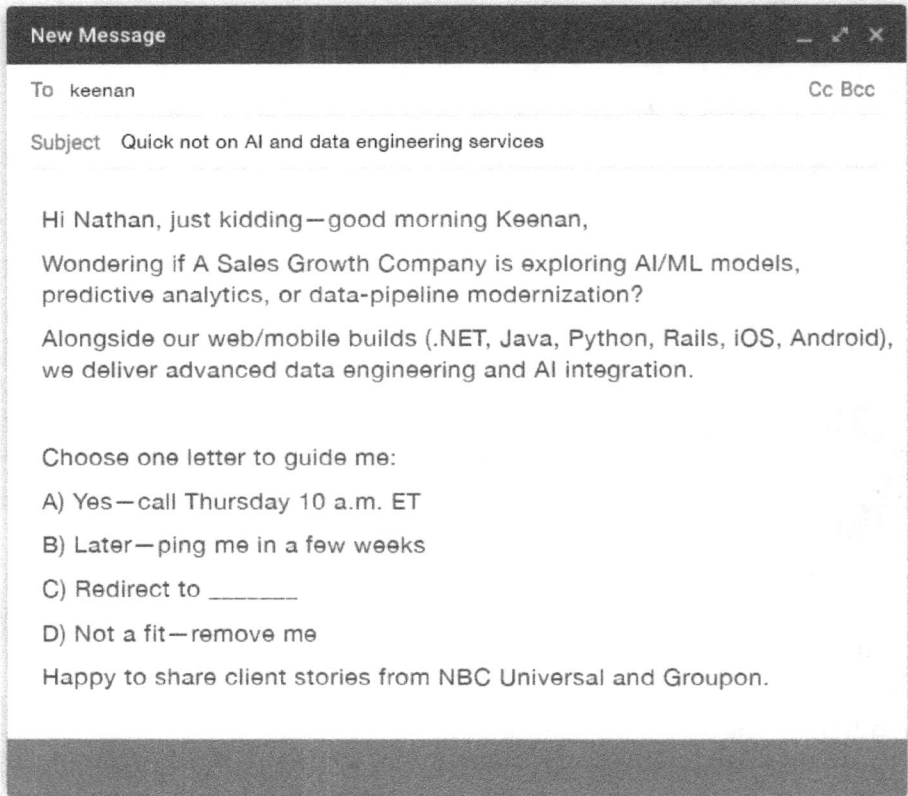

Did you get it yet? Just wait. here's another gem...

New Message — ↗ ✕

To keenan   Cc Bcc

Subject Ever thought about writing a book?

Hey Keenan,

I'm Taylor with Chronicle, a boutique ghostwriting firm out of Texas. We came across your LinkedIn and were fascinated by what you've built at A Sales Growth Company.

We keep an eye out for compelling stories, and yours stood out. We'd be happy to share a complimentary sample chapter to show you what it might look like in book form—with absolutely no obligation.

Would you have a few minutes to connect sometime this week?

--
Taylor
Ghost Writer, Chronicle

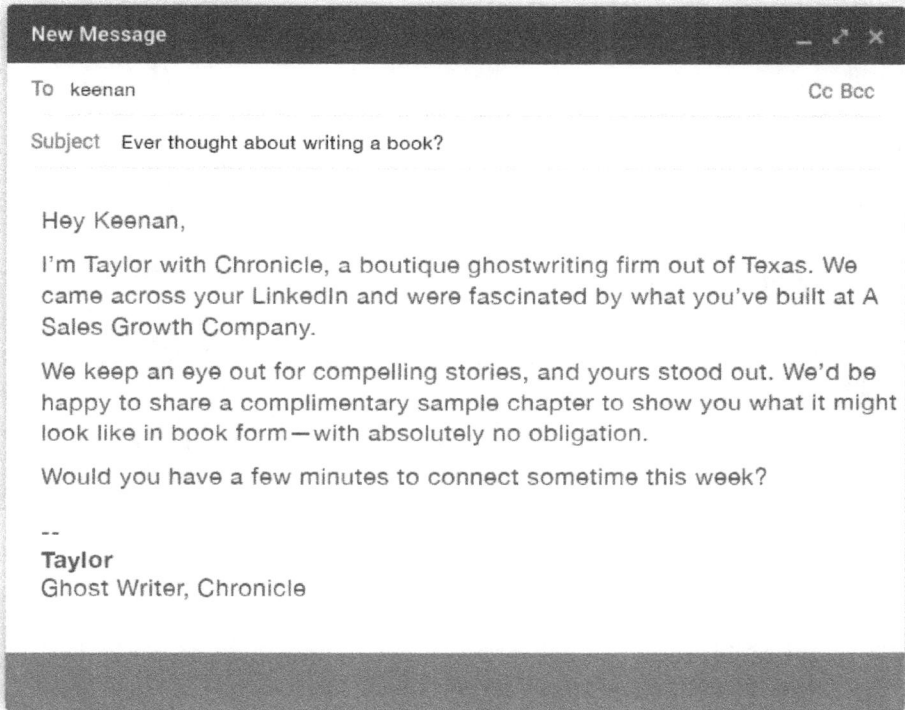

Did it hit you? Keenan has a best-selling book mentioned all over his LinkedIn profile, and this is the email they chose to send him. They clearly didn't read his LinkedIn profile like they said. So, not only is this email not relevant, but they also lied.

Will has seen them too. When he's asked to see examples of people's work, this is what he's received (altered to protect all parties involved):

Flip the page, you've gotta see this...

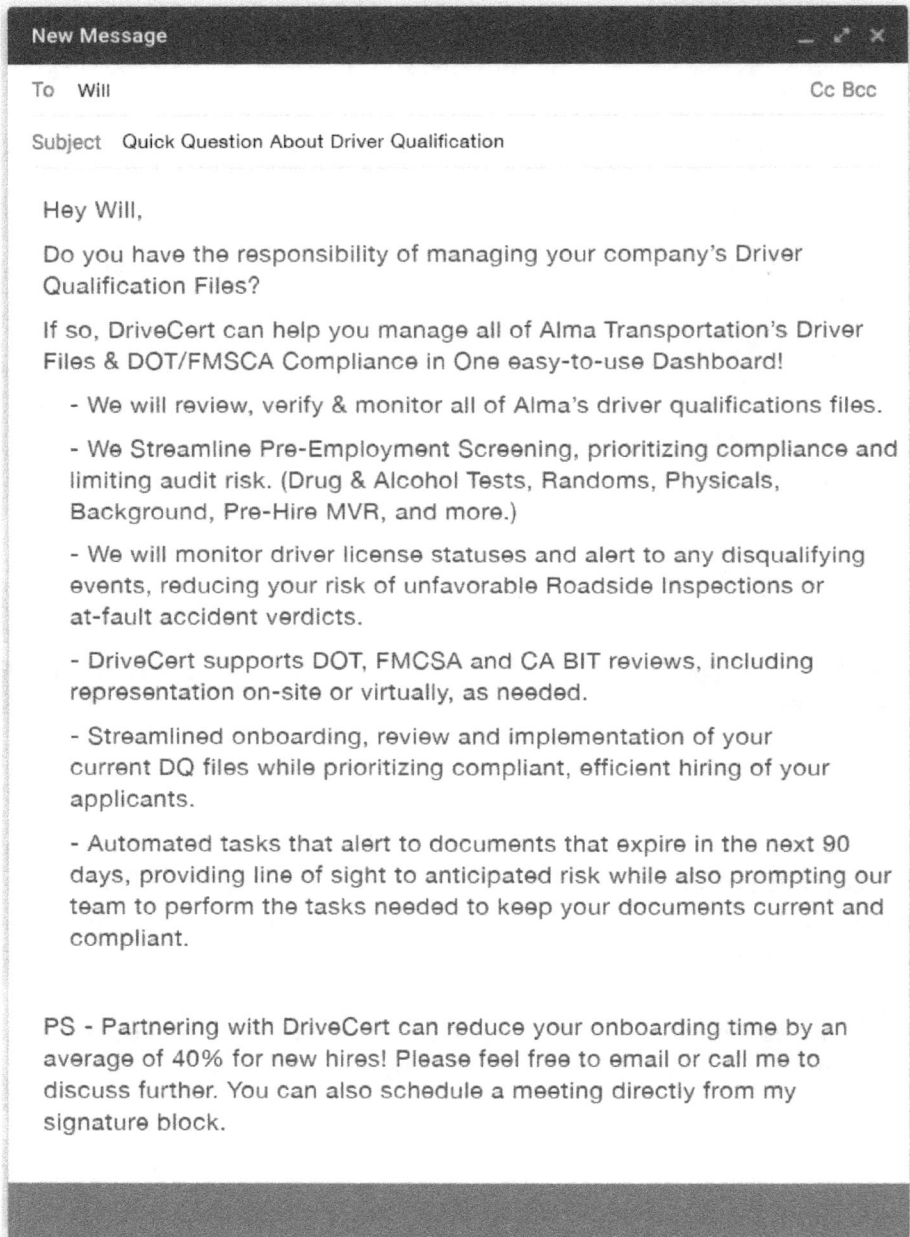

New Message   _ ⤢ ✕

To   Will   Cc Bcc

Subject   Quick Question About Driver Qualification

Hey Will,

Do you have the responsibility of managing your company's Driver Qualification Files?

If so, DriveCert can help you manage all of Alma Transportation's Driver Files & DOT/FMSCA Compliance in One easy-to-use Dashboard!

- We will review, verify & monitor all of Alma's driver qualifications files.

- We Streamline Pre-Employment Screening, prioritizing compliance and limiting audit risk. (Drug & Alcohol Tests, Randoms, Physicals, Background, Pre-Hire MVR, and more.)

- We will monitor driver license statuses and alert to any disqualifying events, reducing your risk of unfavorable Roadside Inspections or at-fault accident verdicts.

- DriveCert supports DOT, FMCSA and CA BIT reviews, including representation on-site or virtually, as needed.

- Streamlined onboarding, review and implementation of your current DQ files while prioritizing compliant, efficient hiring of your applicants.

- Automated tasks that alert to documents that expire in the next 90 days, providing line of sight to anticipated risk while also prompting our team to perform the tasks needed to keep your documents current and compliant.

PS - Partnering with DriveCert can reduce your onboarding time by an average of 40% for new hires! Please feel free to email or call me to discuss further. You can also schedule a meeting directly from my signature block.

New Message   — ↗ ✕

To   Will   Cc Bcc

Subject   Supporting Your Business Growth with IT Services

Hi Will,

I hope you're having an awesome day! :-)

I'm reaching out because I wanted to see how we can help you overcome any IT-related challenges and provide support to grow your business. At REDACTED Technologies, we specialize in providing a range of IT solutions designed to simplify your operations, enhance efficiency, and drive success.

Here's a quick look at how we can support your business:

Dedicated Web Servers: Secure, reliable, and customized to meet your exact needs.

Cloud Hosting Services: Scalable solutions that evolve as your business grows.

Managed IT Services: We take care of your IT infrastructure so you can focus on what matters most—growing your business.

Email Solutions: Safe, seamless email management for better communication.

Backup & Disaster Recovery Solutions: Protect your business from the unexpected.

Data Center Services: High-performance hosting and storage for your peace of mind.

I'd love the chance to chat more and explore how we can make your IT environment work even harder for you.

If you're open to a conversation, just let me know your availability, and I'll be happy to schedule a Google Meet to discuss further.

Looking forward to connecting and finding ways to help your business thrive!

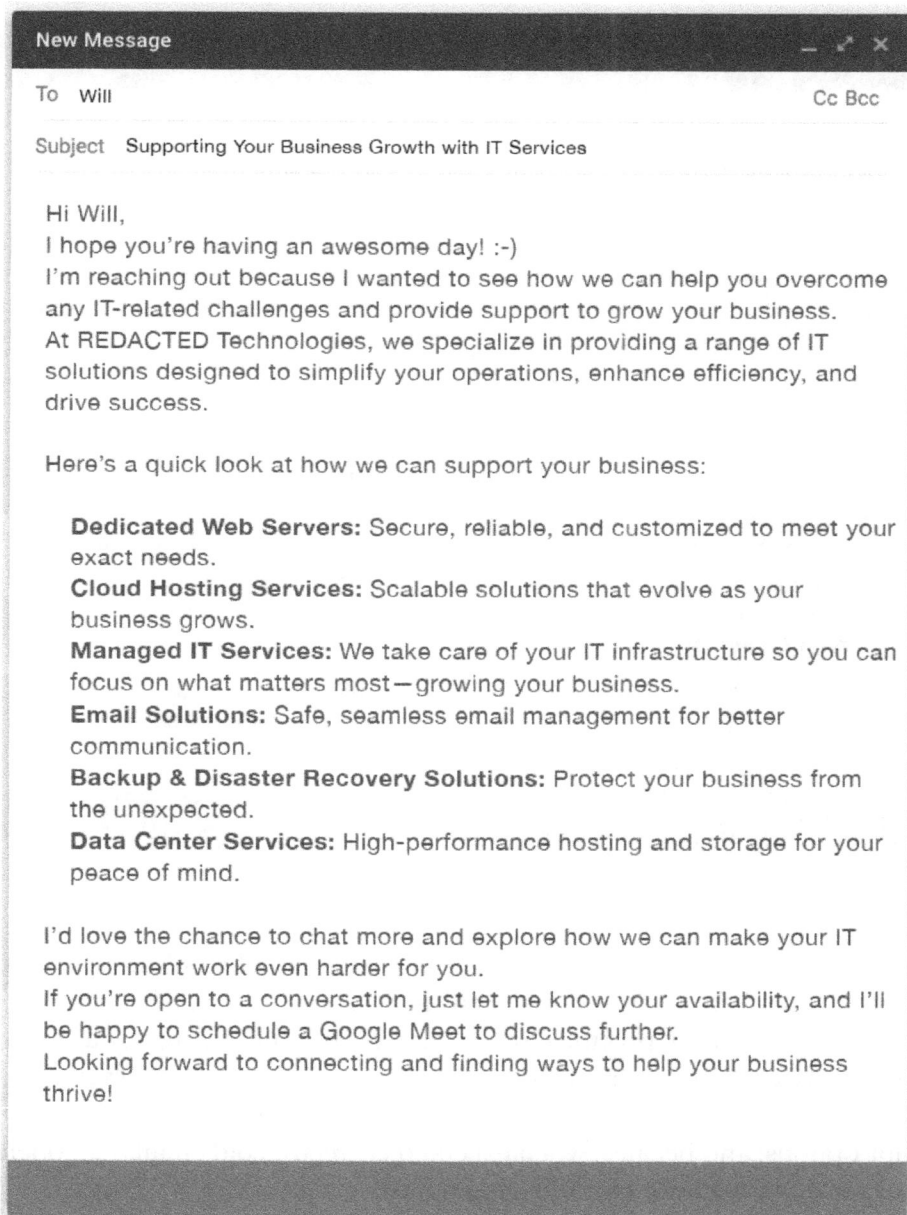

Keep going, there's more...

New Message _ ⤢ ✕

To   Will   Cc Bcc

Subject   Exploring Potential Partnership for 2025 CIO/CISO Events

Hi Will,

I assist with overseeing the CIO/CISO portfolio in the Northeast. While researching potential organizations to engage with in 2025, I came across COMPANY and was instantly impressed.

Given this alignment, I'd like to explore the possibility of having COMPANY sponsor one of our Assemblies or Roadshow Dinners in 2025. This would be a great opportunity for you to expand your presence in the enterprise space and build valuable connections with key decision-makers.

Since we haven't worked together before, you may not be familiar with REDACTED. I'd be happy to set aside some time to walk you through our event formats, agendas, attendee profiles, and thought leadership opportunities regardless of whether you're interested in sponsoring at this time, I'd still appreciate the chance for a brief conversation.

I've set aside time on my calendar for February 26th at 11:30 AM ET and sent over an invite. If that time doesn't work, I'm happy to be flexible :).

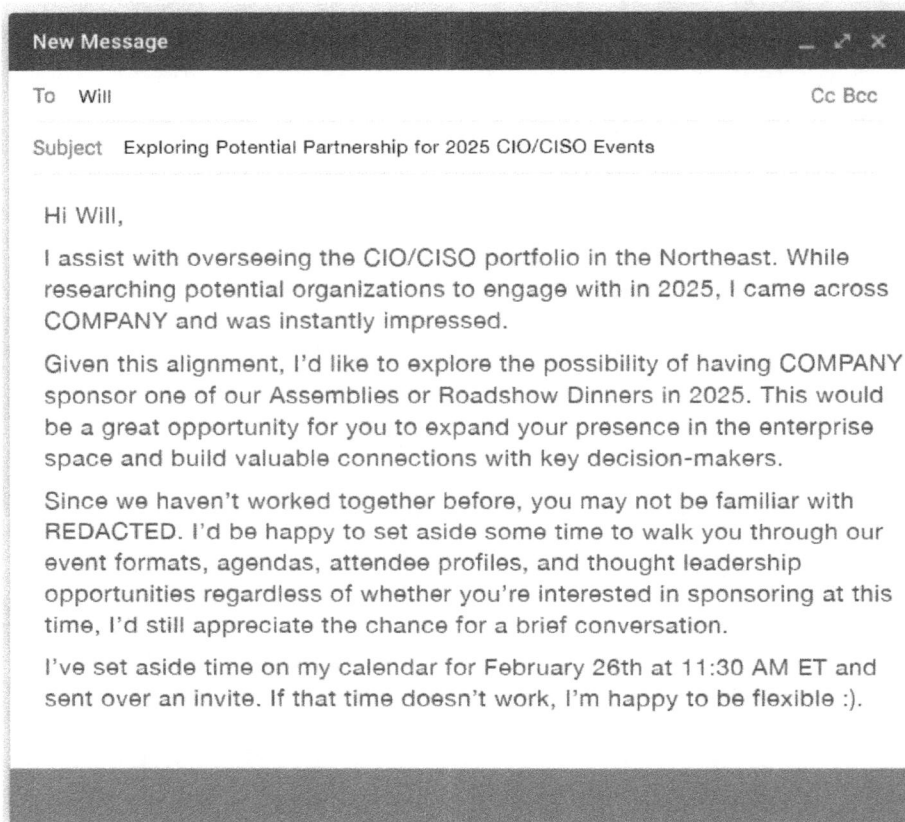

Can you see why our buyers are checked out? There's no value in any of these! And we've sprayed so many of these emails out into the world, we're on the precipice of disaster. If we don't figure out a better way to reach our buyers through their inboxes, emails will never work again. And that would be a low-key fail, because we never want to limit our options, and because when executed correctly, cold emails can open up great opportunities for sellers and buyers.

Fortunately, we're here to teach you that better way, one that lets you craft personalized, targeted emails that will break through the boredom and skepticism of your buyer, and compel them to consider what you have to say.

Some of you have never seen a great cold email (don't argue; you haven't), so we'll start there. But before we begin, you need to learn the building blocks of a great cold email. There are nine, and they're all equally important. Some may be familiar, as they appear in *Gap Selling*, but we added some more to keep things interesting.

THE NINE BUILDING BLOCKS OF A GREAT COLD EMAIL

1. **INTRIGUE.** We covered what makes something intriguing in Chapter 12. Translated to an email, it's all about interrupting patterns. Does your email match the pattern of a bad email, or does it surprise, jarring the OFC and triggering the ACC to force your buyer to take a closer look? To know, you have to know a bad cold email when you see one. If you read the examples we provided above, but weren't sure what made them so terrible, look at them again and see if you can spot the following mistakes:

   - They're unoriginal, following everyone else's template.

   - They state the obvious.

   - They focus on the product and the solution instead of the problem and its impact on the recipient.

   - They confuse humor and fun with gimmicks, hacks, and corniness.

   - They're not specific, instead addressing a broad set of problems that could apply to anyone.

   These are all super-common mistakes. When you avoid the obvious, insert compelling storytelling, and stay problem-centric, you break the buyer's expected pattern and create intrigue. Remember, intrigue—which makes buyers look—is only the first sale you're trying to make with your outreach. The second sale is interest—which makes people act. All the elements that follow lay the groundwork for that second sale. Intrigue should be packed into every piece of your email.

2. **RELEVANCE.** A relevant email immediately answers the buyer's question, "Why me? Why now? Why does this matter to me or my business specifically?" Too many emails are obviously automated and of zero interest to the person reading it—i.e., it was sent to the wrong person—or poorly targeted—i.e., it was sent to the right person but about the wrong subject.

Establishing relevance starts with the first line of your email. So from now on, you'll no longer waste precious time and space with a snooze-inducing start like "Hi, Todd! My name is Emily Banks."

DON'T GREET YOUR BUYER. When nanoseconds count, skip the niceties and get to the point. Fast.

DON'T INTRODUCE YOURSELF. That's what an email signature line is for. Besides, if you're introducing yourself, right away you've made your email about you, not your buyer.

Instead, you'll use the first line of your email to make an observation about your buyer or their company. This will make it clear you've done your research and deeply understand the issues your buyer is facing. Turn back to Chapter 6 if you need ideas on how to get to know your buyers and where to dig up information about their problems and priorities, how they measure their success and failure, and the responsibilities of their job and seniority level.

For example, if you're selling cybersecurity, and you send an email to the admin of a company talking about their risk-reduction strategy, you're done. You just proved you have no idea what your buyer does. But if you write that same email to an IT director, you might hold their attention long enough to see if the rest of your email follows up with more relevant information.

Your observation must indicate clearly and specifically why you've chosen to reach out to your buyer. Some examples:

- It looks like Acme just hired its 20th employee.

- Saw you're running the store on Shopify.

• Noticed you pushed some changes to your site this month.

Many sellers make the mistake of confusing relevance with personalization. Personalization is showing your buyer that you know something about them, like when Kevin Chambers mentioned Greene King in his cold email to Will to show that he'd read all of Will's LinkedIn bio. Acknowledging what you know about people—congratulating them on a new marriage, mentioning a shared obsession with the same sports team—is a personalized approach, and it's a good one so long as you got the information from their own shared content or publicly posted bio (anything else, and you'll give off stalker vibes). It shows you're human and interested in connection. But relevance is something else. You create relevance only when you can tightly tie your product or service to your buyer's job, problems, and goals. If you don't know anything specific about your buyer, lean into your extensive knowledge about market trends, changes in the field, legal rulings, organizational hierarchy, or industry news.

One more thing. Identifying a problem your buyer is likely facing isn't the same thing as tearing them apart for their failures or flaws. Don't write something like this, which is not only awful for its messaging but also awful for being chock-full of grammar and punctuation mistakes:

*Give 'er a turn to see what **not** to do...*

New Message — ⤢ ✕

To   Will   Cc Bcc

Subject   I Hate Your Website But Love Your Potential

Hi Will,

Apart from your website's obnoxious colour schemes (I mean it looks like a gender reveal) what exactly do you have that stands out?

For someone in sales one thing that I don't get from your work is

> **1) Clarity of product:** I get it, you help people sell, you help people put themselves on the map, but your sales website isn't selling your product it's selling....YOU. I get it, personal brand makes the man but that's what your own socials is for. When I visit your website, honestly the first thing I saw was well tshirts not even in your iconic colour scheme.

> **2) Difference:** I checked out your testimonials, people mention humor, how you offer personalised advice and honestly that's pretty good. Excellent. But what I don't see are numbers. I couldn't find results. None of them mention a single statistics on a proven increase in their sales after training with you. If it happened why not advertise it? Unless it didn't happen.

> **3) Social media:** Your Instagram grid shows random ass things. Memes are good, but you hop on one you don't hop on the other. The ones you do hop on I have already seen out there. But then you also post the classic LinkedIn video content that almost every sales pitcher out there is already posting. Why try to change it up when you have not mastered either?

And that's why you need me. I have 20 things that you can change with your strategy, email me back to find the other 17, that is if you want to make more clients.

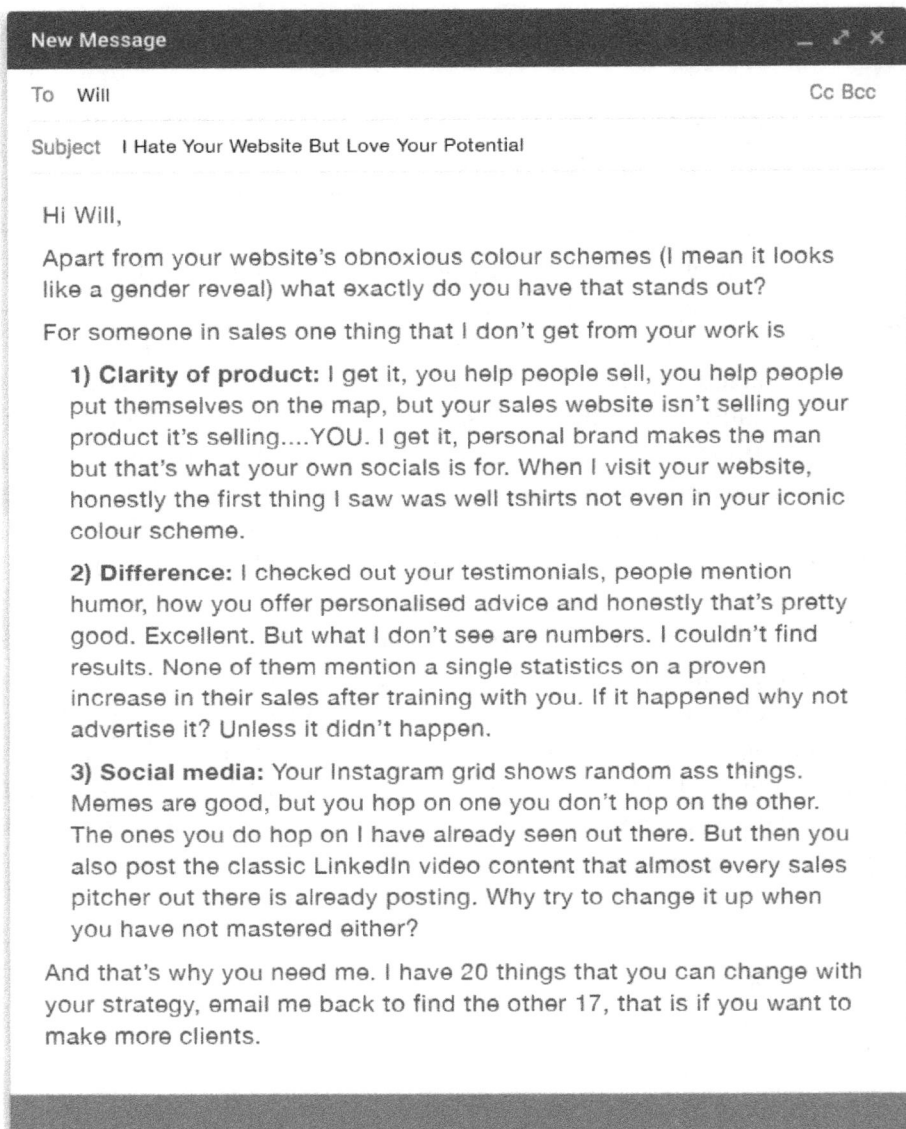

Don't insult your buyer—even if you think you're being funny—don't condescend, and don't trash their work or their efforts. It's the fastest way to turn people off. This is business, not a Comedy Central roast.

3. THE BRIDGE. A great email contains a well-conceived logical bridge, a segue that ties the facts you know about your buyer to a pain point you suspect they may be experiencing (even if they haven't realized it yet), and that your product or service can help them solve. For example, if you sell a social media management platform, you could say something like this:

"If you're running multiple brand accounts across 3 new platforms [the bridge], you're probably spending too much time jumping between dashboards instead of focusing on engagement."

Or

"Your team is now posting daily on Instagram and LinkedIn, and the increase in engagement shows this is working well. While those likes and comments look good [the bridge], a lot of people in your position find they're under constant pressure to prove ROI from campaigns that don't always convert cleanly."

Following up with the openers we suggested earlier, we could say something like this:

"It looks like Acme just hired their 20th employee. Congrats! Most small business CFOs I speak to tell me that's the tipping point where their finances became unmanageable in spreadsheets."

"Saw you're running the store on Shopify. How are you liking it? Many e-commerce businesses find it a really easy and good place to start, but find themselves overpaying on fees as their business starts to take off."

"Noticed you pushed some changes to your website this month. I've heard from other retailers that it can be tough to know if these changes are having a positive or negative impact on sales, especially in the short term."

The best emails are both personalized and relevant, but please don't force the issue by stretching to connect two completely unrelated topics or hitting your buyer with corny junk.

Do:
"I loved your last video announcing your promotion to CMO and your objectives for 2025. While the new job is impressive, I'm even more impressed that you filmed the video while balancing a teething baby on your lap! Respect. It's possible that in your new role you'll be fielding marketing requests from every department. We've seen how this can quickly turn to chaos and slow down your ability to be responsive and deliver. I'd love to talk to you about how we can help."

Don't:
"Congrats on the new promotion! I'm impressed that you filmed while balancing a teething baby on your lap. You know what else is teething? The market for talented people like you. I'd like to tell you about how we position people like you for great things."

Seriously. Don't.

You want to use your knowledge of the industry and deductive reasoning skills to highlight an issue that could make your buyer stop and recognize themselves—"Oh, shit, yes, I deal with that all the time!"—or stop and introduce an element of doubt—"Oh, shit, could that happen to me?" In other words, you're helping them clearly see their problem.

4. **PROBLEM.** The problem you mention in your email must also be one that you list in your PIC. Your tone should be believable, credible, and judgment-free. Don't make a definitive or diagnostic statement, such as, "You're under pressure to post more. That means your team is prioritizing quantity over quality, your voice is inconsistent, and you're going to lose staff to burnout." That will put people on the defensive. Instead, guide your buyer to see what you see, like this:

"We find that social media managers who feel the pressure to post more often can usually get their team to successfully build momentum but then run into problems with stress and burnout as everyone frantically tries to keep that momentum going. As the likes rise, their director or VP of marketing, or even the CFO, may ask for proof that the engagement boosts the bottom line to justify their investment. If social media managers can't produce, budgets can get cut, and all that hard work can go to waste."

Another way to highlight a problem would be to ask a provoking question, which can get your buyer to think in a new way, or recognize an unrealized potential gain:

"You've built a social media audience most brands dream of, but here's the real question: How many of them are paying you"

Finally, you can reveal a problem, establish relevance, *and* boost your credibility through social proof. Mention how other clients like your buyer have used your solution to help them fix problems like the ones your buyer is facing. For example:

"Dunder Mifflin and Wayne Corp were both able to solve their payroll headaches by adopting our finance software that incorporates payroll into the rest of the business's finances."

"Mugs-a-Million were overjoyed when they switched to our platform built for more mature online businesses and saved 5% on their transaction fees without losing any functionality."

"Our customer Peak Ketchup found real-time website analytics allowed them to make changes before they missed out on sales."

You don't have to go into product detail or explain how you helped these customers. That will come later. For now, the fact that other clients have trusted you proves you have experience and builds your buyer's confidence that you can handle their issues.

5. **OFFER.** You've made an observation. You've established a problem. Now give your buyer something they want.

   You're eventually going to ask your buyer to act—by scheduling a meeting, downloading a chart, or maybe agreeing to a demo. So you have to make them an offer they don't want to refuse, something that's valuable enough to compel them to say, "Yes." If you've researched your buyer well enough, you'll know what that is. Would they value a resource, some expertise, an audit, an evaluation, or insight into what their competitors are doing? Would they prefer a video or an overview? Figure that out, and you'll spark their interest. Keep your offer easy to fulfill and easily deliverable. You want to guarantee that they'll walk away knowing something they didn't know before, so it feels like time well spent.

   Keep in mind that what works today might not work tomorrow. The key to a great offer, aside from being valuable, is that it's unique, socially proven, and safe. The problem is that once sellers figure out that an offer works, they send out more and more of the same. For the buyer, what once seemed intriguing and surprising now seems stale and generic. You have to stay ahead of the trends and think creatively.

6. **THE ASK.** Whatever it is you want your buyer to do, it needs to be frictionless, and it needs to be clearly worth their time. Remember the offer-ask ratio we discussed in Chapter 10: Offer − Ask = Value. Your ask can't be more valuable than your offer. If your offer is weak, even asking for five minutes of someone's time will feel like an imposition. Make your offer valuable, and it'll be much easier to get the time you need to show your buyer how you can help them.

   Make it hard for them to say, "No." Go for low-friction asks:

   • Should I send it?

   • Worth your time?

   • Interested in hearing how other companies did this?

7. **READABILITY.** Is your audience CRO or an enablement person? Manager or techie? You want to build credibility with your reader, so you need to speak in their language, at their level, about what they care about.

- **Talk like a human**, not a robot or thesaurus. You want to come across as knowledgeable but not arrogant. Your tone should be confident, curious, conversational, and friendly. It's okay to be funny! If you can find your buyer speaking on YouTube, mirror their type of humor and sensibility.

- **Don't use useless or overplayed adjectives.**

- **Avoid empty buzzwords** like "innovative," "paradigm shift," and "best in class."

- **Skip the corporate clichés.** You don't ever need to circle back, move the needle, reach for low-hanging fruit, or promise synergy.

- **Use jargon and abbreviations only if you're confident your buyer frequently uses them in their own correspondence and conversation.** But be careful. Do this right, and you'll create an immediate sense of recognition and build your credibility. Do it wrong, and your email will get immediately swiped to the trash bin.

- **Don't write anything too formal.** No, "Dear Madam," no, "Allow me to introduce myself." This isn't the Gilded Age. Executives want respect, but as we've already explained, they also need you to get to the point, and fast.

- **Don't ever, ever, EVER start with**, "I hope this email finds you well." Nothing telegraphs "SALES EMAIL! WASTE OF TIME! DELETE!" like that tired, robotic, empty pleasantry. Spare us, please.

8. **FORMATTING.** As you write, think about how your email will look.

- **Keep your sentences short and concise** to keep your message easily digestible. No one's up for a novel, even the most avid reader. Fifty to 100 words should do it.

- **Chunk your text into short paragraphs**, maximum of one or two sentences each.

- **Double space** in between each to create lots of white space.

- **Optimize your email for mobile.** For example, make sure that your subject line is short so that it doesn't get cut off in the inbox preview. Also, check that your preheader text—those few preview words that show up in gray beneath your emails when read on mobile—is compelling. You'll recall that we insisted that you stop greeting your buyer and introducing yourself in the first line of your email. If it reads, "Hi, Todd! My name is Emily Banks," that's what your buyer will see, and you'll have wasted an opportunity to spark intrigue and prove that your email is worth opening. Emails that are crafted with mobile in mind see 83% more replies.[55]

9. **SUBJECT LINE.** In Chapter 10, we discussed how your subject line sets the tone for your whole email and is critical for sparking intrigue. It needs to announce your topic, stand out, and activate the ACC to signal, *Hey, pay attention!* And one other thing—it should be written last. You can't write a clear, accurate, ACC-tickling subject for an email if you don't know what's in it yet.

Once you're ready to write your subject, keep these tips in mind:

- **Keep it short.** One-to-three-word subject lines are best. You build intrigue with less information, not more.

- **Don't use numbers**

- **Don't use buzzwords**

- **Don't use sales or marketing language such as:**
  - Boost
  - Optimize
  - Leverage
  - Unlock
  - Elevate
  - Transform
  - Drive Results
  - Empower
  - Scale
  - Enable
  - Maximize
  - Game-Changer
  - Seamless
  - Synergy
  - Turnkey
  - Revolutionary
  - World-Class
  - Disruptive

PUT IT ALL TOGETHER

Here are two examples of good problem-centric emails:

Now it gets good

New Message _ ⤢ ✕

To Naveen   Cc Bcc

Subject Sackville Smile Center

Hey Naveen,

Noticed 2-3 areas on your Google Business page that could be hurting
your chances to be seen by new patients.

Likely causing new patients to see Sackville Smile Centre before they
get to your practice.

Good news they're quick fixes that could have a big impact.

Worth me sending a video highlighting what these are?

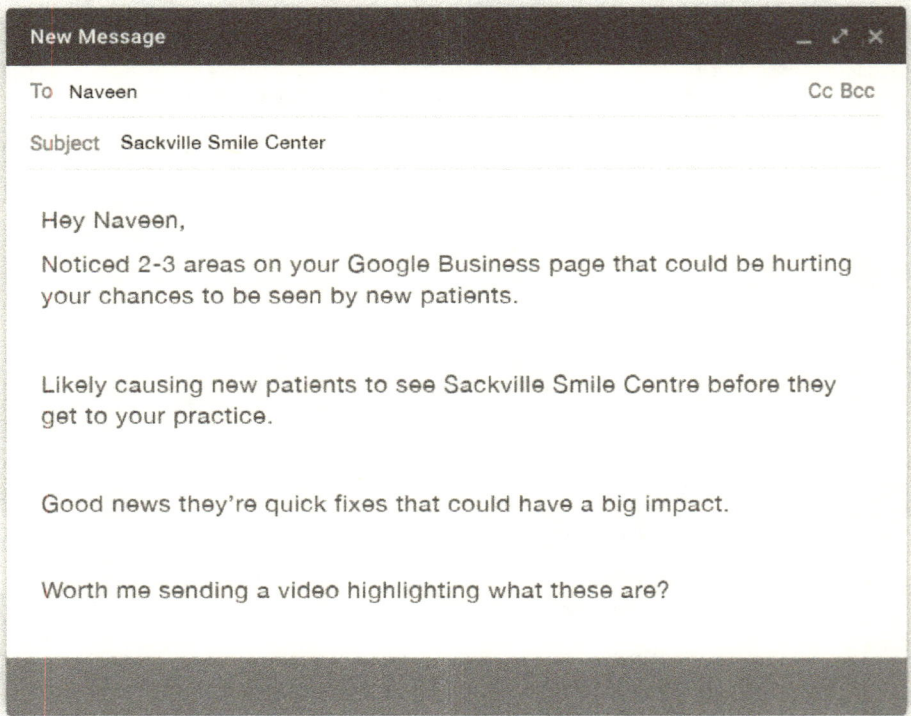

More over here ↗

New Message	_ ⤢ ✕
To Maya	Cc Bcc

Subject Advocacy program

Heard from one of your folks that you're kicking off an employee advocacy program this quarter, Maya.

Whenever teams roll these out, the first few weeks usually feel great. Lots of momentum, tons of posts. However, around week 5, things tend to slow.

Internally the program shifts from "fun new initiative" to "that social thing we tried" pretty fast. Once it gets that label, support from other teams can cool off and future projects tied to organic reach end up getting budget-scrutinized.

When I've seen this happen, it's almost always because the regular employees didn't get the kind of scaffolding that keeps non-power users contributing.

A med-tech group used a 5-point framework to keep 80% of their employees engaged past month 6 (easy tweaks, big impact).

Want me to send it over, or are you already feeling good about your plan?

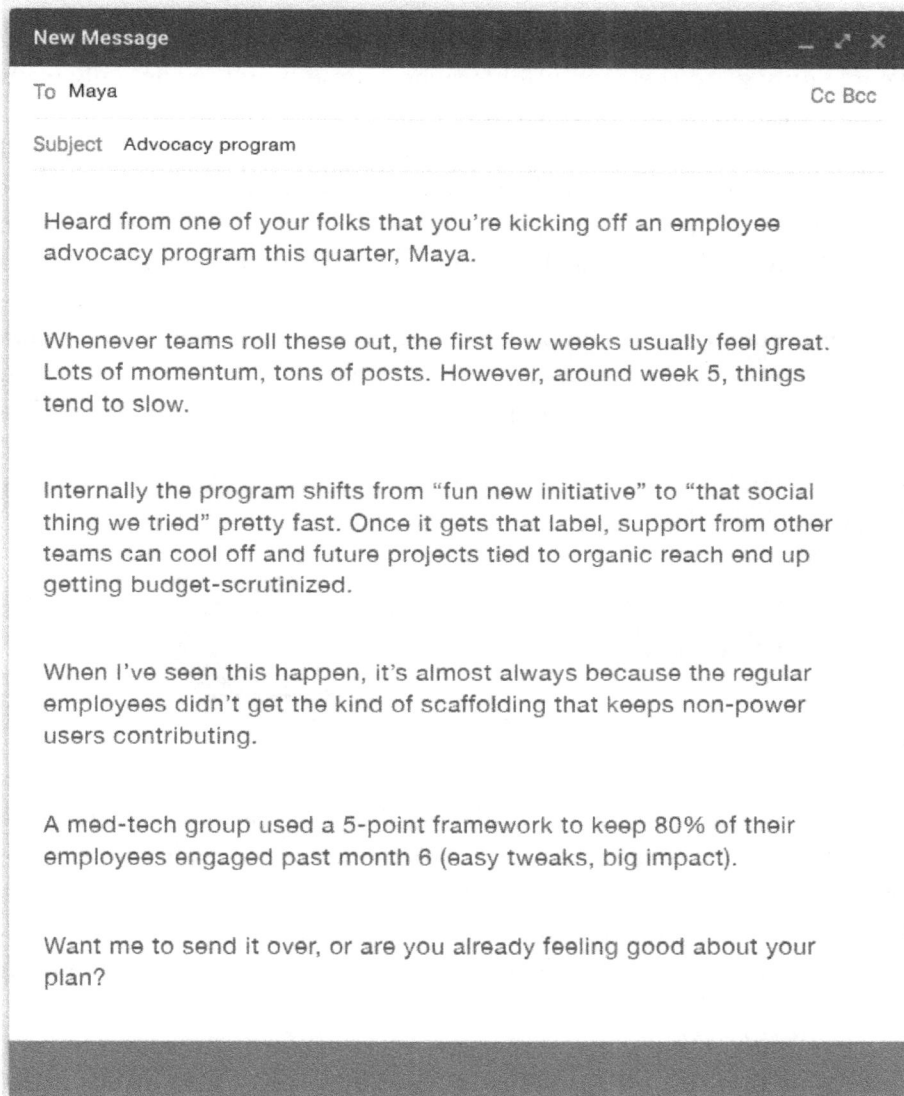

DELIVERABILITY

We didn't number this one because it's boring, operational stuff, not an email element, but you still need to think about it.

Deliverability is paramount. It doesn't matter how short your email is, how specific or relevant it is, or how well it could activate your buyer's ACC—if your email gets caught up in your buyer's spam filter instead of their primary inbox, it's unlikely they'll ever see it, much less open it. People only go to their spam folder when something they actually want doesn't show up. You can't take that risk.

There are steps you can take or discuss with your IT team that will help you protect your domain reputation (the trustworthiness of your email address) and avoid spam sinkholes. In the past, we might have offered advice that included reducing the number of emails you send out, sending them over a period of time and not all at once, and limiting your attachments. The problem is, the guidelines that ensure email deliverability change practically by the minute, so anything we tell you here could be obsolete by the time the book goes to press. Our solution for keeping you up to date is the QR code below. As things change, we'll refresh the information so that no matter when you pick up this book, or check the code, the information will be accurate.

For up-to-date guidelines that ensure email deliverability scan here

FOLLOW-UP EMAILS

You want to keep your email short, not just because of buyers' guppy-level attention spans and better readability but because you want to leave things unsaid. Intrigue draws people to you. When we first introduced the concept in Chapter 10, we said that it's about striking a balance between hoarding your candy, which keeps buyers from seeing that you have something they want, and spilling it all at the front door, revealing everything at once and removing any incentive to keep talking to you.

The truth is that the vast majority of buyers won't respond to your first email, even if they're interested. And that's okay. It may take a second email, possibly a third, and maybe even a few other forms of outreach and up to eight touchpoints[56] (more on touchpoints later) to get any sign of life from them at all. But repeating yourself ad nauseum won't help. Think about it: If your buyer wasn't intrigued or interested enough to reply to your first email, sending out the same thing again and again sure won't do the trick either. Nor will flooding their email with the ever-annoying, "Bumping this up to the top of your inbox!" or "Did you have a chance to read my email?" Unless your email landed in their spam box, it's unlikely you weren't met with silence because your buyer didn't see it at all; it's because they (or rather, their OFC) saw it there among the dozens of other emails they got that minute, mentally declared it unimportant or irrelevant, and dismissed it.

But if you kept your email short, you've left yourself plenty of runway to try again. Because, remember, you did your homework. You know this buyer and their company. You've observed their symptoms and catalysts. The problem you originally wrote to them about isn't the only problem they're dealing with but one of several, perhaps even many. Now you have a chance to provide new information, focus on different challenges, or make a fresh observation.

So here's how that might look if you were selling to professional service businesses, and targeted a growing law firm:

OG Email

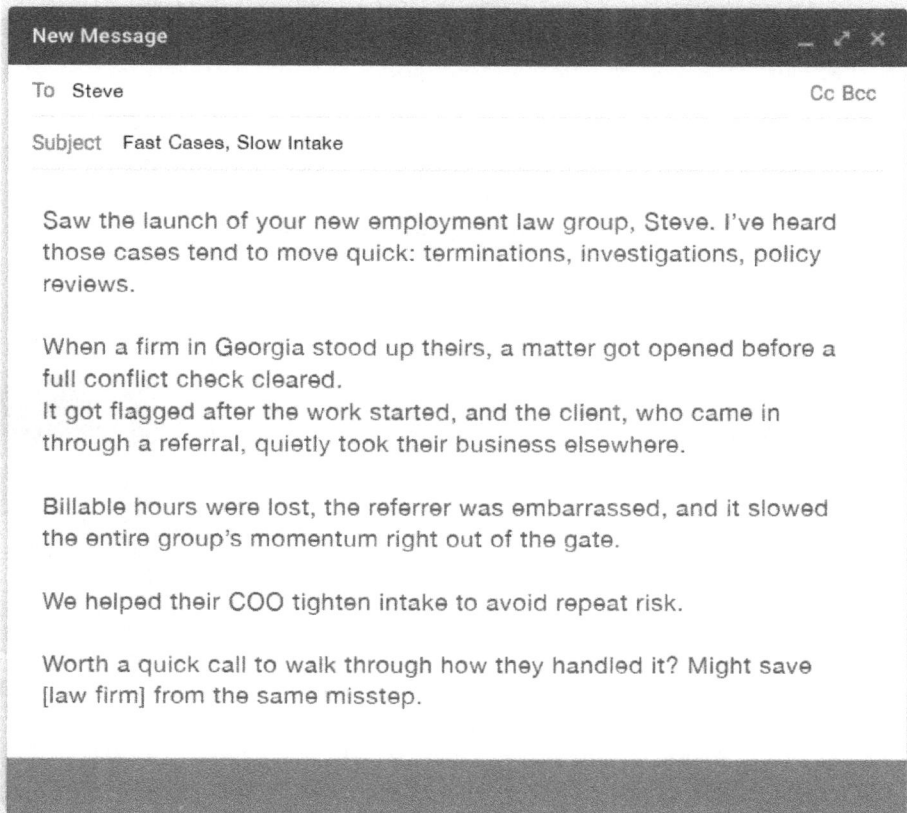

New Message

To Steve   Cc Bcc

Subject Fast Cases, Slow Intake

Saw the launch of your new employment law group, Steve. I've heard those cases tend to move quick: terminations, investigations, policy reviews.

When a firm in Georgia stood up theirs, a matter got opened before a full conflict check cleared.
It got flagged after the work started, and the client, who came in through a referral, quietly took their business elsewhere.

Billable hours were lost, the referrer was embarrassed, and it slowed the entire group's momentum right out of the gate.

We helped their COO tighten intake to avoid repeat risk.

Worth a quick call to walk through how they handled it? Might save [law firm] from the same misstep.

FIRST FOLLOW-UP EMAIL

They didn't respond in spite of this being a great email. That sucks, but it comes with the territory. But the good reps, gap-prospecting reps, know what to do, which is one of three things:

1. **Reiterate** your first email with a little more context that offers some insight into *how* you help solve problems.

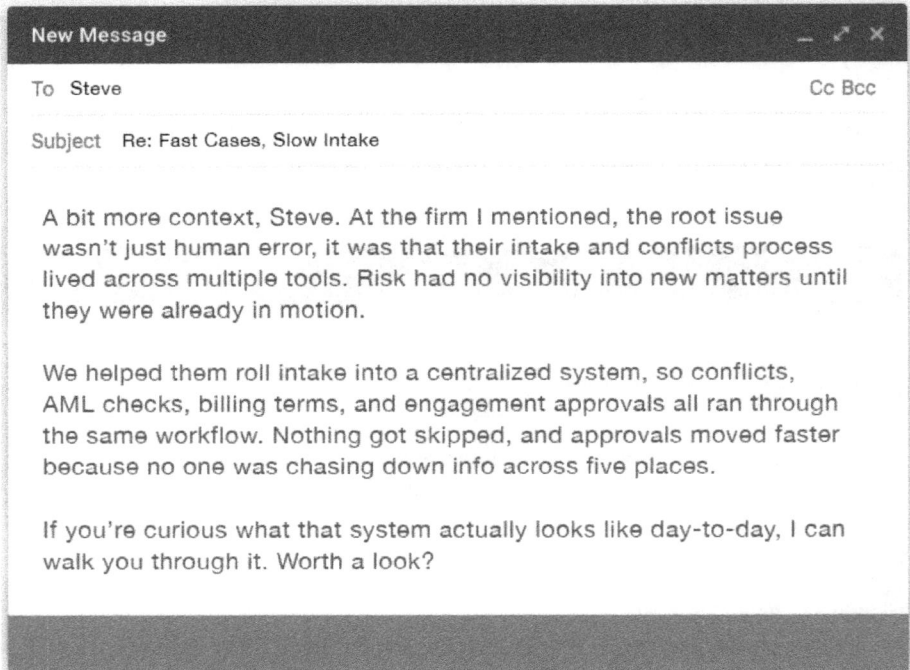

New Message   _ ↗ ✕

To Steve   Cc Bcc

Subject   Re: Fast Cases, Slow Intake

A bit more context, Steve. At the firm I mentioned, the root issue wasn't just human error, it was that their intake and conflicts process lived across multiple tools. Risk had no visibility into new matters until they were already in motion.

We helped them roll intake into a centralized system, so conflicts, AML checks, billing terms, and engagement approvals all ran through the same workflow. Nothing got skipped, and approvals moved faster because no one was chasing down info across five places.

If you're curious what that system actually looks like day-to-day, I can walk you through it. Worth a look?

---

2. **Change the offer.**

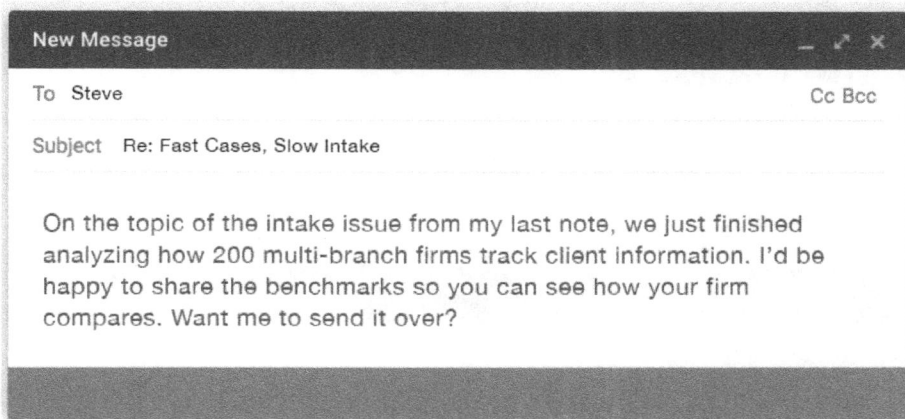

New Message   — ⤢ ✕

To Steve   Cc Bcc

Subject   Re: Fast Cases, Slow Intake

On the topic of the intake issue from my last note, we just finished analyzing how 200 multi-branch firms track client information. I'd be happy to share the benchmarks so you can see how your firm compares. Want me to send it over?

Note that your subject header will stay the same with every email until you start a new thread. It's never "Checking in," or "Circling back."

3. **Add a gift.** While it's not recommended for your original email, you can feel free to add a video, pdf, gif, or image offering a visual example or presentation of what you're talking about to your follow-up emails.

You can also do more research into your buyer's industry and present them with valuable third-party content they might have missed, like a white paper or industry analyst report, or a LinkedIn post by an influencer in their field or market. Explain why this content may be useful to them and how it relates to the problem you wanted to discuss. By sending them content created by a third party, you're building trust and breaking their expected pattern (what vendor shares any content but their own?). It's just another way to offer your buyer value, jolt their attention, and provide another way to absorb your message.

New Message   — ⤢ ✕

To   Steve   Cc Bcc

Subject   Re: Fast Cases, Slow Intake

Attaching an intake workflow that other firms are using as a baseline. Might be useful if you're thinking about tightening yours up before volume ramps.

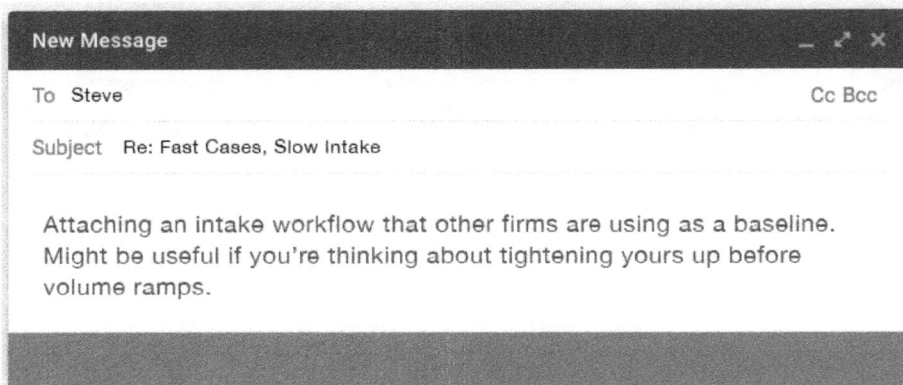

If you still don't hear back from the buyer, it's not over.

It's not over yet

SECOND FOLLOW-UP EMAIL

Bring up a different signal or problem that you've inferred.

This is starting a brand-new inquiry. It stands to reason that if, by now, your buyer didn't open the first email, it may be that the same subject isn't going to prompt them to open another email on the same topic. So start a new thread.

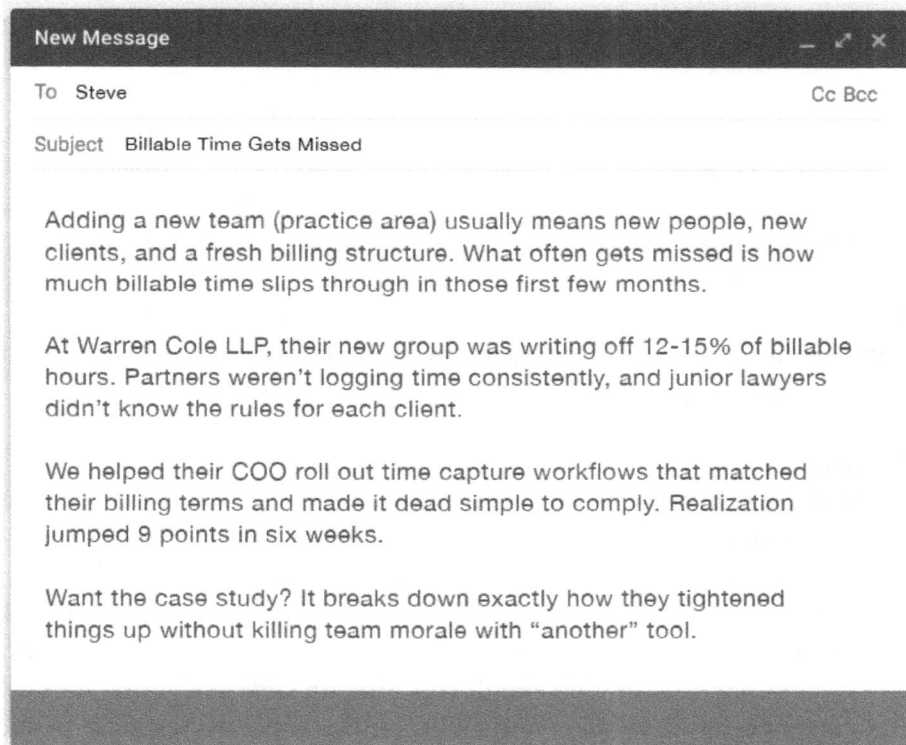

New Message _ ↗ ×

To Steve   Cc Bcc

Subject   Billable Time Gets Missed

Adding a new team (practice area) usually means new people, new clients, and a fresh billing structure. What often gets missed is how much billable time slips through in those first few months.

At Warren Cole LLP, their new group was writing off 12-15% of billable hours. Partners weren't logging time consistently, and junior lawyers didn't know the rules for each client.

We helped their COO roll out time capture workflows that matched their billing terms and made it dead simple to comply. Realization jumped 9 points in six weeks.

Want the case study? It breaks down exactly how they tightened things up without killing team morale with "another" tool.

In every email, use intrigue to compel your buyer to move toward the next call to action.

OBJECTIONS

Sometimes you'll get a reply that isn't the one you want. It's still not over.

Let's say you got an email from a buyer telling you they're not interested. You now have an opportunity to get more information. Give them a call straight away and ask questions to better understand their response. If unsuccessful, you can send a reply:

> "I appreciate you letting me know. Can I ask just one question, is it that [problem] isn't an issue for you, you're not the right person for this, or is this just a bad time to be in touch?" The reason I ask is we found that when a problem(s) like this exists it can cost [insert measurable impacts] if left unaddressed."

With this reply, you're making sure they actually read your first email and understand what problem you raised. You're making sure their "no" is a real "no," not a knee-jerk response. It also helps you better understand their context. Maybe solving this problem isn't a priority right now because they have something more pressing they have to deal with, and in six months they'll be more open to having the conversation with you. It also ensures they know what they are saying "no" to. And finally, it allows you one more chance to prove that you've done your research, and you didn't randomly choose them but sought them out because you understand their job and their business and want to help.

ON NOT GIVING UP

If emails aren't working, there are many other channels you can use to try to catch a buyer's attention, and a way to put those "touches" together into a compelling sequence. We'll talk about those in Chapter 18. But it's important to say here that if you keep bombarding buyers with dozens of emails, you're probably going to get blocked forever. So if you send out a variety of emails touching on different problems and contexts, offering new offers and CTAs, and you get no response at all, it's probably time to stop. But stopping doesn't mean giving up. Instead, you might target someone different at the company and come back to this individual a few months later when you've got something new to talk about. Maybe something will change at their company, or some new regulations will be passed, or you'll notice a new symptom or catalyst that makes it easy to justify reaching out again and gives you a perfect entry back into the conversation. You could let your buyer know your intention with an email like this:

New Message   _ ⤢ ✕

To keenan   Cc Bcc

Subject RE: Fast Cases, Slow Intake

Given the new law practice & team growth, I thought client flows might be top of mind. Am I off base or would this be a better conversation for Jane over in finance?

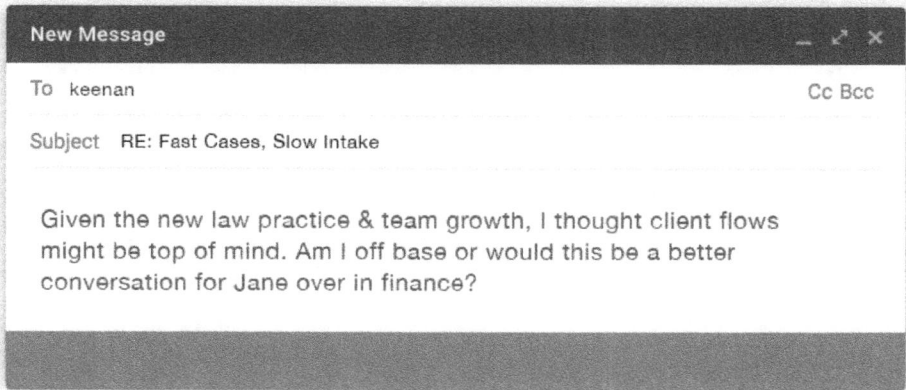

You're not saying goodbye forever, just for now. Your buyer won't be surprised to hear from you again and may even respond more favorably the next time your name pops up because it will be familiar.

HOW TO WRITE A KILLER COLD EMAIL

Okay, now that you know what goes into an intriguing, sticky, attention-grabbing email, how do you write it?

You don't.

We're not going to teach you how to write your email. We're going to teach you how to create it.

CHAPTER SIXTEEN
PROMPT YOUR WAY TO THE
PERFECT COLD EMAIL

We're willing to die on this hill: No rep or enablement team, SDR, or anyone selling anything should ever, ever, ever, ever manually write another sales email again. You're not good enough. You're not creative enough. You can't possibly learn enough about your buyer's business fast enough. And you'll take too long. In short, you'll never be able to come up with an ACC trigger as fast as AI can.

Instead, you need to write the perfect prompt that will allow your AI assistant to feed you a solid email, then use what you know about perfect emails to create it—to edit and fine-tune it so that it's perfect for your buyers. This chapter may be worth the entire cost of the book in your hands.

The Perfect Prompt
In Chapter 8, you uploaded your PIC, and in Chapter 13, you used your AI chatbot to research and analyze problems, catalysts, and symptoms to help you build and refine your target list. That process alone taught your AI a lot about your business, and if you used AI for work before that, it now knows even more. The process has also ensured that YOU know your business, your buyers, their problems, and your offers inside and out. You're about to see how that deep knowledge pays off.

We said that to write the perfect email, you needed to write the perfect prompt for AI. But we're not going to teach you how to write the perfect prompt; we've already done that work for you. Yup, you read that right. No need to grind through countless hours trying to figure out the best prompt(s). In the age of AI, some things just make more sense than others, and this is one of them. So here it is. You're welcome. ;)

Note: Throughout this book, we've tried to stay true to our own personalities and bring you the same lightness and fun attitude we bring to our clients and to our work. In this chapter, however, it's important that you see how the prompts are universally applicable, no matter your market or field. We promise to dish out more snacks and dessert once we're sure you've absorbed this super-nutritious, power-packed prompting pedagogy.

To save you the effort of typing all that out, scan this QR code. It will take you straight to the prompt as written on the next page. Then with the exception of the four inputs in the beginning, you can just copy and paste the text into your AI.

COLD EMAIL MASTER PROMPT

Ready when you are.

You are a B2B cold email strategist. Write short cold emails that sound like a real human typed them quickly, not like marketing copy or AI.

Goal
Generate replies, not polish.

Inputs (required each time)
Audience: company type + website + role + LinkedIn profile
Signal: observable, verifiable change, action, or symptom
Offer: low-lift asset (guide, checklist, playbook, case study, 1-min video)
Proof (optional): peer role + company type + specific outcome

Tone Rules
Curious, peer-to-peer, non-accusatory
No certainty about their situation; imply, don't declare
No flattery, no hype, no obvious opinions

Hard constraints
No greetings
No em dashes
No blog-style subject lines
No buzzwords or filler
No staccato one-line rhythm
From 50-120 words
White space every 1-3 sentences
No meeting ask in the first email

Structure (must follow this order)
Subject line: Short, natural, activates the ACC, creates intrigue, non-salesy.
Opening line: Start with the signal written like an observation, not a conclusion.
Problem frame: Hedge slightly to avoid accusations. Connect the signal to a possible root-cause problem. Use a small, believable scenario. Avoid "you are" language.
Impact / Stakes: Show what could happen if this stays unsolved. Keep it realistic, grounded, and role-appropriate (use proof if provided).
Offer + CTA: Offer something useful even if they never buy.
Ask: End with a binary, low-friction question.

Output Instructions
Three subject line options of varying length
One email body (≤120 words)

The email should feel helpful, slightly imperfect, and written by a human in a hurry.

You, the seller, provide these prompts each time

INPUTS

The only piece of the prompt you need to customize every time you start your outreach is the four inputs. Be as specific, precise, and detailed as possible. For example, for Audience, you'd input VP of Sales, not just VP. For Signal, you wouldn't include "Hiring account executives" but rather, "Hiring six account executives with full cycle (prospecting) responsibilities." The better the input, the better the output will be.

REVISE THE PROMPT

Here's where your deep understanding of the nine building blocks of the perfect email will come into play. Just as the invention of spell-check didn't eliminate the need to proofread our writing, AI doesn't eliminate the need to apply human thought and creativity to our work. It's just a tool, one that can make mistakes. It's going to be especially weak at weighing the psychological and emotional factors we've discussed that influence how buyers respond to messaging and at infusing your out-reach with the qualities that make you, you. It hasn't lived what you have, so it can't draw from your experiences to help you connect with your buyers. Nor has it lived what your buyers have, so it can't draw from their experiences either. It has never felt frustrated, worried, scared, stressed, or pressed for time, so it can't feel empathy, and when it tries, it will likely sound canned. It doesn't know what it's like to be ambitious, hopeful, and eager to see its hard work make an impact. Its humor is derivative, not fresh and original.

You can, however, turn the prompt into your own unique creation that sparks intrigue and draws interest by using the checklist below to assess your first draft and make revisions.

COLD EMAIL SCORING & RE-PROMPTING GUIDE

For each category, score the first draft of your email 1-5. If any element didn't earn a 5, use the **Re-Prompt Cue** to tell AI exactly what to fix.

For example, if your subject line scored 2, you would write in AI:

- **Subject line scored 2:** "Rewrite subject line as 1-4 words, human, peer-style. Use a micro-scenario or curiosity gap, not a headline."

- 194 -

If your Problem Framing scored 3, you would write in AI:

- **Problem scored 3:** "Add a concrete micro-scenario the buyer can imagine. Make it believable and uncomfortable, but not melodramatic."

1. **SUBJECT LINE**
   - **Score 1-2:** Too generic, salesy, or blog-like.
     - *Re-Prompt Cue:* "Rewrite subject as 1-4 words, human, peer-style. Use a micro-scenario or curiosity gap, not a headline."

   - **Score 3-4:** Some intrigue but still templated.
     - *Re-Prompt Cue:* "Tighten subject to feel like an interruption, not marketing copy."

   - **Score 5:** Short, human, attention-worthy.

2. **OPENER**
   - **Score 1-2:** Generic greeting ("Hope you're well").
     - *Re-Prompt Cue:* "Start directly with the observable trigger/event. No greetings."

   - **Score 3-4:** Mentions them but weakly tied.
     - *Re-Prompt Cue:* "Make opener concrete, show you noticed something real about them or their company."

   - **Score 5:** Immediate, relevant, human.

3. **RELEVANCE**
   - **Score 1-2:** Could be sent to anyone.
     - *Re-Prompt Cue:* "Anchor message in their role and current trigger. Why them, why now?"

   - **Score 3-4:** Light tie-in but shallow.
     - *Re-Prompt Cue:* "Deepen the link between the trigger and their job-to-be-done."

- **Score 5:** Laser-targeted, role-specific.

4. **BRIDGE**
   - **Score 1-2:** Abrupt jump into pitch.
     - *Re-Prompt Cue:* "Smoothly connect trigger > root cause > business impact before mentioning solution."

   - **Score 3-4:** Some logic but still forced.
     - *Re-Prompt Cue:* "Make the flow consultative, not promotional."

   - **Score 5:** Flows naturally.

5. **PROBLEM FRAMING**
   - **Score 1-2:** Vague, abstract, or product-centric.
     - *Re-Prompt Cue:* "Add a concrete micro-scenario they can imagine. Make it believable, uncomfortable, but not melo-dramatic."

   - **Score 3-4:** Problem is clear but still generic.
     - *Re-Prompt Cue:* "Sharpen the example so it feels situational."

   - **Score 5:** Vivid, memorable, human.

6. **INTRIGUE**
   - **Score 1-2:** Flat, no tension.
     - *Re-Prompt Cue:* "Inject subtle discomfort—reputational risk, FOMO, or doubt. Keep it credible."

   - **Score 3-4:** Some curiosity, but low emotional pull.
     - *Re-Prompt Cue:* "Make the consequence feel personal and near-term."

   - **Score 5:** ACC activated—they *feel* the risk.

7. **OFFER**
   - **Score 1-2:** Just a meeting/demo ask.

  - *Re-Prompt Cue:* "Replace with a tangible, low-lift asset (checklist, playbook, case study, short video)."

- **Score 3-4:** Generic or low-value resource.
  - *Re-Prompt Cue:* "Make the offer specific and framed as immediately useful."

- **Score 5:** Strong, valuable, easy to accept.

8. **ASK (CTA)**
   - **Score 1-2:** High-friction (30-min call).
     - *Re-Prompt Cue:* "Rewrite CTA as binary, low-friction yes/no. No meeting ask."

   - **Score 3-4:** Lower friction but vague.
     - *Re-Prompt Cue:* "Make the ask crystal clear and role appropriate."

   - **Score 5:** Simple, binary, natural.

9. **FORMATTING & READABILITY**
   - **Score 1-2:** Wall of text, robotic.
     - *Re-Prompt Cue:* "Add white space, vary sentence length, remove em dashes, and make it scannable on mobile."

   - **Score 3-4:** Readable but stiff or generic.
     - *Re-Prompt Cue:* "Loosen rhythm, add slight imperfection, make it sound like a human typed it quickly."

   - **Score 5:** Easy to skim, natural, human.

WATCH IT WORK: SAMPLE DRAFTS AND REVISIONS

Below are six examples of what happened when we fed our AI chatbot the master prompt with a series of customized inputs. Read along to see our thought process as we read and revised.

MASTER PROMPT #1

INPUTS

- **Audience:** CRO, 500-person tech company, with a 60-person sales team
- **Trigger/Event:** They're hiring account executives with full cycle (prospecting) responsibilities listed in the job ad
- **Offer:** A rep lead identification workflow checklist
- **Proof:** Thousands of tech companies using ZoomInfo

AI produced a first draft.

FIRST DRAFT

New Message   — ↗ ✕

To   Keenan   Cc Bcc

Subject   Empty Pipeline Seats

Saw you're hiring AEs and making them prospect, too.

That works, but it also means every new hire is starting from scratch on who to chase. Half the time they burn the first quarter digging through old lists, asking around for accounts, or chasing ghosts that never buy.

At another 600-person SaaS org, the CRO told me his reps were losing 6 weeks just figuring out targets. He fixed it with a simple workflow from ZoomInfo that thousands of tech teams use to front-load account identification.

I've got the checklist he used. Would it be useful if I sent it your way?

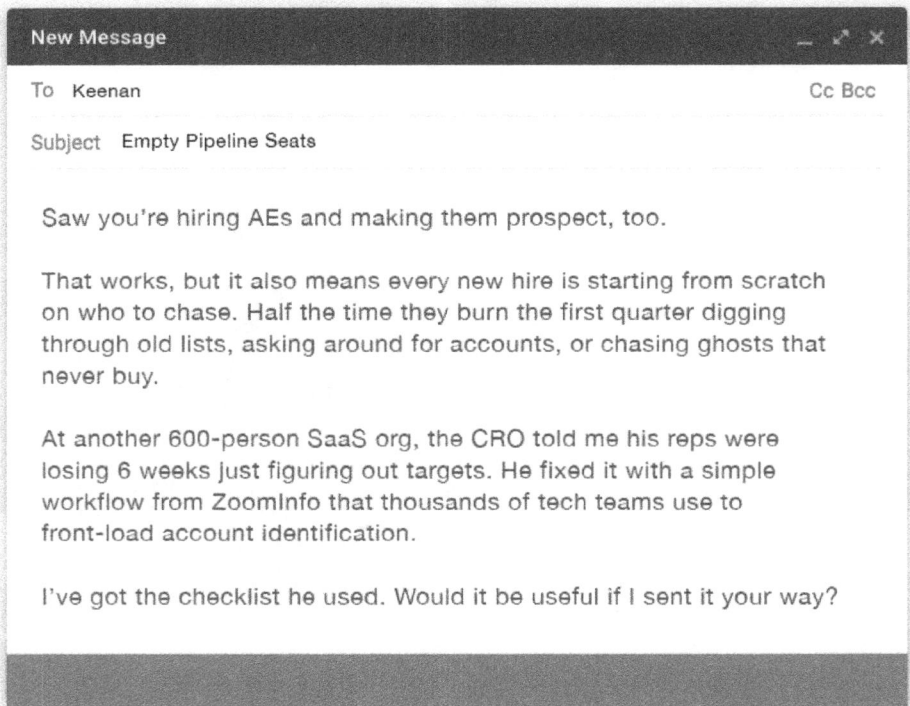

Do you see what we see? We thought the prompt AI gave us was great overall, but after reviewing it with the checklist, we realized that the issues it addressed seemed a little low level for a CRO. So we re-prompted.

Re-Prompt Cue:
"Needs to speak more to the responsibilities of a CRO."

AI produced a revision.

REWRITE

New Message   _ ↗ ✕

To   Keenan   Cc Bcc

Subject   Quota math off

Saw you're hiring AEs with full cycle responsibilities. That tells me coverage is stretched, and every rep's pipeline quality now makes or breaks the forecast.

The risk is simple: half those hires spend Q1 prospecting blind, quota math slips, and your CAC creeps up while the board expects the opposite.

A CRO at a 500-seat tech company ran into the same thing and cut ramp time by six weeks using a ZoomInfo workflow thousands of sales teams lean on.

I've got the checklist he used. Want me to send it over?

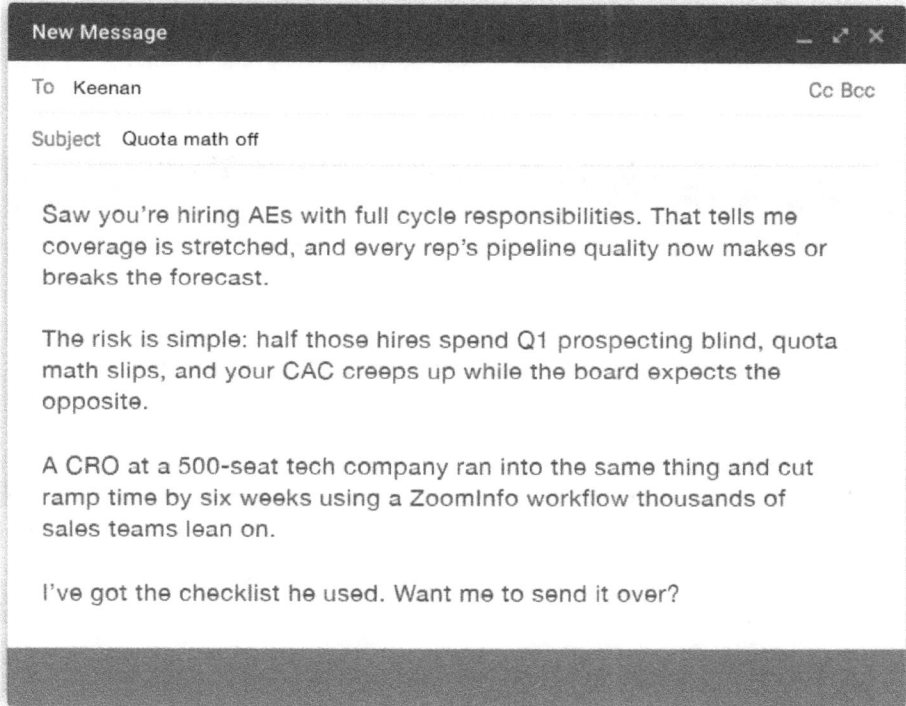

Do you see what we see? We like this one better. This version addresses the issues that matter to a CRO and therefore has a higher chance of connecting with our intended audience.

Master Prompt #2

Inputs

- **Audience:** Director of Sales at a 200-rep SaaS company
- **Signal:** Just doubled SDR headcount after a funding round
- **Offer:** 2-minute breakdown video on how peer teams manage call analysis
- **Proof:** VP at a 200-rep SaaS team cut ramp time 29% by flagging top calls daily

AI's First Draft

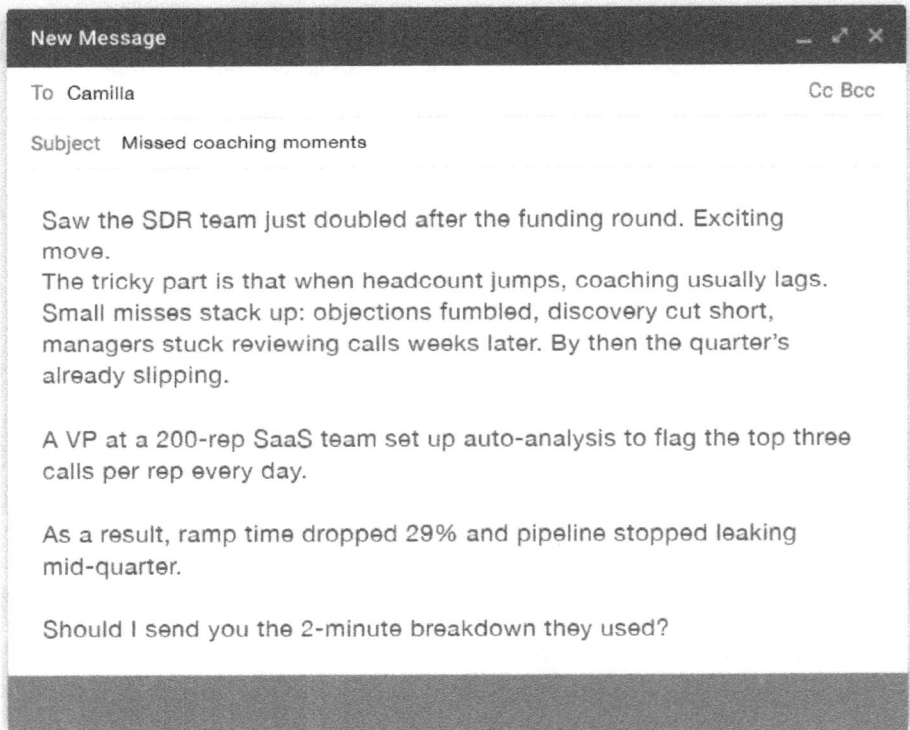

New Message   _ ⤢ ✕

To Camilla   Cc Bcc

Subject   Missed coaching moments

Saw the SDR team just doubled after the funding round. Exciting move.
The tricky part is that when headcount jumps, coaching usually lags. Small misses stack up: objections fumbled, discovery cut short, managers stuck reviewing calls weeks later. By then the quarter's already slipping.

A VP at a 200-rep SaaS team set up auto-analysis to flag the top three calls per rep every day.

As a result, ramp time dropped 29% and pipeline stopped leaking mid-quarter.

Should I send you the 2-minute breakdown they used?

Do you see what we see? Nailed it right out the gate. This email recognizes the problems and speaks to the actual target. It's realistic and follows a logical train of thought. It's relevant and uses a good example of social proof. We saw no need for a re-prompt.

MASTER PROMPT #3
INPUTS
- **Audience:** CFO of a 300-store retail chain
- **Signal:** Store closures and cost-cutting announcement in the press
- **Offer:** 3-line audit checklist to spot hidden fees
- **Proof:** CFO at a 250-store chain discovered effective fees 24% higher and saved $410K in one year

AI's First Draft

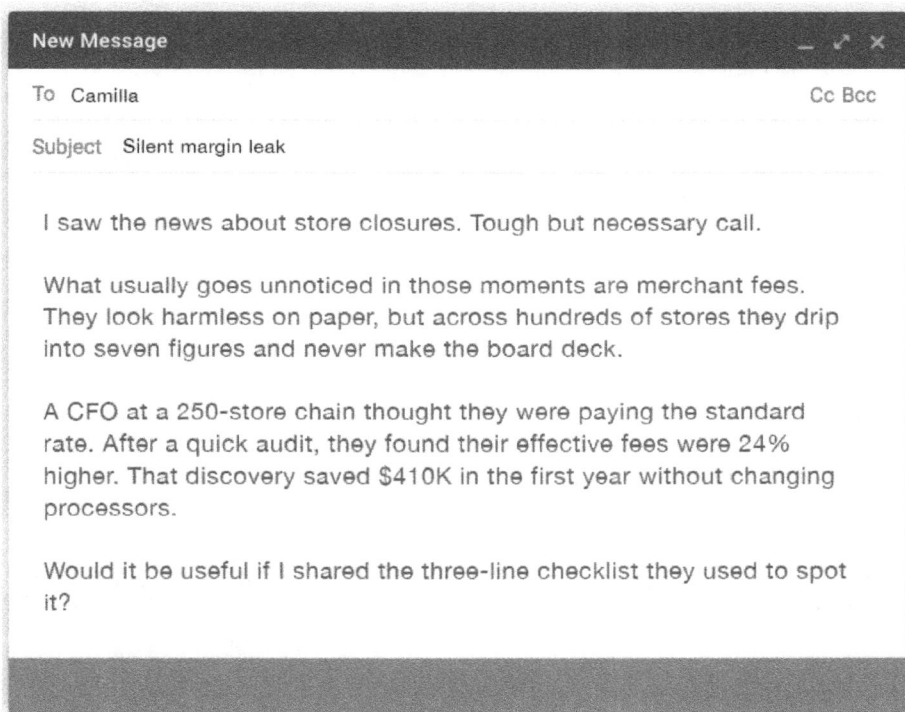

New Message	_ ↗ ✕
To Camilla	Cc Bcc
Subject Silent margin leak	

I saw the news about store closures. Tough but necessary call.

What usually goes unnoticed in those moments are merchant fees. They look harmless on paper, but across hundreds of stores they drip into seven figures and never make the board deck.

A CFO at a 250-store chain thought they were paying the standard rate. After a quick audit, they found their effective fees were 24% higher. That discovery saved $410K in the first year without changing processors.

Would it be useful if I shared the three-line checklist they used to spot it?

Do you see what we see? Not bad, but "Tough but necessary call" feels condescending.

In addition, we haven't made a connection between the store closures and merchant fees. We're leaving out important information, which is that the store closures are a cost-cutting measure, but so is lowering merchant fees.

Re-Prompt Cue:
"Be less judgmental in tone. Bridge needs to better connect the observation to the problem"

REWRITE

New Message   _ ↗ ×

To Zain   Cc Bcc

Subject Silent margin leak

Saw the announcement on the store closures. When pressure is high to trim expenses, the first place where leadership looks is overhead.

What usually goes unnoticed in those moments are merchant fees. They hide in plain sight, drip into every transaction, and across hundreds of stores add up to seven figures that never hit the board deck.

A CFO at a 250-store chain thought they were paying the standard rate. After a quick audit, they found their effective fees were 24% higher. That discovery saved $410K in the first year without changing processors.

Would it be useful if I shared the three-line checklist they used to spot it?

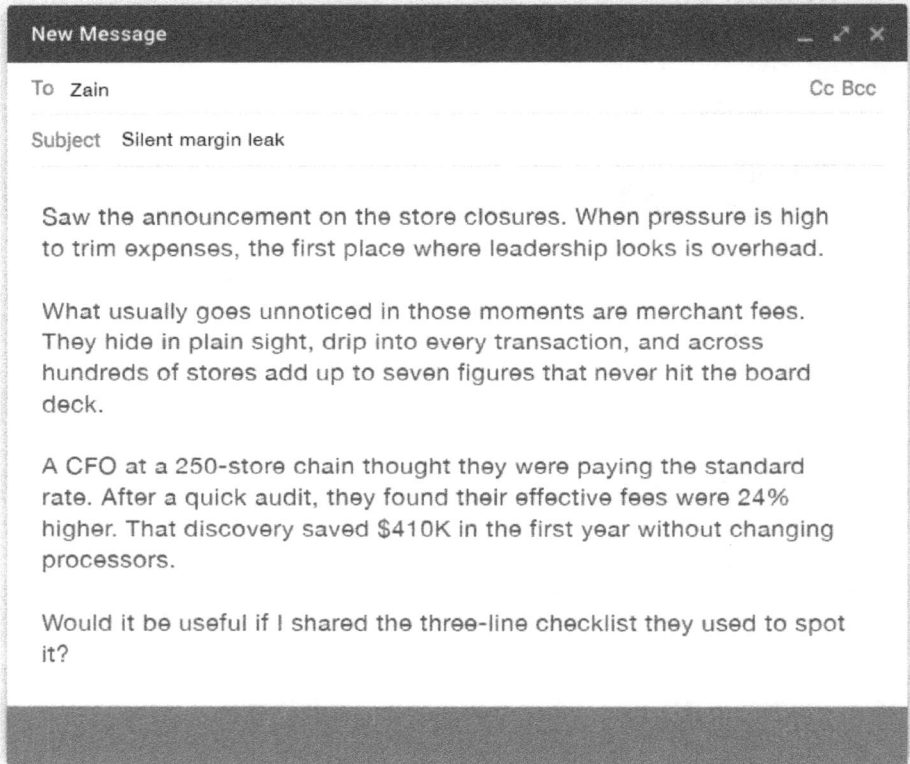

MASTER PROMPT #4
INPUTS

- **Audience:** Head of HR at a 1,000-employee fintech company
- **Signal:** Recent acquisition + LinkedIn chatter showing increased attrition
- **Offer:** 1-page retention playbook
- **Proof:** Fintech HR leader cut regretted attrition by 19% in 6 months using engagement analytics

AI's First Draft

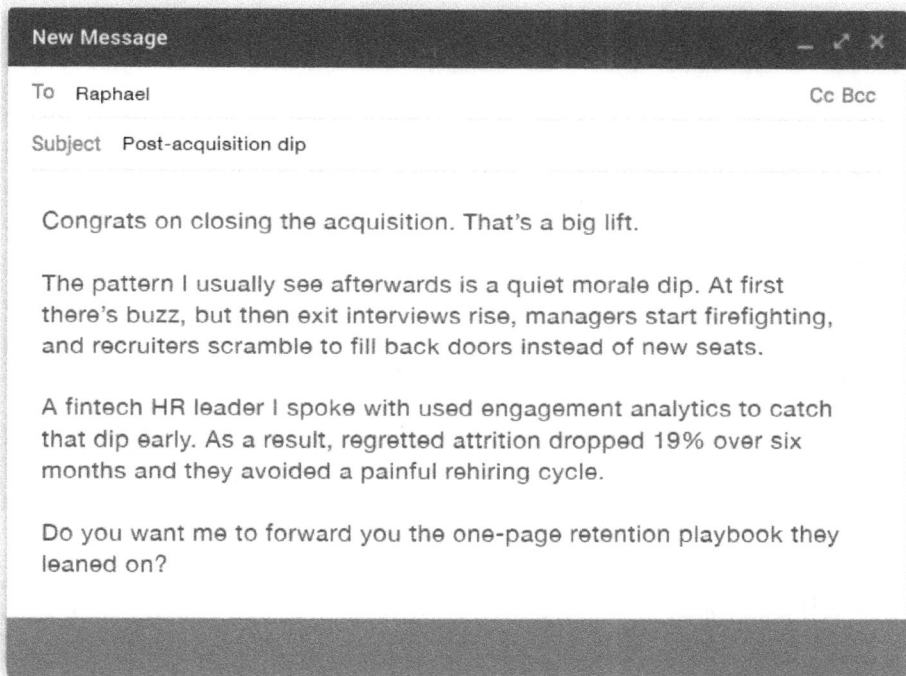

New Message   — ↗ ✕

To   Raphael   Cc Bcc

Subject   Post-acquisition dip

Congrats on closing the acquisition. That's a big lift.

The pattern I usually see afterwards is a quiet morale dip. At first there's buzz, but then exit interviews rise, managers start firefighting, and recruiters scramble to fill back doors instead of new seats.

A fintech HR leader I spoke with used engagement analytics to catch that dip early. As a result, regretted attrition dropped 19% over six months and they avoided a painful rehiring cycle.

Do you want me to forward you the one-page retention playbook they leaned on?

Do you see what we see? This one mentions a root cause and symptoms but fails to point out a business impact or explain why it would be relevant to a head of HR, which is that when people leave a company because of post-acquisition morale dip, you end up spending a ton of money trying to replace that staff. And once again, we're stating the obvious when we say, "That's a big lift."

Re-Prompt Cue:
"Connect to a head of HR-related business problem and impact. Avoid stating the obvious."

REWRITE

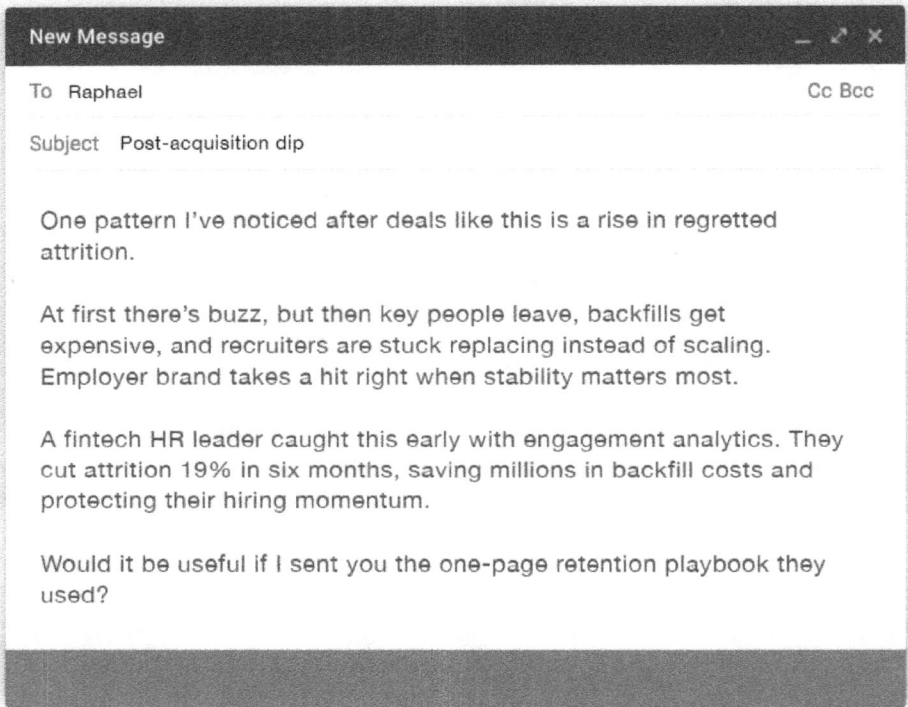

New Message — ⤢ ✕

To Raphael   Cc Bcc

Subject Post-acquisition dip

One pattern I've noticed after deals like this is a rise in regretted attrition.

At first there's buzz, but then key people leave, backfills get expensive, and recruiters are stuck replacing instead of scaling. Employer brand takes a hit right when stability matters most.

A fintech HR leader caught this early with engagement analytics. They cut attrition 19% in six months, saving millions in backfill costs and protecting their hiring momentum.

Would it be useful if I sent you the one-page retention playbook they used?

Master Prompt #5
Inputs
- **Audience:** CMO at a mid-market consumer brand
- **Signal:** Product launch with visible 3x jump in content volume (social/blog)
- **Offer:** 3-check asset flow guide
- **Proof:** CMO peer cut prep time 31% in the first quarter after centralizing assets

AI's First Draft

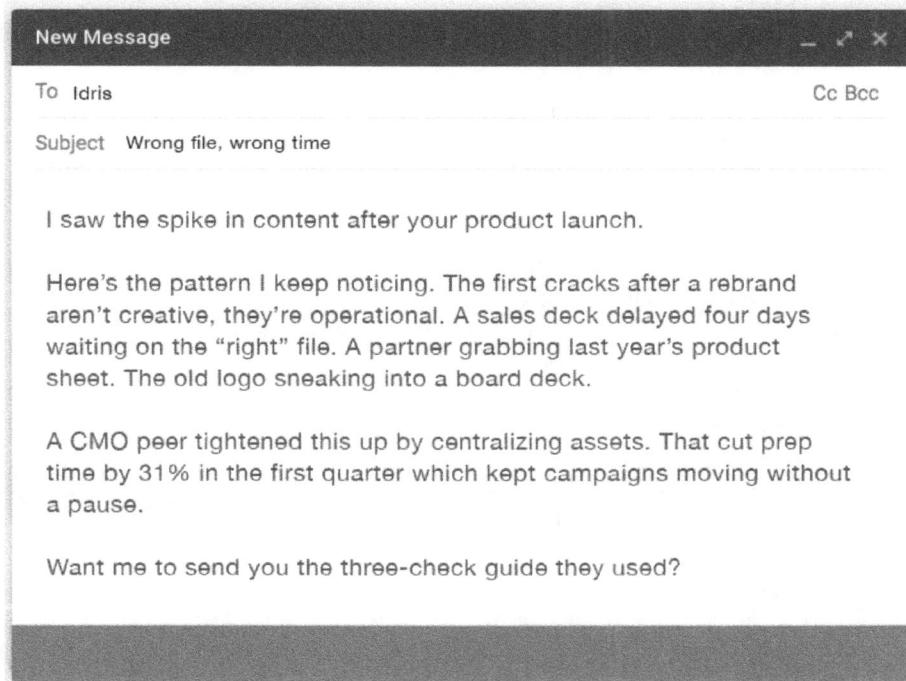

New Message	_ ⤢ ✕
To Idris	Cc Bcc

Subject   Wrong file, wrong time

I saw the spike in content after your product launch.

Here's the pattern I keep noticing. The first cracks after a rebrand aren't creative, they're operational. A sales deck delayed four days waiting on the "right" file. A partner grabbing last year's product sheet. The old logo sneaking into a board deck.

A CMO peer tightened this up by centralizing assets. That cut prep time by 31% in the first quarter which kept campaigns moving without a pause.

Want me to send you the three-check guide they used?

Do you see what we see? This email only lists root causes. Are they missing deadlines? What about how when campaigns start to slip, competitors start eating up your market share?

Re-Prompt Cue:
"Clearly state the impact."

Rewrite

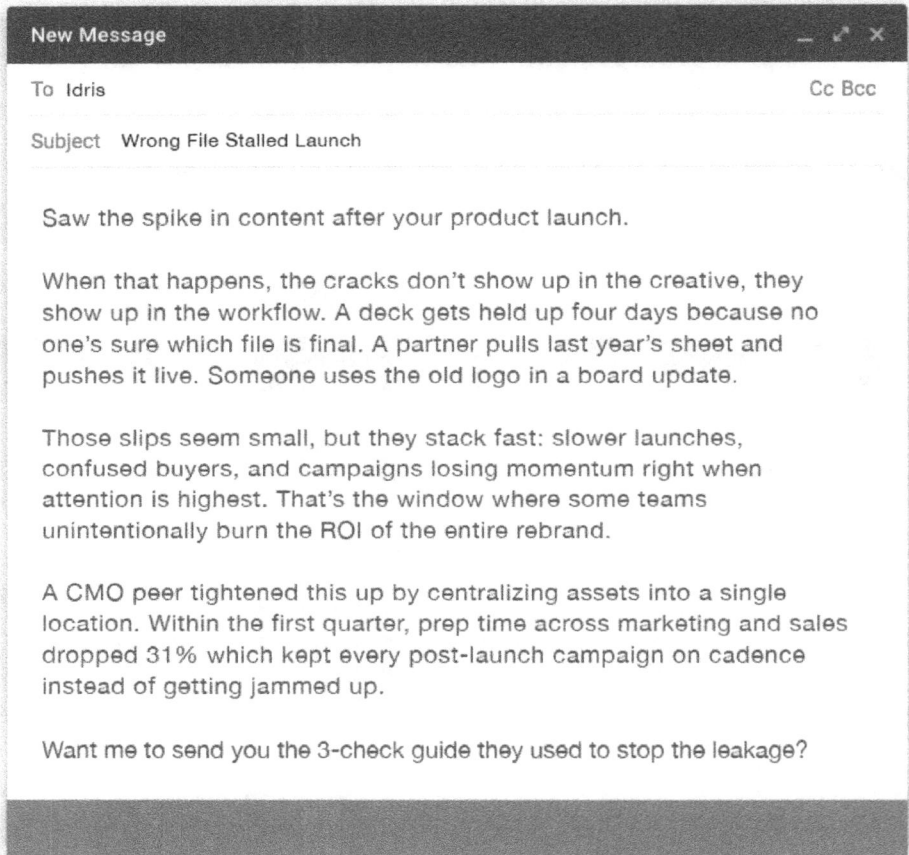

New Message — ↗ ✕

To Idris   Cc Bcc

Subject Wrong File Stalled Launch

Saw the spike in content after your product launch.

When that happens, the cracks don't show up in the creative, they show up in the workflow. A deck gets held up four days because no one's sure which file is final. A partner pulls last year's sheet and pushes it live. Someone uses the old logo in a board update.

Those slips seem small, but they stack fast: slower launches, confused buyers, and campaigns losing momentum right when attention is highest. That's the window where some teams unintentionally burn the ROI of the entire rebrand.

A CMO peer tightened this up by centralizing assets into a single location. Within the first quarter, prep time across marketing and sales dropped 31% which kept every post-launch campaign on cadence instead of getting jammed up.

Want me to send you the 3-check guide they used to stop the leakage?

Make It Yours!

We get that there are aspects of these emails that are subjective, and that we're going to adjust tone and language to fit our style, which may not match yours. Ultimately, you have to feel like the emails you're sending out sound like you and reflect your personality. But making sure you've built in those nine essential building blocks is non-negotiable. AI can't do it alone. Blend style and substance by giving your message your unique human touch and doing the deep thinking outlined in the earlier chapters of this book, and see how many more of your prospects stop, listen, and respond. The more context you give your AI tool of choice on your tone, product, customers, and the problems you help solve, the more accurate the output.

At its core, the formula you'll apply to your cold calls and emails will in essence and function give you the same script Will used to earn a 25% close rate when he went door-to-door selling "No Soliciting" signs. Let us show you:

STEP	SCRIPT	BREAKING IT DOWN
1	"Hey, I was chatting with a couple of your neighbors, and they told me they get a ton of sales reps knocking on their door, trying to sell stuff like pest control, solar panels, that kind of thing... Do you get a lot of that, too?"	"Hey, I was chatting with [other titles in industry], and they told me [problem keeps happening]... Is that something you [experience or see], too?"
2	"How many would you say per week?"	[Does this problem happen often]?
3	"Wow, and does that disturb you? Get on your nerves?"	[How does the problem affect you]?
4	Alternative response: Later, after talking to more neighbors, instead of asking how the problem affected people, Will started sharing what others had told him—"That's a fair amount. I hear those disruptions can distract people trying to work, wake up napping kids, or set the dogs off. Does any of that get on your nerves?"	"A lot of folks find that this problem can cause [impact]. [Can you relate]?"
5	"A lot of folks on this block have posted signs that say 'No' to try to prevent these interruptions. Is there a reason you haven't tried that yet?"	[How have you already tried to solve this problem]?
6	"Well, that's why I dropped by. I spotted you didn't have a sign yet. Are you open to checking out a couple of the signs I've got?"	"Well, that's why I dropped by. [I spotted this particular catalyst, symptom, or problem, and we've been helping clients prevent those by offering this solution]. Are you open to [learning more about how they do that]?"
7	*Handle objections as necessary*	

Problem before product or pitch, every time.

CHAPTER SEVENTEEN
OTHER MEDIUMS TO CARRY YOUR MESSAGE

Your buyers are like Kim, who works in Times Square in New York City, steeling herself before pushing through her office doors onto the sidewalk. All day the tourists throng, but the crowd grows exponentially bigger at night, when the square's enormous LED screens radiate like a five-block hit of digital caffeine, Coke, and Adderall. Add the foot traffic from people leaving their offices and arriving for their pre-theater dinners, along with navigating the Times Square pedestrian plaza and sidewalks, can feel a little like running across a battlefield. Instead of mines or soldiers, Kim dodges sightseers spinning like open-mouthed moths in the bright-as-day glow, costumed superheroes cozying up for pictures, and gawkers taking videos of the Naked Cowboy. Kim keeps her head down and tries to ignore the mayhem around her. A barker calls out, asking if she's interested in a comedy club performance starting in an hour. She accidentally catches the eye of a costumed Hulk who turns in her direction, and she speeds up. She scoots past the jewelry sellers, the t-shirt vendors, and the small group clustered around a game of three-card monte, the thrower's voice rising from the center in rapid patter, "Find the queen, find the queen, watch close now, double your money!"

Arriving near the corner where a right turn will take her away from the noise and chaos, Kim is close to breaking free when she hears a high, pure note among the shouts and honking horns. The unmistakable sound of a sax playing John Coltrane's version of "My Favorite Things." Ahead of her, the busker, tall and lean in a porkpie hat with a little feather tucked in the band, stands close to a wall, swaying as he plays. At his feet lies an open case waiting to catch a few stray bills and coins, partnered with a sign displaying a payment app QR code that reads, "No Cash? Scan me!" As much as Kim looks forward to getting home, she pauses to watch and listen. The iconic image of a handsome musician trying to make it in the Big Apple reminds her of how lucky she is to live and work in the city that never sleeps. The music melts away her irritation and fatigue. As she pulls out her phone to scan the QR code, she notices another message on the sign: "Hear me play Thursdays this month at Lulamaie's Lounge." Kim and her girlfriend, Tori, went out a lot when they'd first moved to the city but had long ago fallen into a routine of take-out Thai and streaming movies. She'd been wanting to get out more, and Lula's was an institution. When she got home, she'd talk to Tori about going this week.

Like Kim forced to navigate Times Square to get home from work, buyers aren't on their social media business accounts to engage with strangers and are definitely not there to buy stuff they don't need. They're there to enhance their knowledge by consuming a thought leader's post or to post their own content, sell their products, network, job hunt, or hire new employees. No one goes there hoping to be pitched. So if sellers want to get buyers' attention, it won't be by being the loudest person in their inbox. And while creativity will help get the attention, that won't keep it either. Connecting with buyers online in any meaningful way only happens when you figure out how to talk to them about their goals or fixing the problems that weigh on them. In other words, though using social media often feels more casual than email or cold calls, it requires just as much research, planning, thought, and care. Without that, you risk triggering the same kind of fight-or-flight response Kim felt the minute she caught the eye of the Hulk. Instead, you want to be the cool jazz player, giving Kim what she needed, in the format she needed, even before she knew she did.

For the rest of this discussion, we're going to assume that you've already built a robust prospecting list and that you're targeting the appropriate people. List ready, you'll start by figuring out where your buyers are most active on social media and how they and their industry use those channels. Then you're going to tweak your problem-centric, relevant message so that it's optimized for the format and culture of that particular site or platform. That can sound daunting, but if you take the following advice, you'll stand out both in message and form.

Let's examine the most popular channels and discuss how to use them for outreach that doesn't piss off your buyers (more than they already are; see Chapter 4).

LinkedIn

LinkedIn is the obvious choice for many buyers to gather, consume information, and communicate because it was built to be a business platform. But while many buyers have set up pages, not everyone is active. Medical professionals and small business owners, for example, often have pages but may not interact with the site much, or check in at all, because they get better results on their Facebook business page or Instagram accounts. A lot of people just use LinkedIn as a digital CV and to direct people to their websites and contact information. The first step you're going to take is to make sure that you don't look like one of them.

Glow Up Your Profile

People should be able to learn as much about you on LinkedIn as you'd like to learn about them, so you want to create a robust, energized LinkedIn presence. Compose your LinkedIn page thoughtfully, and you can tame your buyer's fight-or-flight response before they even open your message.

- **Photo.** Your profile photo should be a high-quality, smiling head-shot—no weirdos, no robots, no dull expressions, but no forced cheerleader smiles either. It should say, "I'm confident and friendly and I love what I do." This image is going to be attached to all your engagement on the site or app, so make it speak volumes without a word.

- **Headline.** Along with your profile photo, this is the first thing buyers will see when you ask to connect or send a DM. Don't scream that you're a salesperson! We're not encouraging you to mislead or be disingenuous. We are encouraging you to instead talk about how you help people or the type of networking you do. It's the difference between lecturing and inspiring. For example, when composing your headline, don't describe yourself as "SDR at Save Money Financial." That tells everyone you're here to sell something. Instead, you might write, "Stop overpaying on subscriptions - Helping companies save 25% on IT Contracts without lifting a finger." You get up to 220 characters in a headline—use them. And by inserting a vertical bar, you can show two sides of your identity, such as your actual title and a playful or profound description of what you do.

If your buyer decides to check out your page before they read your message, make sure everything there inspires confidence.

- **Banner.** Create an eye-catching, colorful banner using graphics, a photo, a photo with text, or any other relevant imagery that tells people more about you as a person or a business.

- **About section.** Include brief, specific information about yourself and your business. Tell a good (short) story if you can, and show off your personality. This is the place where you do get to talk about yourself, but always in a value-forward way. Making yourself approachable and authoritative will put people at ease when they come to visit your page.

- **Featured.** You can feature your favorite content front and center in the Featured section. Add timeless or relevant LinkedIn posts, LinkedIn articles you've written or in which you're mentioned, links to external websites or press, or images and videos you've created.

- **Activity.** You want buyers to see an active page full of recent, interesting posts, comments, videos, and images, all evidence that you're a real person out there discussing important issues with other professionals. The more LinkedIn Groups you join, the more thought leaders and companies you follow, and the more actively you comment on and react to posts, the more approachable you'll appear. In addition, staying active will ensure that your Highlights section automatically populates, which adds visual interest to the page and builds cred.

How to Outreach on LinkedIn
Don't:

Use InMail, the premium feature that allows you to DM LinkedIn members even if you're not connected to them. It costs you money, and it's ineffective. Why? Because the only people who use InMail are salespeople, so the moment a buyer sees one, they assume it's a pitch (patterns, remember?), and they feel confident they can safely ignore it. Sending InMail to an inactive LinkedIn user is a waste of time. If they're not checking their LinkedIn page, your InMail is just going to sit uselessly in their inbox. InMails have terrible response rates.

Do:
Use **LinkedIn Connections**, which will give you full access to each other's pages and contact lists, which can help establish trust when you reach out to a buyer.

Most people aren't in the habit of accepting every requested connection, though, so you need to make sure you don't look or sound like a salesperson. However, Will and Keenan disagree on the best way to do this. It boils down to notes.

To Note, or Not to Note
In Will's experience as a buyer, the only people who include notes with their connection requests are those trying to sell something. The notes are usually bland and generic too, like "I see we swim in the same waters," or "We have mutual connections!" A note like that is worse than no note at all. Will's position is that a note will be a red flag signaling that you want to pitch unless—big caveat—you can establish familiarity by referring back to a meeting or some other time when you and your buyer would have crossed paths or communicated.

Instead, let your profile do the talking. Your headshot, headline, and mutual connections will be visible to the buyer when you make the request. That's why you want to make sure what they see is excellent quality and carefully designed to say a lot about you with a little vibe and few words. This approach also serves as an easy test to find out if a buyer who doesn't regularly engage on the site is even active on LinkedIn. If they accept, you've got an open line to communicate, and you're golden. If they don't, they're either not interested or they never come to LinkedIn, but you haven't wasted much time finding out, especially since you didn't spend a second thinking about what to say in an accompanying note.

To Will's mind, there's especially no reason to write a note if you've been putting out lots of content and building a brand on LinkedIn. If your buyer doesn't know who you are and wants to learn more about you before accepting, they can always look at your page.

Keenan, on the other hand, has a different perspective. He won't accept any connection without a note unless he can see by their title that there would be mutual benefit or interest, or unless he has already dropped comments on the buyer's page to show he was interested in what the buyer was saying and posting. But even then, most of the time, he thinks it's more personable to include a note explaining why you're interested in connecting. However, the reason can't be about you. No "I'm building my network," or "I'm looking for like-minded people." Instead, make your interest about *them*: "Keenan, I read *Gap Selling* and I'm excited to read *Gap Prospecting*, hoping we can connect here." Or, "Keenan, I saw your video on dealing with objections, and it's changed the game for me. My sales are up 10%."

The key is to provide a valuable reason for them to connect with you. When you write, "I'm growing my network," you're putting yourself first and asking a complete stranger to help you. Why? Why should they care? Why should they use their limited number of connections to push or fulfill your selfish agenda? Give them a reason to want to connect with you that they feel benefits them.

If you can't figure out a way to make your interest about them and not about you, don't bother with a note at all, like Will said.

ENGAGE, ENGAGE, ENGAGE

You saw that two out of three of Will and Keenan's caveats regarding notes hinged on whether there was prior contact between buyer and seller. Ideally, if your buyer is active on LinkedIn, the day they see an invitation to connect won't be the first time they've seen your profile picture or your name. You don't have to wait to have a first-degree connection to talk to people. Get in there! Don't be a creepy stalker, but do follow them and engage with their content through reactions and comments. If a topic comes up in which you're extremely well versed, jump into the conversation with their other commenters and followers, always keeping things respectful, polite, and pleasant. Join the same groups and attend the same events, and engage with their posts or comments there. If they post a photo of an event that you attended, you can comment that you enjoyed meeting their team, or say something about what was memorable or that you especially appreciated. Engaging before connecting is like the difference between being DM'd by a total stranger who spotted your picture and being DM'd by someone you met at your spouse's company holiday party or your kid's sports event. It's a familiarity play that builds familiarity in an unthreatening way and, again, shows your buyer that you're a real human being with similar interests as theirs. Then, if you choose to write a note, you can say, "Hey, I enjoyed discussing that topic with you and would love to connect."

We realize that we're asking a lot. If you're reaching out to 100 people per day, it's going to be hard to engage like this with all of them. Do your best, and it will pay off by differentiating you from every other generic seller. If the goal of prospecting is to help, the initial point of contact can't feel like you're trying to get something out of your buyer. It has to come from a place of real interest and commonality.

CONNECTION REQUEST ACCEPTED. WHAT NOW?

If you've taken away anything from this book so far, it won't surprise you to know that the answer is definitely not to pitch. That's the biggest mistake sellers make on LinkedIn.

The other big mistake people make is copying and pasting cold emails into their LinkedIn messages and treating the platform the same as an email inbox. LinkedIn is much more of a social media platform than a correspondence platform and should be treated as such. LinkedIn messages are the equivalent of DMs, so the formatting rules for communicating on text, Facebook Messenger, or Instagram DMs apply here too.

Your goal isn't to sell; it's to start up a conversation. Keep your text so short, your buyer won't have to scroll to read the whole thing. That means keep it to about 50 words, two paragraphs, with lots of white space.

Now, Keenan and Will do this next step a little differently. Will likes responding with the equation:

Observation about the buyer/buyer's company and how it made you infer the buyer might be facing certain problems or priorities
+
Question to confirm whether your hypothesis is true

Keenan, however, isn't comfortable with this. He feels responding with questions about a buyer's business immediately after a connection request looks like a veiled attempt at a sale, and they can see right through it. So he prefers to acknowledge the newfound connection and express appreciation before getting down to business with something like this:

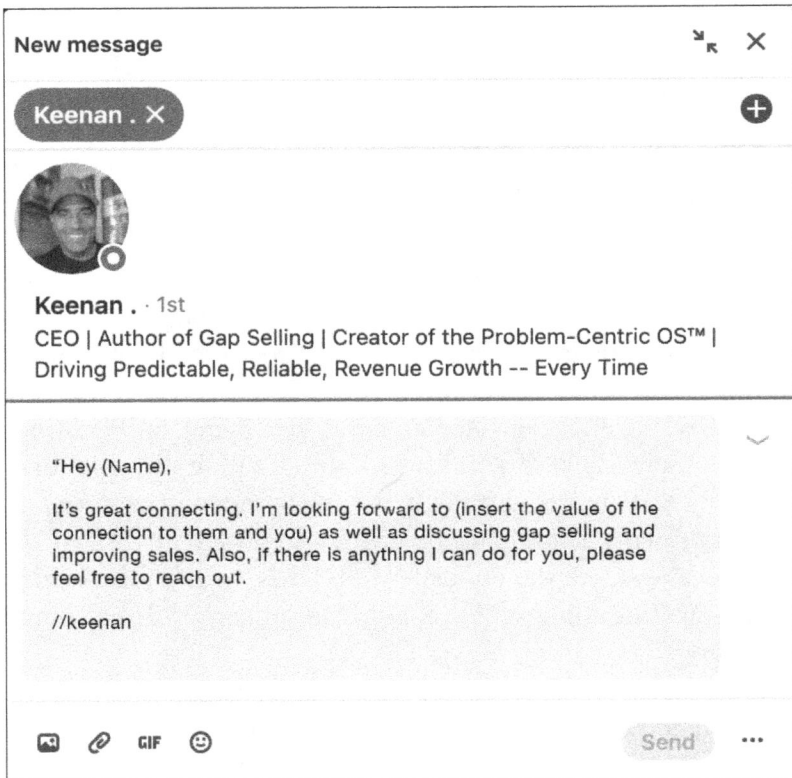

And then, a few days or a week later, Keenan will reach out using the same equation as Will.

How does that equation translate to a message? Like this, for example:

- If you're selling website design services, you might say, **"Hey looks like your website is hosted on Shopify. Are you happy with its conversion rate?"**

- If you're a recruiter, you might say, **"Looks like you're hiring for a senior business development manager. Are you finding the applicants for that role are qualified?"**

- If you're a video editor, you might say, **"Hey, it looks like you're doing a lot of text posts right now. Have you ever considered doing videos?"**

- If you sell some kind of employee benefits or insurance solution to HR people, you might say, **"Hey, it looks like your company's almost doubled in size in the past year with all that growth. Have you taken a look to see if your employee benefits provider is still the best for your size of company?"**

Observation + question. Notice that we haven't even hinted at an offer. You're just trying to get a response. The conversation should feel more like what happens on a dating app than in a corporate exchange.

IF THEY DON'T RESPOND

Try again. However, if you handle this poorly, such as by reaching out again too soon or too often, you could wind up blocked. But you can also make this your chance to shine by doing something unusual and original. After an appropriate amount of time (we'll talk about cadences and sequencing in the next chapter), reach out again, this time explaining why you're asking your question in the first place. To add some spice and variety, you can try some of the ideas we suggested in Chapter 14 and attach an attention-getting and maybe even informative extra element into your DM, like a PDF of an industry report, an image, or one of LinkedIn's built-in GIFs.

And if you really want to stand out, you could try using some tools that as of this writing are seriously underused: LinkedIn voice notes and in-platform videos.

SUPERCHARGED LINKEDIN FEATURES: VOICE NOTES AND VIDEOS

Voice notes and video are fantastic new ways to communicate that spark intrigue. They're conduits for your message that have the benefit of also giving you an unprecedented way to share your personality, warmth, and sincerity, even without building a brand on YouTube. Bonus, they're a godsend to anyone who's iffy on spelling and punctuation!

These features are so powerful, according to Will's research, they can yield response rates of 30-40%, yet most people don't even know they exist. That's because they're mobile-only, not easy to find, and for now, difficult to automate. That's a really good thing. It means that when they're received, people know you're targeting them personally, and that to you, they're not just an anonymous, faceless data point in your massive prospecting blitz. It also means buyers don't receive very many. By their nature, LinkedIn voice notes and videos show that you've spent time and effort on your outreach. Get good at this, and you'll immediately stand out from anything else in your buyers' LinkedIn inbox.

Like all DMs, these are intended to be casual and breezy. You don't need a lot of time, and you absolutely don't need to prepare a special setting or backdrop. Will's favorite time to record is when he's out walking the dogs. The unexpected setting is one more thing that helps the buyer's brain notice the expected pattern isn't there and say, "Wait! This is different!"

What's more important than the setting, the lighting, or the sound quality is the specificity of your message. As in all our communications, you'll want to speak directly to the problems your buyer is likely facing. The buyer shouldn't even question that the message you're sending was created uniquely for them.

VIDEO

Many women say they prefer using the voice option because they feel like they have to put on makeup and mess with filters if they're going to record a video. You don't. Just find a well-lit spot and be yourself. Here's how:

1. Open the LinkedIn Mobile app.

2. Tap the Messaging icon (the little speech bubble with the ellipses) at the top right of your screen.

3. Select the person with whom you want to start a conversation.

4. Tap the paper clip to the left of the text space (on Android, look for a + menu).

5. Tap "Take a photo or video" to photograph or record through the app (you could also click "Media from library," if you decide to pre-record a video).

6. Flip the camera so it's facing you, click the video icon, and start recording.

VOICE NOTES
1. Follow instructions 1-3.

2. Tap the microphone icon on the right side of the text space.

3. Put a smile on your face because it will add warmth to your voice, and tap the blue button to record.

Regardless of which medium you choose, try to record in one take—flubs and all—and keep things short, 30 seconds or even less. You have the option of recording up to a minute, but don't. Remember, people are busy, and you can probably say what you need to in 30 seconds. The shorter you keep things, the greater the chance people will listen to you all the way to the end.

Here's How a Message Might Sound:
"Payton, noticed your company just got funding to grow product functionality. Looks like you might be using a SQL setup that can make scaling new features, handling data variety, or running real-time workloads feel like duct-taping a rocket ship mid-flight, because

infrastructure debt begins to compound. Curious, have you given thought to data architecture as you continue to grow? Let me know. Happy to share how DataBaked has given product teams flexibility to iterate faster without those schema or scaling headaches."

Before sending, add a brief line of text to let the buyer know why you're sending this follow-up, something like "For some more context."

Then repeat. Work your way through your prospecting list, recording a fresh message for each of your targets, making sure to project the same energy, positivity, trustworthiness, and sincerity during the last one as you will in your first one.

How to Scale

You can't scale this strategy, and that's the point. It works because it takes work, and the buyer knows it. That's why it's worth practicing and getting good at it. Most people just won't put in the effort, which gives you an edge at a time when every edge counts. This is your chance to explain the problems you solve and introduce yourself in an informal, hopefully entertaining way. It allows you to build rapport and trust, proving you're a real human who's thoughtfully, intentionally hoping to speak to buyers about real issues that matter to them.

When they see how much work you've put into getting to know them, and that you don't see them as just another potential dollar sign, it helps lower people's guard. You don't fit the pattern of what they expect from a sales professional, and that alone can increase the chances of getting a reply. The format allows you to fully be yourself without the tension of wondering if the buyer will hang up, interrupt, or get angry. Same goes for them—it's a frictionless, risk-free, quick way for them to hear you out.

And they often will. LinkedIn voice notes and videos might not be scalable, but their response rate makes up for it. You can make 200 outreaches in a day and book four appointments, or you can send 25 voice notes or videos in a day...and book four appointments. Quality almost always outshines quantity.

Because you can't scale this, and because it's so personal, we use this approach to target the best of the best prospects. Make a separate list of the 25 to 50 companies that best fit your ICP and have the potential to be the largest or most valuable customers, and use that list for this strategy. It makes the effort worth it and provides the best ROI for your time.

Facebook and Instagram

All the same rules apply to Facebook, Instagram, and any other social channels with the option of direct messaging. Don't ever overstep and seek out your buyer's personal pages, but if they're active as a business or business creator, engage, engage, engage to raise awareness and show interest. When the moment is right, and the relevant opportunity presents itself, send a short, text-like message to start the conversation using the same framework as described above for LinkedIn. Focus entirely on something specific you've observed or seen them discuss, or even discussed with them on their or other mutuals' pages, provided you can draw a direct line between that and your buyer's potential problems.

For example, let's say you're a CRM provider, and a law firm primarily known for family law announces on their page that they're opening a division in labor and employment law. You need to consider what you understand about the business, how it measures success, and what problems such an announcement would infer. How would the absence of a CRM in an expansion contribute to problems around billing hours—the only thing law firms really care about? Well, what does it lead to if a firm doesn't have a CRM its partners can use to record who they've spoken to, details on clients and referrals, how they're selling their legal services, and what they think they're going to sell in the future? What if they do have a CRM, but they're not using it right now because it's not working for them? Both scenarios result in missed opportunities to upsell, missed chances to cross-sell between the different practices, and inaccurate forecasting, all of which affect billing hours. Adding a new division is just going to make those big issues bigger. Plug that observation into the first part of your equation. Add it to a question that gets to the heart of the problem, and you have your outreach:

> "I see you've expanded your services. Do you find that each practice is able to clearly see which clients the other practices are speaking to right now?"

It's an easy yes-or-no question, but likely not one the buyer has considered yet. These types of questions force buyers to stop and think about issues that may not be top of mind, and that can get the conversation rolling.

Video Emails

We highlighted the big advantages of mastering LinkedIn videos—they're fast, they build upon previous online interactions, they're unexpected—but there are downsides to the medium too. Not every prospect is on LinkedIn. Not every prospect is receptive to the casual, informal tone and format of DMs in LinkedIn or other social media channels. Not every prospect who has social media accounts checks them. However, almost everyone uses email for business. It's still the professional standard, and to some feels less intrusive than a DM. Fortunately, thanks to third-party messaging tools developed expressly to help salespeople create short, personalized videos, there's a way to spark the intrigue of a LinkedIn video using the familiar conduit of email.

In some ways, this kind of video offers even greater advantages than the DM type. They share important similarities with, yet are also extremely different from, other channels and platforms channels we've already discussed.

Like live cold calls, video emails give you a chance to project warmth, authority, confidence, and personality, but without the risk of interrupting the buyer or making them feel awkward.

Like email, video emails allow the buyer to control when they decide to receive your message. It has the added benefit that the video's thumbnail can be customized so that the buyer immediately sees something deeply relevant or recognizable, visual proof that this isn't just another generic, mass-produced piece of junk. They differ from plain text emails in that they're still wildly unexpected (for now), thus interrupting the buyer's mental autopilot and making them stop to take a second look.

And like DMs, the format of a video email is super short and informal and lets lets your personality and authority shine, with the big difference being that you can customize the thumbnail your prospect sees before they click on it, and on what for some is still the most familiar, trustworthy platform.

HOOK YOUR PROSPECT BY HYPERCUSTOMIZING

The key to making your video emails irresistibly engaging is to create intrigue through customization, and you can do that even before they watch the video. There are several techniques:

If, for example, your research revealed that your prospect is hiring for a role that's particularly hard to fill, and that's why you've inferred they could use your help, you can use a video platform (current popular ones are Sendspark, Loom, and Vidyard) to project a screenshot of the buyer's job posting announcement behind you as a backdrop. As Will's colleague Tyler Lessard (author of *The Visual Sale*) puts it, creating a visual personalization hook is just one way to lean into the crux of what makes video emails work, which is the ability to show, not tell. It's an immediate visual signal that proves to your prospect that you've done your homework, you're coming prepared, and this message is all about them.

Then, just hit record, and start talking. In this example, you might say (in the brightest, most authoritative, confident, smiling, and personable way):

"Hi! I noticed that you're hiring a number of new folks for your dev team, and on your website (shown in background), I saw that some of the engineer roles you're looking to fill require experience with Scala. Super niche skillset! With the average time to fill for general eng roles being 53 days, I figured those roles might be particularly sloggish to source candidates for, putting projects in jeopardy. Worked a similar role (Scala/Spark) for a streaming client recently, and have a couple of candidates who could be a fit. Worth me sending their backgrounds?"

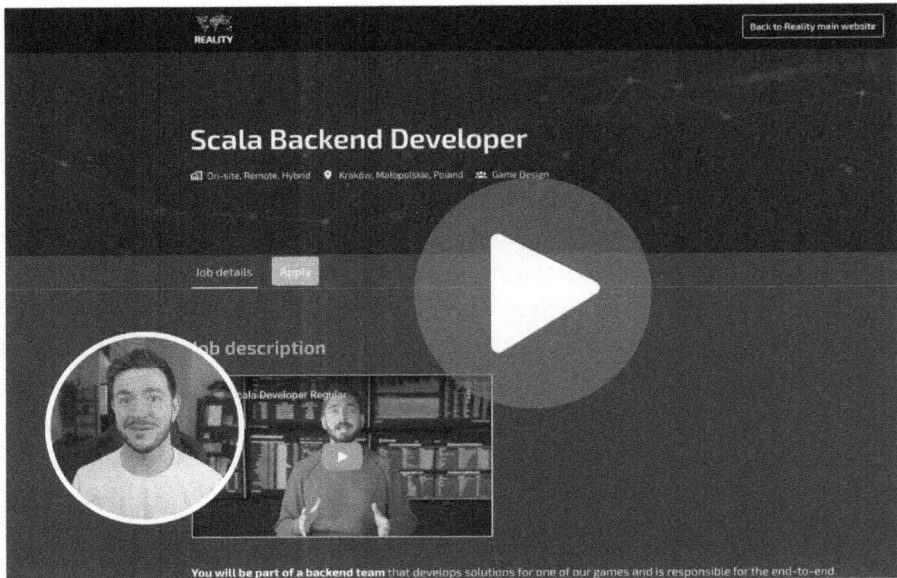

Imagine what an impact seeing their own website—or their LinkedIn page, or a tweet they posted, or any other super-specific image of their own work or words—as your backdrop on your video would have on a prospect, and how fast they'd be able to figure out why you're reaching out to them without even having to ask. It instantly connects the dots between the problems you're walking them through, and you, the person who's suggesting you might be able to solve them. Meanwhile, there you are in a video overlay, talking directly to them, moving, smiling, waving your hands or pointing to things in your backdrop, and being human. That sense of being spoken to directly and personally, of being taken seriously, is powerful stuff, often powerful enough to compel buyers to decide you're at least worth a response and maybe even learning more about what you have to offer

To add even more visual interest, your backdrop can scroll, so you could show them multiple pages on their website, or switch among various images, draw onto your images, insert animated graphics, or add other videos or photographs.

ADD BRIEF CONTEXT
You don't want to send your video email in a vacuum. In the body of

your email, add a few words of context like "Question about your Scala role" to ensure your buyer knows it's not spam, and to heighten their curiosity and intrigue, maybe add an extra-condensed version of the observation you make in the video itself and an explanation that you made this 16-second-long video just for them. That way they know it won't be a time-suck if they click.

Then, underneath the video, ask a question that can only be answered if they watch the video. For example, "Is that something you'd like me to send over?" Your buyer sees a picture of their own site or something otherwise important and relevant to them and only them. You're implying you've spotted a potential problem. You've created a scenario that's very likely going to make your buyer's ACC spike: *Heeeeeey, pay attention! And force them to weigh the cost of action versus the cost of inaction. Oh, shit, I'm hiring for Scala, and it's taking too long. Can this seller shorten the process for me? If I don't act on this email or phone call, can I live with the outcome? Will I regret it?*

If you've done your job well, they'll click to make sure they don't.

Tips for Perfecting Your Videos

Practice, of course. It can take filming up to 100 videos for it to feel natural, but given how many times you're going to use these for outreach, you'll get there in no time. Use videos internally with colleagues or your boss, if you can, to build in practice time.

Don't strive for perfection. It's okay to flub. Any time spent on TikTok should tell you no one cares anymore about perfection. Should you be precise, polished, and personable? Yes, of course. No one is going to respond well to a slob who doesn't seem to know what they're doing. But perfect? Nah.

Use your hands. Be animated and engaged.

Use good lighting. Buy a ringlight, or film in front of a window that provides plenty of sunlight.

Trade Shows

Arjun woke up to his alarm with a jackhammer inside his brain. A few snooze-button slams later, plus some painkillers chugged with water, he was in the shower, letting the hot water clear his head and wash away the aftereffects of last night's trade show afterparty. As he got ready for another day on the trade show floor, he tried to remember the name of a guy he'd spoken with the day before who seemed like he'd be the perfect fit for his services. But it wouldn't come to him. He went through all his badge scans in his CRM, trying to find the name, and finally found it. Elle! That's right, it was Elle. Okay, now, what was it Elle had said that made it clear Arjun should reach out again? Arjun tried his best, but the memory of the conversation wouldn't come. He couldn't remember a damn thing. That's okay, Arjun thought. He'd email Elle the same email he sent all his warm prospects, and it would be fine. Surely Elle would remember him.

If you go to a trade show, don't be Arjun. In a world that's increasingly run online, people are finding that in-person events can be a huge opportunity to connect. Unfortunately, most sellers, like Arjun, waste them. They take days out of their calendar to attend and scan 1,000 badges and shake a million hands, but they don't take notes, and even if they don't party too hard like Arjun, they forget who they spoke to or what specifically they spoke to people about. This leads to bland, generic follow-ups, which means all their time and effort, and money if they traveled, were for nothing. Because Elle isn't going to remember what she talked about with Arjun when she sees Arjun's email in her inbox. However, she will take the time to reply "Unsubscribe," just like she will with most of the other vendor follow-ups she receives.

It's absolutely worth stepping out of your office and taking a break from calls or sending emails for a few days to attend a trade show if you have the opportunity, but it's a complete waste if you don't do it the right way.

BEFORE YOU GO

Check who's attending the trade show and make a list of your ideal prospects. Reach out to them by email, cold call, or social media (people often post about their upcoming appearances at events), focusing on their problem as always, but adding that you're going to be in the same place at the same time, and maybe it would be a good chance to talk. Preload your calendar before you leave, setting up as many appointments at the trade show as possible. It's a much better play to spend a few days jumping between back-to-back lunches and coffees with prospects than standing by your booth, anxiously hoping the right targets come to you.

While you're at it, if there are after-events, rsvp to or preregister for these events so you have an idea of what your evening calendar will look like ahead of time.

Next, practice your gap-selling elevator pitch. Remember, a gap-selling elevator pitch is problem-centric. It leads with the problems your buyers run into, not what your product does. Be ready to give people a brief overview of the problems you solve and the people that you help, one that encapsulates who you are and why you do what you do in just a few seconds, and delivers it in a way that leaves a strong impression.

AT THE EVENT

Keenan didn't want to include this section because the information is so damn basic. Like total "duh" stuff that everyone should know already. But after hearing some stories, and knowing that many people are addicted to their phones to the point their social skills are suffering, we're throwing in these reminders. Trade show etiquette matters, so get it right.

If you've taken the preliminary step to book meetings, you won't be prospecting once you get to the event. But when you're not in meetings, you'll be working a booth or walking the floor, networking and shaking hands.

If you're working a booth: Don't sit down, and don't get engrossed in your phone or laptop. You're there to talk to people, so look and act like that's what you want to do. That said, it can be uncomfortable for people to approach a booth when you're the only one there. They know they're going to have to talk and won't be able to take their time looking at your materials before deciding if they want to engage. Don't be afraid to make eye contact or call out to people as they walk by.

Whether you're at your booth or walking around, you're going to open the lines of communication as usual, focusing on your prospect, not yourself. Be real! Show interest in your buyer and get them talking. Ask lots of questions. Eventually, they'll ask you what you do, and that's your opening to use your elevator pitch, something like "People come to me when X is going wrong, or Y. Can you relate to any of those?" Then shut up. Let them talk.

Only when they've fully answered the question should you speak up again, and that's with something like the following: "Would you be curious to learn more about how we've helped other people solve that issue?"

If the customer can relate to the problems you mention, if at all possible, immediately get them on the calendar for the following week, right then and there. They're going to be hit by a tidal wave of follow-ups when the event is over, and if you wait, you'll be just one of about 50 other vendors trying to reach out to them. If you can't book the meeting right away, at least get their mobile number and shoot them a quick text immediately to open a direct communication line. "Hey, Kai, great talking with you. I've made a note to reach out tomorrow to schedule a call so we can discuss [whatever it is they told you they needed help with]."

Important! Don't move on to the next prospect until you've taken notes about what just happened. Scribble in a notebook, type something up, or use the voice recorder on your phone to quickly rattle off the prospect's name and all the details of the conversation you just had, and especially anything funny or memorable that happened during your time together.

Follow Up
When you do follow up, you'll mention those details from the conversation you had to show you were listening, build familiarity, and remind them why they were interested in talking to you in the first place. For example, "When you dropped by the booth last week at the trade show, you told me that you experience [their problem] and that it adds up to a lot of lost revenue over the year. Still interested in having a conversation about this?"

If your prospect can't relate, that's an opening too: "Do you know anyone else who might relate to those problems?" Leave no stone unturned.

Referrals
Every seller spends every day speaking to prospects who know other people just like themselves. And those other people can probably relate to the same problems as your prospects. Requesting referrals is a phenomenal way to grow your pipeline by doing very little work. All you have to do is ask.

That's the problem; most people don't ask. Maybe they're afraid of pushing their luck if they made the sale, or they just don't know when or how to ask, or maybe they're afraid to hear another no. That last one especially doesn't make any sense, because even if your solutions aren't a good fit for your prospect, that doesn't mean they aren't a good fit for your prospect's colleagues or other people they know.

Just ask.

When?

Every time. Ask when buyers agree to a next step and when they don't agree to a next step. Ask when you book, ask when they buy, ask when they don't buy. If the buyer says they're not going to move forward with you, they'll be pleasantly surprised and relieved that when you respond, you're not trying to talk them into changing their mind. Just say something like "I appreciate that what I have here isn't a fit for you. Is there anyone else you might know who's struggling with these issues that might benefit from talking to me?" You're still focusing on the problem and the value that you can bring to a buyer, even if you know it isn't the buyer right in front of you.

GIFTING

We'd only suggest this option if you want to break into really big, important accounts or someone you're extremely interested in. It's a good way to get people's attention, but it only works when it's done in a thoughtful way, which is a challenging thing to scale. The juice has to be worth the squeeze.

The key to gifting is that it's not about the gift—it's about the connection. For example, Will once had an important prospect that he'd tried reaching by email, phone, and LinkedIn, but nothing had worked. Meanwhile, Will's CEO was getting impatient. Why hadn't he brought in this client who'd once been their biggest spender? Under pressure, Will started trawling the prospect's social accounts and noticed he'd written a post about his son going on a mission to Fiji. So along with a nice note reminding the prospect why he thought it might be worth the buyer's time for them to talk, Will sent the prospect a handmade wooden photo frame from Fiji. This time, he got a response: "That's the nicest thing anyone's ever sent me. Let's chat."

One of Will's friends makes it a habit to engage with people's socials, take note of something they're interested in, like hiking or pot-

CHAPTER SEVENTEEN -

tery, and send them a book about that interest, along with a short note, something like "Hey, I saw you like New Mexican traditional pottery. I saw this book and thought of you. I've reached out a few times to talk about audit-readiness being slowed down by scattered journal entries. Hope we can talk soon." It's an inexpensive but thoughtful, memorable gesture.

Now, the above example is appropriate when reaching out to any accounting department. And books are always classy. We're pretty sure, however, that no one wants or needs a mug with their name on it. Don't send people crap that's just going to get thrown in the landfill. No one wants or needs a $20 gift card, especially the people who run the kind of big accounts that you're most likely going after if you're thinking about sending a gift. That's what your great-aunt sends you when she doesn't know what you actually like. You're going to look especially pathetic if you send an executive even a $100 gift card. Don't take this road unless you have the means to make it pay off big. For example, in his book *How to Get a Meeting With Anyone*, Stu Heinecke writes about Dan Wald-schmidt, a turnaround specialist who, to connect with "VIP prospects," would send custom-made swords engraved with the prospect's name on the blade, accompanied by a note that said, "What you're going through is war...if you ever need additional warriors, I've got your back." He claimed to have a 100% response rate.[57] No one had ever seen anything like that before. Talk about intriguing. In these scenarios, you've got to go big, so make sure the cost will be offset by the wins.

In-Person Drop-Ins

We're in such a disconnected, impersonal world now that analog interactions make an impression and have many charms. It would never hurt to reach out to key accounts showing a catalyst or symptom and say, "Nice win on the 102 project! A few of the crews I work with have found that projects like that tend to twist up the communication between office and field teams. Which have led to project delays and uncomfortable budget mishaps. I'm going to be in Houston next week—would be a shame not to connect while I'm there. Fancy a lunch? Happy to bring some examples of how construction firms have kept their teams aligned." The worst they can do is ignore you or refuse, right? This can be especially effective if you're selling to service-based businesses in which the owners

- 230 -

and managers aren't tied to their desks, reading emails and looking at their phones all day, and who are accustomed to seeing vendors every now and then, like mechanics, chiropractors, or restaurant managers. If you have a key account, you should always take the opportunity to ask if you can drop by to say hello if you're in the area.

Everything, Everywhere, But Not All at Once

When Keenan started out, he prospected through snail mail and the phone. You're probably not ancient, though. You can prospect through phone and email and LinkedIn and videos and voice notes and social media and tradeshows *and* snail mail. Use all your options!

It's a lot, for sure, and it can probably seem overwhelming. For example, you know that wherever your buyer spends the most time online is where you should be getting to know them too. But then what? Which medium do you start with? So many choices! That's what we're going to cover next. You know how to use these channels; now we're going to teach you when and how often to use them.

CHAPTER EIGHTEEN
PLAN THE PERFECT SEQUENCE

L et's talk potatoes. Yes, potatoes. Almost everyone loves them, but not everyone loves every type. And even if they love a certain potato, no one wants to eat the exact same thing every day. It's boring. Facing the same dish day in, day out could even turn a person off potatoes forever. So if you're serving potatoes to buyers, you want to mix things up to keep their interest and meet them with whatever they're in the mood for at that minute. Some people love french fries but not mashed potatoes. Some people crave their potatoes baked and loaded, others simply boiled with a little salt. Yet there could come a day when your buyer is open to a bowl of potato soup or gnocchi, latkes, or poutine (O Canada!). They're all potatoes but in completely different forms.

Our point is, of course, that you want to treat your outreach like potatoes. Using each available channel where you believe your buyer will be most responsive or will spend the most time provides you with more chances to break the patterns they expect to see. Variety triggers your buyer's metaphorical tastebuds—and their actual brain chemicals!—and gives you multiple opportunities to send a message that might resonate. The best way to increase your odds is to master the art of sequencing—planning the number of touches you're going to take over a period of days or weeks to give you the best chance of reaching your prospect in the format, at the time, and in the order most likely to break through to your buyer and grab their attention.

How Many Touches Make the Ideal Sequence?

Enough to get noticed, not enough to get blocked. There was a time when we would have strongly disagreed on how often that is. In Keenan's early selling years, when he had to prospect every day, he'd be on buyers like glitter at Coachella until they told him no, no matter how long it took. It worked for him then. Today, he still doesn't think you should give up until you hear a definite "no," but because we have many more outreach options, dogged persistence looks and feels a little different to buyers.

Will's opinion is that most sequences are too long, and that the best sequence is done in a short burst of three weeks, ten to 15 touches. After that, even if you haven't heard a definitive "no," stop.

However, don't stop forever. Simply put that prospect on the back burner, and re-target them again in the future

In the end, Keenan and Will are saying the same thing. Until you hear from the prospect, don't give up. You don't know why your prospect isn't responding. Sure, they may have deleted your message if you targeted poorly, if your message is so vague the prospect doesn't understand what problems you solve or what you want them to do, or, most importantly, if you didn't explain why the message should matter to them. But their silence may have nothing to do with you at all or the message you sent. They may understand the value of what you're offering, but it's just not relevant to them right this minute. Or they're overwhelmed with other things right now and don't want to take the time to think about it. They may even be interested but keep forgetting to get back to you. In these cases, your prospect would probably appreciate the reminder that you're still out there, ready to help when needed. Don't take silence for disinterest. Silence doesn't always mean no; it could just mean not right now. You want to keep on keeping on, but be smart about it. Brute force is no longer effective.

BEST PRACTICE

You're going to take four steps on **DAY 1**.

1. Start with a cold call. It's the fastest, most direct way to connect and find out if you and the buyer are a good match. Best case scenario, they pick up the phone right away, you get your answer, you never send an email or DM, and you've saved yourself a bucket of time. But let's keep it real, that would be like winning the lottery. It's probably not gonna happen, so be prepared for the slog.

   Next-best scenario is still pretty good. If they don't pick up, leave them a voicemail, following the five rules of cold calling we listed in Chapter 14, as well as the advice there on proper voicemail length and delivery. But you're not leaving the voicemail with a request that the buyer call you back. Focus on building the connection. The voicemail is there only to give them a heads up to look for the email you're about to send. If they hear the message, they'll remember you when they see the email in their inbox; if they don't see it, and they're intrigued, the voicemail will serve as a prompt to check their spam folders. Either way, you're increasing the possibility that they'll open the email.

2. Send an email that incorporates the nine building blocks of a great cold email as outlined in Chapter 15, one that makes an observation, suggests a problem, proposes an offer, and asks whether the buyer finds any of this relatable.

3. If you've seen your target engage on LinkedIn, or have reason to think it's likely they're active there, make a LinkedIn Connection request.

DAY 2: Focus on other prospects and activities

DAY 3: Make another phone call. Don't leave a voicemail. In fact, you may never leave another voicemail with this prospect, because people can get really peeved to find their phone full of you there repeating yourself (seriously, watch *Swingers*). You can call as much as you want, as long as you're changing your number at least once a week to keep it fresh and avoid being the person who has called six times, but realistically, you probably don't want to make more than two to three calls per week.

DAY 4: Focus on other prospects and activities

DAY 5: Write a follow-up email. Think of your emails in terms of threads, the same type as you've seen on social media, in which a single post might devolve into several sub-conversations, each one focusing on different aspects of the post, or coming at the topic from different angles. Each email in a "thread" should refer back to the previous one.

So for this second follow-up email, you'd use the same subject line as you did in your first email, give a little context, talk about the problem again, maybe share a resource that you alluded to in your first email, and finally, ask if this problem sounds like something they'd like to discuss further with you.

So your first thread could look like this:
Email #1: Observation, problem, story, ask
Email #2: Recap, provide resource, refer to story, ask

DAY 6: Focus on other prospects and activities.

DAY 7: Try the phone again. Don't leave a message.
If your LinkedIn Connection request was accepted, send a LinkedIn message using the guidelines described in Chapter 17.

DAY 8: Focus on other prospects and activities.

DAY 9: If you haven't received any response from your first two emails, it's time to start a new thread with an email making a new observation, suggesting a different problem, and proposing a different offer. Change the subject line to reflect the new content.

DAY 10: After this many outreach attempts, it's likely the prospect has noticed you and hasn't seen fit to respond. Maybe it's because what you're offering isn't relevant, but it's equally and maybe even more likely that they just don't trust that you're not trying to scam them. They have no way to know if you're someone who'll be worth their time. A LinkedIn video or voice note could make all the difference here, proving that you're not just spamming indiscriminately but have taken the time to get to know the buyer and understand their needs. Use the guidelines for making your recordings and attaching the appropriate contextual message found in Chapter 17.

DAY 11: Call again. Don't leave a voicemail.

DAY 12: Focus on other prospects and activities.

DAY 13: Send a follow-up email to the first email that launched your second thread. Try to jazz this up with a brand-new offer. So your second thread might look like this:

    Email #1: Observation, problem, story, ask
    Email #2: Observation, problem, provide resource, ask

Below is a sample sequence to show you how all of that might look:

DAY 1

STEP #	ACTIVITY	WHAT TO SAY
1	Call	
2	Voicemail	"Hey, Brian, don't worry about giving me a call back, I'm shooting you an email with more context that will have the subject line 'Credit card errors.' It'll be coming from Will over at SLAYPAY."
3	Email	**Subject: Credit card errors** Saw reviews saying Thompson Holidays' site isn't accepting some cards and, in a few cases, charged people twice. That usually points to homegrown processors running out of runway. When that happens, IT ends up firefighting: refunds stacking up, reconciliation getting messy, and execs asking why conversion is slipping even as traffic holds steady. Aer Lingus hit the same wall. After moving off their legacy stack, failed payments dropped to 0.5% and finance regained control of reporting. I've got a white paper that benchmarks payment failure rates across travel and other industries. Could be useful to see where you stand even if nothing changes. Want me to send it over? – Will
4	LinkedIn	Connection Request

DAY 3

STEP #	ACTIVITY	WHAT TO SAY
5	Call	No VM

DAY 5

STEP #	ACTIVITY	WHAT TO SAY
6	Email (same thread as first email)	**Subject: Re: Credit card errors** Attaching the benchmarking data so you can see how Thompson stacks up against peers. Helpful to know if those failed payment reviews are noise or a real gap. Aer Lingus cut failures to 0.5% in 3 months with SLAYPAY, no downtime, no website rebuild. I can walk you through how they pulled it off. Worth a chat? – Will

DAY 7

STEP #	ACTIVITY	WHAT TO SAY
7	Call	
8	LinkedIn Message (if accepted)	Looks like you're running payments on your own system, Brian. Are you seeing payment failure rates above or below 2%?

DAY 9

STEP #	ACTIVITY	WHAT TO SAY
9	Email	Subject: Card data risk If Thompson's homegrown system is handling card data before it gets to partners, the purge process alone can create risk. One slip, and it's not just hours of cleanup; it's a GDPR fine that can wipe out profit from a whole season. Tablet Hotels solved this by removing card data from their environment entirely while still securely passing it to OTAs and channel managers. Side benefit, their PCI audits stopped being a fire drill. Want me to record a quick video with an example of how they set that up without overhauling their stack? – Will

DAY 10

STEP #	ACTIVITY	WHAT TO SAY
10	LinkedIn Video/ Voice-note	Script: "Hey Brian, for context on that last message: I asked because I spotted Thompson may be using a homegrown system for payment and credit card processing. Given that some reviews online point out declined transactions and double charges, I thought this might be causing some headaches over there. SLAYPAY has worked with other European travel giants like Aer Lingus to reduce their failed transactions to less than 0.5% while maintaining security. Think something like this would be worth a chat? Let me know" Text: "Context on my last message about failed payments"

STEP #	ACTIVITY	WHAT TO SAY
11	Call	

DAY 13

STEP #	ACTIVITY	WHAT TO SAY

12	Email (Second email in the second thread)	Subject: Card data risk
		    On the note about data risk, SLAYPAY handles that by capturing and tokenizing card data before it touches your systems, then transmits it straight to OTAs and partners.
		    I recorded a short video walking through the process so you can see exactly how it works in practice:
		VIDEO LINK + THUMBNAIL
		Look like anything you've explored before?
		– Will

DAY 15

STEP #	ACTIVITY	WHAT TO SAY
13	Call	

14	Email (Third email in the second thread)	Subject: Card data risk
		    Reached out a couple of times because I thought payment failures or GDPR/data handling might be top of mind, given Thompson's setup with partner airlines and hotels.
		    Would it make more sense to connect with Jane in Sec Ops about this, or is this just not a top issue for the entire Thompson team right now?
		– Will

All along, keep an eye out for opportunities to engage with your buyer on social media, responding to things they post, liking and commenting, or talking to other people within their circle who they trust, or who are at least reputable. The hope is that your buyer will notice you, that you'll make a good impression and build trust, and that your name will become familiar enough that they'll recognize it when they see it pop up in their email or DM.

THE BREAKUP EMAIL

If you've called, left a voicemail, emailed multiple times, tried to connect on LinkedIn, sent a video, shared a few personalized resources, and done everything except stand outside your prospect's office with a boom box (j/k—folks, don't do that; and if you don't get this reference, go watch *Say Anything* with John Cusak). It's time to stop doing what's clearly not working. Send one last email as part of your second thread using the framework we suggested in Chapter 15, letting the buyer know you understand that the issues you're raising are clearly not of interest to them right now, but you'll check back in the future to see if anything has changed.

Then before you sign off, what will you do?

You'll ask for a referral, which we said you should do each and every chance you get. It's easy: "Would it make sense for me to speak to [name of their colleague]?" Give them the chance to point you in the right direction.

Sometime in the future, maybe three to six months from now, you might research this prospect again and make a new observation or spot a new catalyst or fresh symptoms that you can help them solve. In that time, you could work with clients who will challenge you in unexpected ways, add to your wealth of experience, and give you new things to talk about. It ain't over 'til it's over.

CHAPTER NINETEEN
STOP GETTING STOOD UP

You did your research, you targeted appropriately, you mapped the problem and centered it, you created sticky outreach that broke through the prospect's OFC and activated their ACC, you were empathetic, you paid attention, and you booked a meeting! Let's gooooo!

And the buyer ghosts you. Damn it, you skipped lunch for this!

While there are no authoritative statistics on the current no-show rate for prospecting meetings, anecdotally, almost every seller who does outreach will tell you it's happened to them, so whatever unpleasant feelings bubble up as you sit there staring at your Zoom room reflection, take some comfort knowing that you're not alone. That said, it happens to some sellers less than others, because there are things that can be done to prevent no-shows. Let's talk about them.

WHY DO PROSPECTS FLAKE?
The primary way to prevent no-shows is to understand why a person would agree to a meeting in the first place when they have no intention of showing up.

REASON #1: They wanted to get rid of you.
What's the goal of selling? It's not to book a meeting; it's to get to the truth and help people. Yet many sellers get so anxious about meeting quota, they become fixated on getting a meeting on the books and compromise their ability to gap prospect. It takes patience, but they've got none. They think they're following all the rules, but, in fact, they've gone product-centric. They don't confirm that their target is actually reso-

nating with the problem. They get pushy. And if they stop listening too, they're cooked. We've heard sellers on the phone with prospects who said something like "I'm not the right person to talk to about this," and instead of asking who the right person would be, the seller replied, "Let me just put you on the calendar, and we'll figure it out." If the buyer wasn't brave enough to just hang up the phone right then and there, what were they supposed to do? They rolled their eyes, sighed, agreed to the meeting, and after they hung up, they never gave the seller another thought. We can't blame them.

Only schedule meetings with qualified buyers who can actually benefit from your help AND WHO WANT IT. Anything else is a waste of your time and theirs.

The other two reasons buyers might ghost you are self-explanatory.

REASON #2: **You failed to make the value of the meeting clear.**

REASON #3: **You booked the meeting so far into the future, by the time the day came, the prospect had forgotten why they scheduled it.**

REASON #4: **Something came up that seemed more important or urgent, and they forgot to reschedule.**
A buyer won't forget if you leave them hanging. Miss a scheduled meeting, and it's unlikely you'll ever speak with them again. You can also bet they'll tell colleagues that you stood them up, which could hurt your chances of doing business with anyone else at the company too. But the truth is that there are zero consequences to the buyer for blowing you off. Showing up is your job. What are you going to do if the prospect doesn't show? Tell their boss? Trash them on social media? Neither option would go well for you.

Look, unless you've behaved like a total knucklehead, it's unlikely that the buyer said to themselves, "You know what would be fun? Stringing this seller along just to waste their time." More likely, they got busy and decided that if you really wanted to talk to them, you'd try again. So let's make sure that the next time you do, you can be confident your buyer is looking forward to the meeting as much as you are and minimize the risk that they'll forget. You've worked hard to get them to agree to a meeting; it only takes a little more work to ensure it actually takes place.

How to Improve Your Show Rate

Follow the rules. Check that you're actually gap prospecting. Is your mindset all-in on being helpful, or are you trying to sell the meeting at any cost? Is your list thoroughly researched and fine-tuned? Are you targeting people and businesses showing symptoms or revealing catalysts that made it reasonable to infer these buyers could be facing problems you're prepared to solve? When you finally made contact, did you listen to what your buyer actually said?

Make it okay to say, "No." In dating, desperation is an instant turn-off. Same with selling. If you get pushback or sense hesitation during your call, address it directly. "I'm here to help, not push you into something you don't want. Is the issue that the problem isn't currently near the top of your priorities?" Better to know the prospect's mind now than be left hanging later. Give them the freedom to be honest from the get-go so that you know the information you're working with is accurate.

If they say, "Yes," don't delay. Data shows that if you book a meeting for the day following your initial phone call, the buyer is 90% likely to show up. A meeting booked for the following Monday has only a 70% chance of taking place. And if you book a meeting five weeks later, the chances of the meeting actually happening go down to about 15%.[58] The longer the time between booking the meeting and the meeting itself, the less likely it will happen.

Schedule meetings no later than within two weeks of your initial call or email, and ideally sooner. When setting up the meeting, only give your buyer the option of choosing times and dates within the next two days. They may have reasons for needing to pick a date farther out, which, of course, you should accommodate, but the reality is that anyone who insists on scheduling a meeting weeks or months in the future probably isn't genuinely interested in what you have to offer, unless they're taking a month-long sabbatical or are planning around a long holiday or surgery. People who want what you've got will want to talk to you as soon as possible.

Clarify the agenda and value. When you send the calendar invite, make sure to spell out the purpose of the meeting and clarify the agenda so that when the buyer sees it, they remember the value they saw in agreeing to talk with you further.

Confirm. Two days before the meeting, send an email reminding the buyer of the date and time. Include a recap of what you learned over the course of your initial conversation, list anything else you've noticed about them while preparing for the meeting, and ask them if there's anything else they'd like to discuss. This will help bring the meeting front of mind and increase their sense of commitment to showing up.

IF THEY DON'T SHOW

Send a gentle nudge. After five minutes, send an email with the meeting link and location, letting them know that you're there, ready to chat.

Leave a second gentle nudge. After ten minutes, give them a call. If they pick up, say something like "Hey, [name], we had a meeting scheduled for this time to discuss [topic]. Still got time?" If they don't pick up, leave your buyer a voicemail letting them know that you're still online, waiting to have your scheduled conversation.

Wait. Don't leave the meeting site until it's officially supposed to be over. Get some other light work done but be available in case your buyer shows up at the last second, flustered and apologizing profusely. It does happen. Turn on the "ding" in your Zoom/Teams settings so you don't get caught off guard when they join.

Reschedule. You're going to give your buyer the benefit of the doubt. Maybe there was a family emergency or their boss threw something at them last second. You just don't know. Move the invitation in your calendar forward by two days, and send an email saying, "Hey, I assume something came up today. I moved our meeting to Thursday, 1 p.m. ET. Let me know if that day and time work for you. I hope everything is okay!" If the no-show was unintentional or unavoidable, your buyer will appreciate your decency and likely reschedule. If you don't hear from them, or they decline the invite without suggesting alternate times, your warmest lead probably just became your coldest. It's a bummer, but at least you don't have to spend any more time chasing after them and can move on to someone else who will be more receptive.

Handle disappointment graciously. Stay warm and friendly and make it clear you don't hold a grudge. Sometimes it's while trying to recover a no-show that sellers actually lose the prospect for good. If you send an email that sounds judgy, or a voicemail that guilt-trips, you'll push them away even more. They have zero obligation to interact with you and certainly no responsibility for your feelings. Get a grip. You owe it to yourself and the company you work for to behave with dignity and grace.

Just as you can't let the ghosting that's unfortunately become ubiquitous in dating sour you on dating forever, you can't let no-shows keep you from putting your whole heart and soul into making connections and building relationships with your potential buyers. The world is mean enough as it is—don't add to the negativity. This is where embodying a super-optimistic, helpful, resilient, accepting, mastery-focused mindset can help you win. They're qualities that are not only protective but also allow you to be much more productive. Use your manners, give people the benefit of the doubt, and above all, trust the gap-prospecting process. It's worth the effort.

You know what, though? There is one more thing you can do to make sure most people who agree to meet with you actually meet with you. You can do some math. That's up next.

CHAPTER TWENTY
THE MATH OF MAKING QUOTA

L et's say you decide to run a marathon. That's a 26.2-mile run.

Let's say you want to finish in four hours. You're not aiming to break records, just to complete the race in a respectable amount of time.

To accomplish your goal, you know you need to run 11:27 per mile. (240 minutes / 26.2 miles = 9 minutes, 10 seconds /mile)

And let's say that on the day of the race, unlike most participants, you'll be running "naked,"[59] that is, without a watch that can track your pace, mileage, and other metrics to help you gauge your performance. You'd rather follow your body's cues than have your pace dictated by a piece of tech. Besides, digital clocks will be set up every five miles along the course and at the halfway point. You'll know if you're on pace or need to speed up.

The starting gun pops, and you move forward along with the other runners, like a giant school of numbered fish.

The crowd is tight at first, but you eventually find yourself on the road with some good breathing room between you and a few other runners. You streak past the mile markers but try not to think about how far you have left to go. Much better to think about how far you've come. You pay attention to your breathing, legs pumping, feet pounding. You've got this.

At mile five, you can see on the digital clock that you're right on time, coming in at 45:15. You're feeling good at mile ten, too, just a few minutes off at 1:39. No worries, you can make that up. But as the temperature rises, and your muscles tire, you can feel your body working harder to keep up the pace. By mile 15, you can see you're in trouble. The time should read 22:17. It reads 2:35.

By mile 20, the clock says 3:29. You're now 26 minutes behind. To make your four-hour goal in the next 6.2 miles, you'd have to double your pace to five minutes per mile—Olympian speed. You'll finish the race and be proud that you did, but meeting your goal? Not gonna happen.

We can accept that some runners may have philosophical or personal preferences for opting out of using tracking tech when running a race; if they don't meet their goals, it's a personal disappointment, but the stakes are low. Yet when your livelihood depends on meeting quota, it's insanity to forgo the insight tracking analytics can provide. As the saying goes, you can't manage what you can't measure, and too many sales careers are going completely unmanaged by sellers whose entire prospecting strategy seems to be chasing (leads), charming (prospects), and praying (for deals to close) on repeat.

By now you know that it takes a lot more than that to prospect successfully. But it's not enough to know what to do. You have to know how much you need to do and when what you're doing is working and when it's not. And the best way to do that is to math it out.

Numbers don't Lie

A surprising number of sellers jump into prospecting confusing busyness with effectiveness. They believe that success is simply a matter of staying busy, then wake up at the beginning of the fourth quarter wondering how they got so far behind. Do the math ahead of time, and you'll know exactly what you need to do, and at what rate, before you start. Check your math as you go, and it can tell you early whether you're on track, giving you enough time to adjust if necessary. Without this information, by the time you realize you need to make changes, it might be too late.

Take Annika, who sells services that help recruit test patients to medical trials, for example. When she came to Will for coaching, she was drowning in a multi-million-dollar chasm that had formed between her current sales and her annual sales goal—and she only had six months left to fill it. She thought her problem was that she wasn't closing enough deals. The numbers told the following story:

Annual sales goal: $3M

Sales so far: $400K

Difference between goal and current sales: $2.6M

Average deal size: $100K

Close rate: 20%

Current Pipeline: $500K

Qualification Rate: 25%

Positive Reply Rate: 5%

No marketing department was going to swoop in with a few inbound leads to help fill the deep hole she was in, so Annika was entirely on her own. Is it even possible for someone in this kind of pickle to turn things around in time? The math will tell us.

We know that for some, high school algebra was a special form of torture. Don't sweat it. We've done our best to write this part of the book with the math-phobic in mind, so that no one's ever wondering, "Where the hell did they get that number?"

To start, we have to calculate how much business Annika needed to funnel into her pipeline, at her current 20% close rate, to make up the $2.6M gap between her and her annual goal.

Calculate Required Pipeline

$2.6M ÷ 0.20 = $13M

$13M - $500k=$12.5M

Yikes.
Okay, but thinking proactively, what could Annika do?

1. She could speed-read *Gap Selling* and improve her close rate. But without the pipeline to close she'd still be stuck.

2. She could source more of those $100,000 deals. How many would she need, exactly?

CALCULATE NUMBER OF DEALS NEEDED

$12.5M ÷ $100,000 = 125 deals

Annika would need to generate 125 opportunities, each worth $100K, to make a $13M pipeline.

But there's one more thing to consider. Annika's qualification rate—the number of prospects she meets that she confirms are actual opportunities worth putting in the forecast as a potential deal—was 25%. With that in mind, how many meetings would she have to book to generate those 125 opportunities?

CALCULATE MEETINGS NEEDED

125 ÷ 0.25 = 500 meetings

Woof.

Should Annika give up? What would it take to book 500 meetings? For that, you need to calculate how many outreach attempts she needs to make. We now have to factor in one more number: her positive reply rate, the percent of targets who respond to her outreach with interest in meeting. It's 5%.

CALCULATE REQUIRED OUTREACH ACTIVITIES

500 ÷ 0.05 = 10,000 outreach activities

That's a terrifying number. We can make it look a bit less intimidating for Annika by breaking it down.

Quarterly: 10,000 ÷ 4 = 2,500

Monthly: 10,000 ÷ 12 = 833

Weekly: 10,000 ÷ 52 = 192

Daily: 10,400 ÷ 250 = 40

Can a seller make 40 combined touches per day? Sure, it's possible, depending on how customized the touches are. Relentless and tiring, with a high risk of burnout, especially while managing a pipeline of deals that need closing. For a rep who's also juggling *any* other responsibilities, it wouldn't be.

But Annika wouldn't have to perform 40 activities per day for a full year if she improved some of her original numbers. For example, her qualification number is currently 25%. The average qualification rate is generally 70-80%. That tells us something. Annika is either targeting the wrong people, neglecting to conduct meaningful discovery, or failing to help her buyers see the value in progressing further. If she could manage to increase her qualification rate from 25% to 50%, that would halve the number of meetings she needed to book, which would then require her to make only 20 calls or emails per day. If she could increase her conversion rate from 5% to 10%, she'd only have to make ten. Ten touchpoints per day? Easy!

The key is to get so good at gap prospecting that you can improve every one of these metrics. Far too many people and organizations focus on quantity. More calls, more emails, more, more, more. But if you get really good at gap prospecting, it's not about quantity, it's about quality. Can you improve each of these metrics? Can you improve your connection rate? Can you improve the number of meetings set per call? Can you improve meetings attended? Can you improve your meetings-to-opportunities created? That's the gold. That's the win.

Think about it: If you need 48 sales a year, and you were "perfect," it would only take 48 calls to make quota. That would be batting 1.000. Every call after that 48 would represent a failure, a miss. The goal is to minimize the misses. It only becomes a numbers game if your conversion numbers are off because you can't get people's attention, get them to open and respond, attend the meeting, or become an opportunity. All this is to say that prospecting, like everything else, is a skills game, not a numbers game. Hone your skills, get more hits, and you don't have to make as many calls to close more deals.

CHEAT SHEET

To calculate the number of activities you'll require to meet your goal, plug and chug your own data into the formulas below.

Monthly Goal = Annual Quota ÷ 12

Required Pipeline = Monthly Goal ÷ Close Rate

Opportunities Needed = Required Pipeline ÷ Deal Size

Meetings Needed = Opportunities Needed ÷ Qualification Rate

Activities Required Per Month = Meetings Needed ÷ Conversion Rate

---

Doing the math ahead of time will help you focus and show you what a huge difference you can make when you apply everything you've learned in this book, which ultimately increases your positive reply rate. Start with your goal and work backward to figure out what that reply rate needs to be. The higher the quality of your input, the higher your booking rate. And suddenly, now you don't feel pressure to throw the proverbial spaghetti at the wall to see what sticks. Now you're planning your days out, committing one hour for phone calls, one hour for emails, and a half hour for LinkedIn DMs, which leaves you time to manage deals, attend in-house meetings, or complete whatever else it is you're expected to do in a day. Now, if you're a manager, you can conduct this exercise across your team to set KPIs that roll up to team goals. Now your stress levels are manageable, your income is steady, and you're sleeping at night, no longer worried about how the hell you're going to make quota.

And that's what this whole book has been about—how to make prospecting a promising challenge, not a dreaded chore. Elevate your prospecting skills from the get-go so that you're discussing the right things, with the right people, at the right time, so that buyers can see that it's in their best interest to talk to you. This entire time, our goal has been to help you work smarter so that you don't have to work quite so hard at what is, even in the best of circumstances, an effing hard job. Prospecting isn't for the weak. But if you're up for it, embracing the gap-prospecting mindset and approach is a commitment—maybe the best commitment—you can make to your success and future. Hell, you might not just save your job but all of ours too. The faster sellers adopt gap prospecting, the faster we can start to change buyers' minds about us, our vocation, and our intent, so they won't want to run the minute we show up.

The best sales leaders get more out of their people than they can get out of themselves. —*Keenan*

PART V

BUILDING A GAP-PROSPECTING TEAM

PART V · BUILDING A
GAP-PROSPECTING TEAM

Home stretch, y'all! We toyed with the idea of calling this section "Making Bank with Gap Prospecting" to ensure that all of you read it, even if you're not in a position to build teams yet. But while it's totally possible to gap prospect your way to wealth, to say that's what this part of the book is about would be deceptive and manipulative, and if there's one thing we've tried to hammer into your skulls, it's that the less of that we see in the sales world—or anywhere—the better. So we hope that by now you'll trust us when we say that even entry-level sellers can get a lot out of the chapters that follow. Think about it: If your dream were to play for a certain team, and you found a list written by the head coach outlining exactly what they're going to look for in their next recruits, wouldn't you use that information so you could train to become that player? While these chapters were written to help hiring managers build strong prospecting teams, they can and should be read by all sellers to check that they're developing the strengths they'll need to be any manager's first pick.

In the end, it all comes down to people and the culture you create.

Build a culture of shortcuts, product-centricity, and sales at all costs, and that's exactly what you'll get. You'll burn through customers, constantly chase opportunities, and wonder why growth keeps getting harder.

Build a culture of problem-centricity—one that hires the right people and teaches them how to help—and growth becomes easier. Engagement improves. Trust compounds. You attract and retain customers who actually need what you offer.

The choice is yours.

So are the consequences.

CHAPTER TWENTY-ONE
HIRE FOR WHAT YOU CAN'T TEACH

Many years ago, in the previous century, during an era dominated by MTV, big hair, and shoulder pads, Keenan was a college student. And like most college students, he often stayed out late. One night, he and his buddy Turtle (the OG, long before *Entourage*) were walking back from a party at about two in the morning through downtown Boston. To get home, they had to pass the giant Prudential Center, which serves as a hub for hotels, food courts, shops, and the subway. As Bostonians frequently do, rather than trek all the way around, they decided to cut through its public indoor arcade to the other side of the block. Inside, the shops lining the passageways were dark and locked, but city skyscrapers gleamed above through glass skylights. Passing through the mall's center, they could see the entrance to the lobby of the Prudential Tower, the city's second-tallest building. Being college students with the impulse control of puppies, they decided to test the revolving doors. Turtle went first, and to their shock he easily swept into the tower's gorgeous lobby. Keenan, still hyped up from the party, followed by playing running back, barging through the revolving door, spiking a pretend ball, and yelling "Touchdoooown!" so his voice echoed through the empty space. Just two friends who were young, dumb, and having fun.

A second set of revolving doors on the opposite side of the lobby opened back out to another arcade, where they could continue in the direction of home. As the two pushed through, Keenan relived his football days with another loud "Touchdoooown!" But this time, they didn't just hear his echo. They heard a holler.

"What the fuck you guys doing? Get outta here!" It was the security guard, and he was heading their way. And Keenan...Well, we mentioned puppy-like impulse control, right? Keenan didn't appreciate the dude's tone and decided to say something about it. "Yeah, whattaya gonna do, man? I'll kick your ass!"

He can admit now that this wasn't his finest moment.

Turtle had wisely already started walking away, moving toward an escalator, one of two divided by a wide staircase that would carry them down, out of the building through a wide open-air passageway, and onto the sidewalk. The security guard started talking into his walkie-talkie: "I got some assholes up here...," but Keenan missed the rest of what he said because he lobbed one more f-bomb and ran to catch up with his buddy about five yards from the top of the escalator.

"You're an idiot, man," Turtle informed him. Looking over his shoulder, Keenan could see the security guard behind them, about fifty yards back, but he wasn't chasing. It was over.

Laughing and talking, calm as could be, the two had started the slow ride down the escalator when four cops came running around the corner and into the building through the open-air passageway below. As they looked up at the two friends, without hesitating, Keenan called down, "You better hurry up, there's some guys really fucking with that security guard up there! He needs help!"

"Thanks, guys!" called out one of the guards, and the whole lot of them raced up the stairs in the opposite direction.

Keenan and Turtle stood still without saying another word on that slow-moving escalator until the second the cops were out of sight. Then they ran home as fast as their legs could carry them.

Until that moment, Keenan had spent a lifetime talking his way out of trouble with people who didn't appreciate his energy and spontaneity, but nothing could have prepared him for that moment on the escalator. Yet in an instant, he was able to assess the situation: Those cops are looking for us. The security guard called them. If we get caught, we're screwed. Their expectation is that somebody's hurting their buddy. We need to deflect their attention. That kind of ninja-fast thinking is what we call quick-wittedness—the ability to process information in a high-pressure, unpredictable environment and rapidly come up with an appropriate response.

You can't teach someone to be quick-witted; it's just who they are. Will's like that too. Once, he cold-called someone, and they critiqued his pitch, giving him feedback on what he could have said that would have landed better. Will said, "Thank you, good tips. So can we pretend I did say that and carry on?" He got a laugh *and* a meeting! Quick-wittedness is just one of several inherent qualities that have made us good at what we do and especially effective at prospecting. It's what we look for when hiring for our own teams. We want you to know how to do the same.

You may not be a hiring manager yet and think this chapter isn't for you, but if you adopt gap-prospecting, chances are pretty good that one day you will, in fact, be in a position to hire your own team. It's one thing to gap-prospect yourself, and another thing to get other people to do it with or for you. Following our advice will help you hire badass salespeople like…us!

MINDSET OVER SKILLSET

When building a prospecting team, whether one made up of SDRs, BDRs, or anyone else up the food chain who might be responsible for outbound, we'd encourage hiring managers to look beyond traditional requirements of prior experience, education level, or industry familiarity. Chuck those hiring checklists! You can train anyone in knowledge and process; that is, to use the building blocks they need to sell your product or service. Experience and skill sets are nice-to-haves for new hires, but the must-haves are the inherent qualities you *can't* teach, plus the five mindsets of power sellers we discussed in Chapter 12. Let's quickly recap those first, along with some questions you can ask during interviews to test for these qualities:

Optimism. Clinical psychologist Martin Seligman confirmed for MetLife that when looking to hire outstanding, persistent, productive salespeople, skills only mattered to a degree. More important was the seller's inherent optimism. It makes sense. Optimists believe in their ability to fix their mistakes or improve their circumstances and recognize that hardship or disappointment is only temporary. When the going gets tough, optimists are tougher (with a smile).

> **INTERVIEW QUESTION** "How do you stay positive when things aren't going well?"

Helpfulness. Too many sellers approach prospecting with the mindset of "I need to sell my shit," instead of "I need to find the truth—am I right that you, buyer, have this problem?" The best sellers approach prospects the way a scientist approaches a hypothesis, not as a conclusion to be proven but as a question to be tested. They come in problem-focused, looking for answers, and they're okay if that answer is no.

INTERVIEW QUESTION	"What would you say if someone told you they didn't need our product?"

This one's a bit of a trap

Resilience. The explanatory styles that predict a seller's optimism—how permanent they perceive their failures or disappointments, how pervasive they believe those negative outcomes are, and how personally they take rejection or failure—are also connected to their levels of resilience. When you believe your setbacks are temporary and that redemption is within your control and power, you're a lot more likely to get back up and try again. When you know that failure in one part of your life doesn't predict failure in any other part, it's easier to focus on shoring up what's not working and not get overwhelmed. And when you don't take rejection personally, it's no sweat to keep reaching out to the people your research has told you are likely to need your help. If you're wrong, so what? There's always someone new to talk to.

INTERVIEW QUESTION	"How do you handle rejection, particularly if it was something really important to you or something you really wanted?" (It can be personal or professional, your choice.)

Acceptance. Prospecting is boring, repetitive, and uncomfortable. It just is. So the sellers who do it well are those with realistic expectations who can deal with rejection, monotony, and the grind. Above all, they've got loads of grit, as explained and explored by Angela Duckworth in her book *Grit*, and are willing to put in the extra hard work and practice that's frequently necessary to reach big, fat goals, and that most people just won't do. Gritty people aren't afraid of failure and are motivated by a desire to constantly improve and grow, no matter how good they already are. Gritty people aren't necessarily the smartest or most naturally talented, but they will out-try, outwork, and outperform everyone else.[60]

> **INTERVIEW QUESTION**
>
> "Describe a time you wanted to quit and didn't. What was it? Why didn't you quit? What did you do to motivate yourself to keep going? Did you achieve the goal?"

Mastery-Focused. People who are mastery-oriented are driven to be the best at whatever it is they do. Being the best at prospecting may result in full-to-bursting pipelines, or even eventually closing the most deals or making the most money, but that's not what drives a mastery-oriented seller. Rather, they're driven by the urge to keep learning, to keep pushing the boundaries of what's expected, and to gain a deep knowledge, even expertise, about their field. But that knowledge isn't just theoretical or academic. They use their time prospecting to test what they've learned, constantly tweaking, experimenting, and challenging themselves to improve. A mastery-oriented person is born to be a prospecting superstar.

> **INTERVIEW QUESTION**
>
> "What's the last skill you taught yourself? Or: In the last 12 months, what specific skill sets have you focused on to be a better [SDR/AE]? Why did you choose those skills, what did you learn, and how did you apply them?

Okay, so what other qualities should you look for?

Self-Confidence. Duh, right? Of course you want to look for self-confident salespeople! But not exclusively. There's a certain type of insecure person who can be your secret weapon.

Find the seller with a chip on their shoulder. Keep an eye out for the person who's frequently underestimated and overlooked but who knows they've got greatness inside and is dying for a chance to show it. The person who hears, "You're not good enough to win," and replies, "Watch me." That person will do whatever it takes to prove their doubters wrong, and you want them on your team. Give them the right gap-prospecting training and room to run, and in no time they'll be your Aaron Rodgers, rising from marginalized bench-sitter to MVP and champion. In fact, Aaron Rodgers' words should become the seller's credo: "Find [your] sources of motivation and harness them. Never settle. Never. [It's about] continuous improvement…"[61]

INTERVIEW QUESTION	"What's something that people tend to get wrong about you? Have you ever felt underestimated? How did you prove them wrong? Has anyone doubted you? If yes, what did you do?"

Quick-Wittedness. We talked about this already. It's the ability to process the entire environment in milliseconds and react quickly, or rapidly process an argument and flip that argument in one's favor. Note that being quick-witted isn't the same as being prepared. Preparation is leveraging the information you've absorbed through reading or listening to lectures and podcasts, studying, or past experiences, and applying them to good use. It's pulling together the knowledge you need before making a prospecting call or sending out an email. Quick-wittedness is the ability to respond to a conversation or situation in a way that keeps things going in your favor in the *absence* of preparation, where there's no way you could have predicted how things would go.

How would the quick-wittedness that Keenan exhibited at the Pru apply to a cold call? It's all about synthesizing your knowledge—about your product, about the market, even about human nature—and drawing from it to create opportunities for a conversation. So if a customer said, "I'm already using [other solution]," your brain would start riffling through its memory bank, because unless it's Day One, you've probably heard that before in some form or another, and even if you haven't, you'll naturally be able to keep the conversation flowing with some improvisation. Buyers can sense when you're giving them a canned response to their real, unique concerns.

Quick-wittedness can often be funny, but it doesn't have to be. Regardless, it delivers the electricity and surprise of improv, not a scripted performance. But you have to know shit to be a good improviser—and to prospect. That's why a seller's education should never stop.

> **INTERVIEW QUESTION**
> "Suggest a surprise roleplay. You're not looking for your candidate to give you anything in particular; you just want to see what they come up with on the spot under pressure and see how their brain works in an unexpected situation."

Curiosity. If you're curious, then educating yourself, expanding your horizons, exposing yourself to new ideas and perspectives—including those of your buyer—will be as natural as breathing. Curious people observe the world and take mental notes. Curiosity drives the need to fill the knowledge bank, which gives you the material to be quick-witted. It's critical. In *Gap Selling*, Keenan listed curiosity as one of the nine must-have qualities of a gap seller, but it might be even more important to gap-prospecting. Unlike during a discovery call, which gives you the time to satisfy your curiosity with questions, when prospecting, you've got only seconds to figure out how to connect with your buyer. Sellers need to choose their words extremely carefully, and their curiosity about their buyer, and about their buyer's problems, will help them make sure those words resonate immediately.

Keenan's a big fan of what he calls fearless curiosity, which goes a step further than regular curiosity. Fearless curiosity understands that no question is a bad question, and that being afraid to ask certain questions can undermine your ability to understand a specific environment. Think of the child who is NOT afraid to ask a one-armed woman how she lost her missing limb. Most people never ask because they're afraid of hurting feelings or of creating an awkward situation. The child doesn't. She's fearless, and because of that, she learns the woman had cancer and was proud she survived, and it only cost her an arm. The woman isn't offended—she smiles at the young girl's courage and interest, and now they share a bond. What could have been an awkward interaction instead becomes an opportunity to connect.

The same is true in sales. Fearless curiosity is next-level curiosity. Sellers are often afraid to ask deep or invasive questions that ask the buyer to share stuff that really matters to the business, worried they'll seem rude or intrusive; buyers could get defensive, especially if a question points out flaws in their thinking or logic. Don't let that fear stop you. Getting the information you need to make sense of their environment—just as a child does—is more important than any discomfort you—or your buyer—might experience.

> **INTERVIEW QUESTION**
>
> Take note of whether your candidate is asking *you* questions; it's something all the best ones do. They should be trying to gauge what problems you're trying to solve and explaining why they think they're the best person to help solve them. In other words, they should be gap selling you.

Articulate. Don't ever underestimate the power of speaking and writing well. That doesn't necessarily mean being formal. Your seller wants to use slang? If it's appropriate, let them slay, slap, and flex all they want. They want to play with text-ese? Again, know your audience. Rhetorical power lies in the ability to convey ideas and concepts in a language and style that your chosen audience can easily absorb and understand. An articulate seller is good at drawing parallels that help people see connections they might otherwise overlook.

> **INTERVIEW QUESTION**
>
> "What's something you love to do in your free time? Explain to me how to do it like I'm ten."

High EQ. Sellers who embody the above qualities and mindsets also more than likely have a naturally high EQ. A high EQ is what allows sellers to engage articulately and convey credibility, to explore with curiosity, to put their quick wit to use, and to exude confidence. It's what allows them to build relationships quickly and reflect and manage people's emotions. As people talk, they're able to tap into what buyers are feeling and adjust accordingly. Nothing they do is by rote. When they engage, they intuitively know how to do it in a friendly, warm way that disarms buyers and makes them feel connected, understood, heard, and valued, so they want to listen, and they feel listened to. High EQ is the umbrella under which all the crucial characteristics of star sellers live.

> **INTERVIEW QUESTION**
>
> "Tell me about a time you could tell someone was upset without them saying so. How did you handle it?"

In prospecting, you get 30 seconds, if that, to connect with your buyer. Whether a seller gets that time depends on how well they embody all these qualities we just talked about. Just one or two words, or a turn of phrase, can make the difference between buyers opening an email or dumping it into the trash. Tone of voice, a pause, or a well-timed joke can determine whether you hear, "Yes, I'll give you 30 seconds," or the click of a disconnected call. Every word, every phrase, every cue, every connection decides whether your conversation stops or moves forward.

CHAPTER TWENTY-TWO
MORE THAN MOTIVATIONAL POSTERS—
BUILDING CULTURE

Remember Annika, the struggling sales rep who came to Will for coaching when she couldn't figure out why she wasn't making her numbers? By the time Will met her, unless she managed to raise her qualification or conversion rates, the only way she was going to turn her situation around was to churn out as many activities as possible, day in and day out, and hope that sheer volume would allow her to make enough connections to fill her pipeline. Sometimes that's what you have to do in the short term to save yourself. Maybe she pulled it off. More likely, she lost her job. And that reality begs the question: *Why did she have to come to Will for coaching in the first place?*

The fact that a salesperson had to go outside her company and spend her own money to get the help she needed tells us something important. It tells us her managers failed her and failed to build a strong company culture.

Could Annika's predicament have been her own doing due to laziness or ineptitude? We'll say it could have been *some* of her own doing, and we'll talk more about accountability in a moment. But all of it? No way. The biggest failure wasn't Annika's; it was her managers' for neglecting to help their employee improve her performance *before* her numbers sank so low, Poseidon himself would have trouble pulling them up. Annika wouldn't have needed to get outside help had leadership given her the support she needed to figure out where she was going wrong. That she felt she had to means she didn't get the in-house guidance she needed to correct her mistakes. Since she couldn't turn to other high-performing sellers for advice, it means that collaboration and mentorship weren't encouraged. It means that someone neglected to foster a culture of success.

IT'S NOT *JUST* ABOUT THE NUMBERS

A culture of success in any organization, including sales, doesn't stem exclusively from consistently crushing quota; it's a natural result of leadership that knows how to nurture and develop people and teams. It's the antithesis of the boiler room. If you don't get that reference, there are two versions: old school—salespeople yelling into their phones, frantically trying to beat the clock in a pressure-cooker atmosphere that rewards aggression, manipulation, and sometimes deception, as depicted in films like, well, *Boiler Room*, in addition to *The Pursuit of Happyness* and *The Wolf of Wall Street*—and the modern digital type, with the same high-pressure stress of hitting numbers and beating the clock, except with everyone virtually gathered in a Zoom room where every keystroke is tracked, and the sound of yelling is replaced by incessant Slack pings. In boiler room organizations that still prioritize quantity over quality, failure to meet quota is always considered the salesperson's problem, not the manager's, and if you don't make your numbers within a certain time, that's it. You're out.

But who hired the team? Who saw something promising in their sellers? Who created the processes they were expected to follow? Who set up the onboarding and designed the training? Who gave them the tools or didn't? The manager, the leadership, and the organization. When salespeople fail, it often looks more like a boat running aground than a car crash—you can see them getting into trouble ahead of time, and that if they continue, they're going to struggle to reverse course. But it's the manager who creates the environment in which the sellers set sail. If they failed, and you, the manager, didn't step in to help, that's on you.

In a culture of success, the people in charge of hiring take ownership of it. They put in the effort to cultivate a setting and climate where sellers can thrive (and one where top talent chooses to stay). It's a culture of shared responsibility, accountability, and humanity, where your team's success reflects as much and maybe more about you, the leader, as it does about them.

We're not saying you should aim to create a stress-free workplace. That would be an impossible ask anyway. And we're definitely not saying you should lower your expectations, even if you could control what the company demands from your team. What we are saying is that the old ways of getting people to meet those expectations—threatening, bullying, and micromanaging people through hours of relentless outbound while offering little support and encouragement—don't draw the best out of your sellers. That kind of activity-based management doesn't grow salespeople; it forges robots. It saps sellers of their initiative, creativity, and empathy—all the qualities of a great salesperson. No one can work like a robot for long before burning out, which is why those kinds of workplaces have such high turnover. Anyone who stays risks losing their souls to the maw of productivity-at-all-costs. Take the time to grow a culture of success, however, and you'll not only shore up people's performance in the short run, but in the long run you'll also enjoy a work environment populated by talented, engaged, motivated sellers committed to your collective victory. Investing in a culture of success is a win-win for everyone.

How to Build a Culture of Success

It starts with you deciding what kind of leader you're going to be. There's a name for the management style that uses a system of punishments and rewards to get results, creating an aneurysm-blowing environment that chews sellers up and spits them out. It's called transactional leadership.[62] In a transactional culture, sellers feel like cogs in a wheel. It deprives sellers of ownership over their work, because every step they take is dictated from the top down. But a culture of success is built through **transformational leadership**, a management style that draws out people's best work through encouragement and positivity, not fear and threats. You want people to take it upon themselves to deliver because they believe in what they're doing, not because you're on their ass. Transformational leaders "envision an appealing future goal state for their team or the entire organization and express confidence in followers' abilities to attain this higher-order goal."[63] In other words, they're gap sellers to their core!

Transformational leaders exhibit "four key attributes:" idealized influence, inspirational motivation, intellectual stimulation, and individualized consideration."[64] In essence, those four fancy-sounding I's are reflected in the four simple priorities we've identified in teams with cultures of success—optimism (we know, again??), teamwork, coaching, and accountability. These are the keys to how transformational leaders fuel the kind of energy and empowerment in their salespeople that improves performance.[65] They encourage cohesive, self-motivated teams that work well as a unit and individually because they believe in what they're doing, not because they fear what will happen to them if they don't perform. In the fast-paced, often-defeating world of prospecting, this could never be more important.

In prospecting, the numbers are constantly in the teams' faces; they can't escape them. Rejection is 90% of the day, with reps hearing, "No," getting hung up on, and getting no replies for seven hours of the day. It can be dejecting. But when front line managers embrace transformational leadership, they can see early in a rep's tenure if and where they're making mistakes, help them avoid the mistakes sooner, and therefore minimize the ongoing sting of the job. Transformational leadership allows people to feel safe, supported, and protected rather than always a day away from the unemployment line.

OPTIMISM

We can't beat this drum enough. It's not enough for you to have optimism or to hire for it—you have to encourage it. The #1 thing you can do as a leader is let your team know that you're confident they've got what it takes to be a star player. Remember that popular teacher, the one everyone knew was a hardass, yet whose door was open before and after school for tutoring, and who always had kids hanging out in their classroom during lunch? Kids liked and respected that teacher because they made them feel safe, and because they believed in their students and were willing to do whatever it took to make sure that if they put in the work, any kid could succeed. That's the kind of teacher who can have a lasting impact on a student, who can get them to aim higher than they might otherwise have tried. You can have that same effect on your team when you lead with optimism and seed it through your organization.

The American Psychological Association includes optimism, as well as resilience, hope, and efficacy, as the four requirements for "psychological capital," which over 200 studies have shown promotes everything from "higher job performance (both self and supervisor reported), higher worker engagement, higher job satisfaction," to lower turnover and lower burnout. In addition, your own psychological capital has a positive effect on that of your subordinates. Yep, optimism breeds optimism. It isn't just a skill; it's a belief system—one that allows great leaders to see the extent of people's potential and help them live up to it.

How to Lead with Optimism

- **Redefine the word "no."** Your teams should understand that rejection or refusal isn't a defeat. Rather, "no" is an opportunity to learn and experiment. Negative outcomes are just data points. "Welp," says the optimistic leader, "that didn't work for you, did it? Good to know. What else can we try?"

- Make sure your sellers know that **mistakes are allowed**. You want them to take risks, and they can only do that if they know that even if they don't get the results they'd hoped for, they won't get attacked or penalized.

- **Build their confidence.** Lead with the promise that improvement is always possible: "You haven't made your numbers…yet. Let's come up with a plan to get you there." This kind of encouragement also helps them keep sellers' defenses down, because they know whatever feedback they get is going to be constructive, not punitive.

- **Correct behaviors and habits, not the person.** Failure is just situational. When a rep isn't producing the way they'd hoped, the optimistic leader doesn't say, "Better get on it, or you're outta here." Instead, they say, "I know you're going to get there. Let's talk about what you need to work on. Here, watch me and see if you can spot the difference…" You want to instruct but also give people the freedom to problem-solve on their own.

- **Promote a supportive environment** where team members lift each other up. If you start to hear rumblings of pessimism or negativity, call it out and address it constructively before it can bring down team morale.

- One more thing. To cultivate a sense of optimism, **bring a sense of fun** into your workplace! A team that doesn't have time to laugh together and be human is one that's heading for dysfunction if it's not already there. When the only interaction you have is negative or competitive, you don't develop a sense of camaraderie and teamwork. Think of ways to encourage a sense of fun that doesn't put pressure on anyone (like going to a bar). For example, you could call for midday breaks, when everyone gets to stop calling for 30 minutes and hang out. You can bring in doughnuts or snacks, let everyone take a breather, and have them share the funniest thing that happened that morning—the worst rejection, the oddest customer response, or anything else that adds levity to the situation. The key here is to keep things light. Think of creative ways to pull the stress plug for just a little while, let the team exhale, and have some fun before they get back at it.

TEAMWORK

For a culture of success to flourish, you need a sales group made up of individuals ready and willing to work together. We can all think of phenomenal athletes or performers who burned bright, then flamed out because despite their talent, they were so hard to work with, they brought everyone around them down. In Chapter 21, we talked about two types of self-confidence and how sellers with either can be huge assets to your team. But you want to make sure that the self-confidence you find so appealing in a hire doesn't spill over into arrogance or narcissism. Those people can poison a culture with their ego and negativity and can cost the company money when it has to clean up their messes. Avoid bringing them on board as best you can.

Set the example by encouraging teamwork. Let people know you've got their back.

HOW TO LEAD THROUGH TEAMWORK

- **Be approachable.** You don't have to be anyone's close friend, but you don't have to be their drill sergeant either. Make it clear that your door is always open if they have questions or need advice.

- **Be human**, and let your sellers be human, too. Invest in getting to know your people as people, not workers or employees. Take the time to talk to them. Are they married or single? Do they have kids? What do they do on the weekends? What are their favorite hobbies? What did they study in college? Where did they grow up? Don't interrogate them; this is the kind of information that will naturally come out over the course of time when you have regular, real conversations and when you actually care to learn about people. Investing in knowing your people not only helps build camaraderie and trust, but in the event people are coping with something difficult, it also helps them feel it's safe to tell you. While it would be unprofessional for a seller to let their personal life intrude too much into their work, there will be times when people need to be shown a little compassion. Letting people know that you're not going to hold a bad day or two against them can ease their anxiety and make it easier for them to recharge and come back swinging. Come up with a plan to help them persevere until things are less overwhelming.

- **Commit to your role as team bullshit filter.** This isn't always easy when not only is it your responsibility to present your team to your higher-ups in the best light, but it's also your job to defend those higher-ups' directives or unreasonable demands to the team, even when you think they're crap. It sucks when the CEO is asking for bigger numbers even though you barely squeaked through quota last quarter, or when you have to pick up the slack because marketing isn't doing their job. But it's your responsibility, whenever possible, to limit the impact of that type of corporate BS on your team and protect them from becoming every other department's punching bag. For example, when customer success leaders blame the sales for churn, or marketing leaders complain that Sales isn't taking their crap leads seriously enough, or when Product fails to deliver on their promises, leaving sales to deal with customers who are expecting those promises, or Finance decides to cut budgets or change the comp plan, as professional bullshit filter, you'll stand between your team and the blame games, the mixed messages, and the stupid company politics that have nothing to do with their job—selling.

- **Constantly reinforce teamwork** among your sellers through recognition and rewards. Define it clearly and offer the team examples of what teamwork looks like and what you expect to see. Build teamwork into the evaluation scorecard, so people know that living up to that ideal, and not just hitting numbers, is part of their performance criteria. Create an annual or bi-annual award, along with an award that celebrates teamwork weekly or monthly. Feel free to be spontaneous too. For example, when someone demonstrates the teamwork behaviors you embrace, publicly celebrate them and offer them a gift card to their favorite restaurant or coffee shop. The key is to consistently and relentlessly reward and acknowledge people's effort, giving them many chances to see and understand the culture you're trying to build until they embrace it and even help you build it themselves.

- Encourage people to act on the mindsets that make great sellers great. **Helpfulness**, so they're not just out for themselves. **Acceptance**, so they all have a shared understanding that the work they do is hard and sometimes thankless. Prospecting is never easy in and of itself, but it's a lot easier when you know your cohorts are in it with you, and that you're all rooting for each other.

COACHING

When psychologist Daniel Goleman (of *Emotional Intelligence* fame) asked leaders to rank their preferred leadership style, guess which one was consistently listed dead last? Coaching.[67] We can see why. It takes patience, it's a time-suck, and it doesn't pay off right away. On top of that, many managers who try to coach don't get great results. But that's not because coaching doesn't work. It's because managers aren't trained. Studies have shown that most of those who think they know how to coach aren't as good at it as they think they are.[68]

Coaching is hard because it's not just about teaching people what you know. Rather, it's about teaching people how to learn, or as John Whitmore, author of *Coaching for Performance*, put it, "unlocking people's potential to maximize their own performance."[69] Coaching is a fundamental aspect of cultivating an optimistic, teamwork-oriented prospect-ing environment. It's hard for one to exist without the others.

How to Be an Effective Coach

- **Hire for coachability.** We mentioned this in Chapter 21, and this is why. You can't coach people who aren't curious, humble, and willing to learn. You'll be banging your head on your desk in frustration if you don't start out with a team already embodying a growth mindset.

- **Coach at the individual and team level.** Individual coach-ing is vital—everyone has their unique strengths and weaknesses, and people need time to ask questions and discuss their specif-ic issues. But team coaching normalizes the feedback cycle and helps keep people from feeling like they're being targeted. That said, sometimes the best thing you can do is get pushed into the spotlight. In one of Will's jobs, everyone got a turn in the hot seat, and the manager would play a recording of one of their recent cold calls. The whole group, including the person whose work was being critiqued, would offer their thoughts and feed-back, positive and negative, in real time. The exercise allowed the group to learn from each other's mistakes and ensured that everyone learned how to analyze their work and give construc-tive criticism. Since everyone eventually wound up being the center of attention, it eliminated any stigma from the process, and people were in a much better headspace, enabling them to better absorb the feedback and apply it. There was never any question that the goal of the exercise was to help people im-prove, not embarrass them.

- **Learn the difference between coaching and passing judgment.** Coaching is continuous guidance toward improve-ment; judgment is an assessment against good and bad. Judg-ment feels personal, like an attack, and triggers people's stress response [70] (such as fight-or-flight), which hurts their ability to absorb what you're trying to say. Judgment has its place. But it's not good for coaching. Coaching focuses on behaviors and outcomes—"Here's where I think I see room for improvement," not personal worth—"You're not good at this." Constant judging will crush your team's morale. Don't do it.

- **Catch people doing good.** The whole coaching system should be set up to quickly notice when people are struggling, but remember to also let them know that you've noticed when they're doing something well. A warm "That rocked; do more of that!" can be a major boost to a tired seller's spirit. Don't forget to praise effective behaviors and strategies publicly, not only to give credit to the person who did something good but also so the whole team can learn by example and benefit from it.

- **Ask questions that allow people to figure out the answers themselves.** People are often most committed to ideas they feel were their own over ones they were prescribed. Will's biggest learning leaps occurred when his leaders essentially gap-sold him to the root cause of his problem. Basically, he used the discovery process on himself, which consequently led him to more thoroughly understand and believe in the solution they chose.

- **Create a predictable process.** Randomly popping up to nitpick can make people feel like Big Brother's watching all the time, which is stifling and stressful. And when feedback, especially negative, comes out of nowhere, it feels like an attack, not a learning opportunity. When coaching is expected, however, it's welcomed, not feared. At Keenan's company, managers use the ODP model:

OBSERVE. Watch seller behavior.
Impact: What did the manager see the behavior cause or create? Did it result in the desired behavior?

DESCRIBE. Give objective feedback about what you saw or heard—"I heard you respond in x way"—not what you didn't see or hear—"I didn't hear you ask y." People can't connect to what they didn't do. It's far more effective to highlight what they did do.

Impact: Describe the impact their action had on the environment. What outcome or impact did the action have that was not desired?

PRESCRIBE. Offer clear guidance on what the seller should do.
Impact: Describe the outcomes or impacts the new behavior should elicit or create, and why. Paint a good picture so the rep can see how changing their behavior will benefit them and create the outcomes they want.

After that, managers keep an eye on the seller to make sure they absorbed what they said and apply it appropriately. Then they discuss the results, and restart the loop! It's a system that creates a continuous learning cycle, so that ideas can be easily tested, no one goes on autopilot, and skills are continually reinforced.

- **Implement a predictable, reliable coaching rhythm.** As a seller, you've figured out your most effective prospecting cadence. Now do the same thing for coaching. You can do it daily, weekly, monthly, or quarterly, so long as it's consistent. In our experience, however, a daily coaching session in one form or another is ideal. That doesn't mean everyone gets critiqued every day. For example, you could try a combination like this:

MONDAY: An all-team meeting to review pipeline and booked meetings, and to celebrate wins; discuss problems or obstacles that seem to be getting in the way, parsing between what's a legitimate issue that needs to be addressed, and dismissing what counts as excuses.

TUESDAY: One-on-one coaching with individual sellers, focusing on whether they're on track to meet their personal goals.

WEDNESDAY: Team practice of a specific skill, like cold calling, objection handling, using videos in outreach, setting a good agenda, or questioning techniques, through analysis and role-playing.

CHAPTER TWENTY-TWO

Thursday: Listen to calls or review emails as a team.

Friday: Asynchronous coaching, in which you offer written feedback on calls, sequences, or emails.

Most of these sessions should only take about one hour each, with the exception of the asynchronous review day.

- **Keep coaching even when you're ready to give up.** What if a seller just doesn't improve or doesn't improve enough? Well, you're an optimistic coach, so you know that failure in this job isn't a total failure. A good manager can see and appreciate each team member's qualities and wants them to succeed, wherever they land. In this case, your conversation might sound like this: "I'm sorry things didn't work out here. Maybe prospecting isn't the best fit for you. I noticed these other skill sets where you excel, though. If you're interested, I'd like to explore whether there's another opportunity for you elsewhere in the company. Would you consider customer success, marketing, or some other job if an opportunity were available?" And if you're refused, find out if there's anything you can do to help the seller find the next good fit. When approached like this, firing someone isn't punitive—it's freeing them to go somewhere where they'll be able to thrive.

ACCOUNTABILITY

The biggest thing to remember about accountability is that it has to go both ways. At least, it does if you want to build trust and goodwill. Keenan knows. He was once in charge of hiring a new account executive. His team was down a rep and needed to backfill the position quickly. Keenan's boss was also intent on quickly hiring someone new. Keenan has always understood that hiring the right people was a leader's #1 responsibility, and that getting it wrong kills everything (it's why all the Gap books have and will have a section on what a great candidate looks like). He was doing his best to recruit, but none of the people he'd interviewed up to that point were the right person for the job. But instead of being supportive or talking to Keenan about what he could do to help, the boss just complained about how long it was taking to fill the position. Finally, he offered Keenan an ultimatum: Hire someone within a week, or there would be consequences. Not only that, he suggested (judged) that Keenan wasn't "thinking outside the box." So Keenan gave his boss exactly what he wanted and hired the best of the bad options he'd already interviewed.

As Keenan expected, the dude sucked. He lacked drive, urgency, and creativity, as well as most of the traits we outlined earlier in this section. Once, Keenan found him lounging with his feet up on his desk like he was waiting to be fed grapes. He didn't even last three months. And then bossman had the nerve—the nerve!—to be mad at Keenan for making such a stupid hire. That experience has followed Keenan for 20 years. It shaped his leadership style and led him to develop what he calls the Freedom Box, which we'll explain in more detail in just a bit. Simply put, Keenan believes that we must let people do the job we hire them for in the way they see fit. Give them the freedom to do the job their way. Every person carries different perspectives, skills, and talents. Letting those differences flourish maximizes the diversity of the team and uncovers new and effective ways of meeting the goals.

Keenan's boss didn't let Keenan run his own process, despite the fact that Keenan was making his goals, and, in fact, was well past them. He dictated his decision to Keenan, taking away Keenan's choice, yet held Keenan accountable to the decision. But as this anecdote illustrates, when you take away people's choice, eventually, it'll bite you in the ass.

We all have to look out for ourselves, of course, but when you force people to sacrifice their autonomy and unique approaches for yours, minimize or eliminate their ability to use their best judgment, and then force them to take ownership of YOUR decision, that's not being a leader. That's being a dictator, and no one wants to work for a dictator.

A good manager doesn't say, "Deliver, or else." They say, "I'll deliver so that you can deliver." Two-way accountability builds a fighting, trusting, loyal team that excels long-term.

How to Instill Accountability
- **Don't make people earn your trust; give it freely.** It's a puzzle to us as to why managers wouldn't automatically trust the people they hired. After all, presumably, they saw something in

the seller during the interview process that made them think the candidate could do the job well. Yet it seems that many managers don't trust their teams at all, because a lot just hand out a prescription on how to sell and then spend all their time making sure the seller sticks to it. That's not managing; that's micromanaging. Micromanaging assumes there's only one way to get things done. It robs people of their agency and stifles creativity, wasting a selling team's most precious resources. It makes people feel like cogs in a wheel.

Hire self-motivated people so you don't have to hover over their shoulder (irl or virtually). If you believe in the qualities you're hiring for, you should be able to start the relationship by trusting that the people who embody them are going to do their jobs well.

- **Be predictable.** You make a team stronger if you're specific and transparent from the beginning with your expectations, desired outcomes, and the consequences of meeting those outcomes or not. Everyone should know what their potential earnings and promotional options can be if they do well; be equally clear about the steps that will be taken if they don't, along with the benchmarks they'll need to meet to avoid being let go.

- **Assess behaviors and results:** There are four types of sellers on a team:

  1. **SUPERSTARS.** They have a great attitude, they meet their numbers, and they work well with everyone.

  2. **SHINING STARS.** They also have a great attitude and mesh well with the team, but they're not quite meeting their numbers. You hired them for a reason, though—you can still see loads of potential.

  3. **SHOOTING STARS.** These sellers' numbers are on fire, but they're burning everybody in their orbit. They seem to reject the company values and culture, and they don't play nicely with others. You want to keep them on if you can, but an

attitude adjustment is in order, stat. For the record, there was a time in Will's career when he was one of these. Luckily, his boss gave him a chance to shape up, and he did.

4. **BLACK HOLES.** Nothing's working. Their attitude sucks, they're bringing down morale, and they're not producing. Worse, they don't seem all that interested in improving.

A manager only has so much time and energy to spread around. We offered ideas for how to coach at the group and individual level, but you want to start knowing where your efforts will be best spent. To do that, create a 2x2 Behaviors vs. Results matrix, and think about where each seller on your team belongs. It shouldn't take long, since you're just answering two yes-or-no questions: Is this seller's behavior what it should be? Is this seller's numbers where they should be?

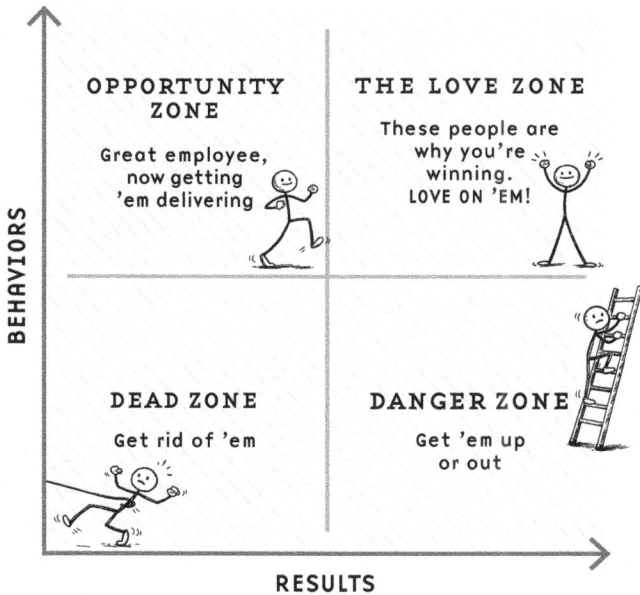

The people who land in the top right are your most valuable team members. Shower them with love, and do whatever you need to keep them happy and feeling supported. The people in the bottom left, you can give them 30 days to get their shit together. The people in the top left (shining stars) and bottom right (shooting stars) are the ones you want to focus on, using the framework below to make them superstars.

Give sellers a **Freedom Box**. You've told everyone what you expect from them, and what will happen if they succeed and if they fail. Now let them do their thing. Literally.

Imagine a box stuffed with every prospecting tool, tactic, and strategy you've ever heard of, and maybe even some you haven't. This is what Keenan calls the metaphorical Freedom Box. Sellers start out with a big, full box and are free to do whatever works best to give them the results they want. If they excel at filling their pipeline through networking events or social media instead of emails and cold calls, don't force them to email and cold call. The only options not found in the box are those that cross ethical or legal lines, or ones that could undermine the team's success as a whole. Outside of that, you can do pretty much whatever you want.

What happens if a seller starts having trouble making their numbers? You shrink the box. Now it's too small to hold all your seller's prospecting options, so you remove a few, usually the less proven or more creative ones. Of course, you talk about it. "I know you've been trying this, but let's give it a rest. I'd like you to shift your focus to this other thing I've seen work for a lot of sellers." You're nudging them a little more toward the tried-and-true basics and installing a few more guardrails. For example, whereas before, if you didn't dictate how many calls they had to make, now you set a minimum.

It's important to give people ownership over their progress and the ability to make their own decisions. These are adults, after all. But you owe it to them to keep supporting them to give them the best chance at success. Ask more questions and request more updates. Keep the communication lines open so they aren't afraid to come to you if they realize they need help. The goal isn't to shame, punish, or make an example out of anyone. The goal is to show them that you're invested in seeing them succeed. Yes, it's more work on your part, and it's worth it in the long run. Many studies have indicated that as long as the job and person are a good fit for each other, it's less expensive and time-consuming to invest in helping an employee improve than it is to fire them and have to go find someone to take their place. In addition, employees who have been coached and who believe that their success matters to you and to the company can become some of your most loyal, engaged team members.

If sellers still don't make their numbers, shrink the box some more. Now you'll empty the box of most options, leaving only a select few inside, as well as explicit instructions on how and how often the seller will be expected to use them. But you're not just going to leave them there to figure their shit out on their own. You're a coach, remember? So together, you plan the steps they're going to take to get the results they need. And then you check in regularly. You're still not micromanaging, by the way. Sellers have to be able to do this themselves, or what's the point, right? But you make it clear that you believe in their ability to turn things around, and you're rooting for them.

Maybe it doesn't work out, and you have the coaching conversation we suggested where you try to help them figure out where they might do better. But maybe they take your guidance and run with it. Either way, you've lived up to your end of the deal and remained accountable to the people you hired through role modeling, establishing a clear vision and collective goal, offering feedback to the team as a whole, and providing support and encouragement to each individual as needed. In addition, the rest of the team will notice that you don't give up on people when they're struggling, and that hitting quota isn't the only thing that matters.

When managers build a culture of success, the salespeople, the SDRs, and the AEs all the way through the customer success team feel empowered, and the business is more effective. Reps don't wallow in failure too long without course correction. Simple mistakes don't morph into defeating habits that undermine outcomes. Rejection is just another change. Being ghosted is just part of the job, and every new email or call is a chance for success. The entire environment is salesperson-centric, where poor fits are removed amicably. Good reps are encouraged, and superstars stay. It's a powerful environment to be a part of, and salespeople need more of it.

People will always perform best in an environment that fosters collaboration, accountability, and transparency. When you think about it, that's exactly what we ask of all sellers at every step of the prospecting process. The best sellers meet their numbers not just because they're competitive, and not just because they want to make money, but also because they're operating with a sense of higher purpose, both to their team and to the buyers they're trying to serve. They believe in what they're selling and in the mission of the product or service. Putting in the work to make your team feel that they're a part of something big, something that matters, results in an environment where the best of the best want to invest their talent and want to stay. That's not just good culture. That's great business.

THE LAST WORD

Remember the time Will went door-to-door, selling "No Soliciting" signs? He was left with some surplus, so he posted one near his front door.

That's right, the man whose mission is to teach people to successfully do cold outreach stuck a "No Soliciting" sign on his own house. (Will loves Alanis Morrisette, but this is actually peak irony, unlike a free ride when you're already there, which is just bad luck.) There's a good reason: He's an easy sell. Even when a door-to-door seller is terrible, Will's heart goes out to them, and he buys. Posting the "No Soliciting" sign was an act of self-preservation and fiscal responsibility.

No soliciting signs work. Through his window, Will has seen people carrying clipboards head toward his house, spot the sign, turn around, and walk away.

About six months before we finished the manuscript for this book, however, Will was working at home when his dog started barking, which usually means someone is nearing the house. Sure enough, he looked out the window and saw a guy getting out of his car, holding a clipboard. The truth is that even with the sign there, if someone rings, Will still answers. Like everyone, he's always a little suspicious when greeting a stranger on his front step, but he's usually friendly. When he opened the door, he found a middle-aged man wearing the typical contractor uniform of a hoodie and cargo pants. *Here comes the pitch*, Will thought.

To his surprise, the seller said something to the effect of: "Hey, man, I was just driving by your house, and I noticed you have a lot of moss on the roof."

He was right, Will did, because his home was in a wooded area, and moss tends to grow in the shade.

"Yeah, I've noticed," said Will.

The seller, whose name was Andrew, continued, "So if you leave it there, it can grow underneath the shingles, which causes leaks. It can cause moisture to become trapped, which causes rot, and it can prevent drainage into the gutters, which causes foundational issues."

Will already knew all of that. "I meant to get up there this summer with some weed killer, or at least just brush it off. But frankly, I've been a bit too busy."

Andrew said, "Well, you can get rid of it that way, but if you want to prevent it from coming back, you can install zinc strips. Zinc is toxic to moss, so if you put those on your roof, you'll never have to worry about it again." He pulled up his phone and pointed to a picture of the product. "You can buy them from the store yourself, but they can be a pain to install. If you're busy, I'm happy to come by with a couple of guys next week and install them for you."

"How much would that cost?"

"$500."

"Hell, yes. Come by next week for sure," said Will.

After they'd agreed on the time and date Andrew would return, Will said:

"I appreciate you ignoring the sign."

Andrew laughed and said, "I don't feel like I'm soliciting; I'm trying to be helpful."

He returned the following week with his crew, cleaned the roof of moss and laid down the zinc strips, and Will paid him five hundred bucks.

Moral of the story: When people believe you're helping them, they *do* want to be bothered.

And that, friends, is the whole point of what we've been trying to tell you. Sellers broke the sales world by doubling down on unethical selling techniques and a shit show of distractions, amygdala-melting intrusions, and channel overkill. As a result, buyers are simultaneously overstimulated and numb to most outreach efforts. When we come knocking, literally or figuratively, their first impulse is to get rid of us before they even know why we want to talk to them. Imagine if Andrew had not ignored the "No Soliciting" sign, or if Will had ignored the ring at the door. It would have cost Will thousands of dollars, and (here's the ironic part) the engagement with the next salesperson that followed would have cost him way more money. Experience has taught our prospects that we provide no value. We've lost their trust. Yet when we're there to help, we can be the best thing that could happen to a buyer.

In the year that it took us to write this book, the amount of crap spilling out into the world actually increased. Thinking they'd found the magic silver bullet they're always hunting for, agencies, sales leaders, and small business founders invested in AI so their teams could further automate their prospecting and blast out hundreds of emails at a time. Some even replaced their SDRs with AI. And all of them have been disappointed. Why? Because you still have to give AI something to work with for it to deliver, and they fed it the same old trash. If you dump in trash inputs, you get a trash output.

But there is a way to kill the garbage monster of old prospecting and gain the trust we've lost. It's to gap prospect, and to do it exceptionally well. That means giving these new AI tools thoughtful, specific prompts, feedback, and context, which requires deeply understanding your buyers, diagnosing their problems, and being crystal clear on which ones you can solve. It demands that you adopt the right mindset, calm your buyers' fears, know how to interrupt patterns, and get creative. It calls for using the proven formulas that lay the foundation to intriguing, interesting cold calls, emails, LinkedIn features, and social media DMs, as well as effective email videos, trade show introductions, referral requests, drop-in visits, and gifts. It means doing the hard, sometimes boring problem-centric work, day in and day out, never forgetting that absolutely not one single buyer gives a shit about you—and that's okay!

Join us in our mission to create a selling environment where buyers want to talk to us because they've come to anticipate a valuable exchange. Gap-prospecting can bring enormous value to both parties right from the start, easing the way to a positive outcome that benefits everyone. Even as the world goes more and more digital, and even with the rise of AI, it's the mostly analog features of gap-prospecting—the humanity, the accountability, the inventiveness, the ethics, and the value-creation—that make it the most effective outreach imaginable.

THE LAST, LAST WORD!

Finally, there will be some of you who are reading this and will be thinking about moving some, if not all, of your outbound to AI. And you're probably thinking gap-prospecting no longer applies. You're thinking, we're moving SDRs and our outbound to AI soon, and the AI will do the work, so this no longer applies.

Welp, that couldn't be any more misguided. Here's the point. AI needs us as much as we need AI. AI needs us to teach it how to sell. Like new sales reps, the companies that teach AI better selling and prospecting techniques will have the better AI agents. Use old, ineffective techniques, and you'll get an AI that can do crappy selling faster than other crappy sellers. Build AI agents taught how to gap-prospect, using gap-prospecting methods, and you'll have a killer AI agent that will outperform other AI agents.

As we're finishing up this book, AI is improving exponentially; and maybe someday, AI will learn a better way to sell, but until it does, gap-prospecting is the only way to outbound, and with humans or AI agents, it's the only method guaranteed to get results.

Becoming a gap (prospecting, selling, or customer success) organization means embedding gap into every part of the org, human or not.

TRAINING

ASALESGROWTHco.

CREATORS OF GAP SELLING

ASG offers a powerful in-person or virtual training program for your sales organization. To train your team on how to execute the gap-prospecting approach and grow your pipeline, click this **QR** code to learn more and schedule time with one of our consultants.

Scan here

ONLINE TRAINING

Wanna get even better at gap selling?
Check out our interactive choose-your-own-journey!

Gap selling online training

SHOUT-OUTS

The Gap franchise would not be where it is today if it were not for the brilliant mind and writing of Stephanie Land. Her ability to get into our minds, navigate through the noise, and coalesce our thoughts on paper is an act of genius. There is no scenario where Stephanie is not part of this team. On behalf of both Will and me, thanks, Steph! You make the process enjoyable and possible.

Thank you to the entire Sales Growth team. You work tirelessly to make this ship sail and we wouldn't be where we are without you.

A big thanks to the people who worked hard to make this book materialize. Your dedication, expertise and knowledge help make our dreams come to life.

ABOUT THE AUTHORS

Keenan is A Sales Growth Company's CEO/President and Chief Antagonist. He's been selling something to someone for his entire life. He's been teaching and coaching almost as long. With over 20 years of sales experience, which he'll tell you he doesn't give a shit about, Keenan has been influencing, learning from, and shaping the world of sales for a long time. Finder of the elephant in the room, Keenan calls it as he sees it and lets nothing or no one go unnoticed.

Keenan's passion for problem-solving reaches well beyond the sales and business world. He is the celebrated author of *Not Taught: What It Takes to be Successful in the 21st Century That Nobody's Teaching You*. The 21st century has ushered in the information age, and with it a new set of rules for success. *Not Taught* shares how the rules of the industrial age no longer work and that if you want to be successful, you must learn the new rules for success.

Father of three amazing girls, PSIA Certified Level 2 ski instructor (see, more coaching), and avid Boston sports fan, Keenan keeps crazy busy when he's not focused on A Sales Growth Company.

Will Aitken is a sales trainer, speaker, and professional button-pusher. Will spent years riding the sales rollercoaster and he's coached thousands of sellers through cold call anxiety, objection panic, and "why the hell won't they respond to my emails" syndrome. Whether it's through his viral content, cold copy rewrites, or live workshops, Will helps sales teams stop guessing and start booking. When he's not helping reps cut through the noise, he's probably deep in meme production or trying to get one of his two kids to stop using his microphone as a lightsaber.

ABOUT A SALES GROWTH COMPANY

A Sales Growth Company is the creator of Problem-Centric Selling and the architect of a modern Problem-Centric Sales Enablement Operating System.

Buying and selling have fundamentally changed. Buyers are more informed, more distracted, and more resistant to traditional, product-centric sales approaches than ever before. The old playbooks—built on volume, persuasion, and pitches—no longer work. They erode trust, flood buyers with noise, and produce weaker outcomes for both sellers and customers.

A Sales Growth Company redefined the selling ecosystem by shifting the focus from products to problems. Through Problem-Centric Selling, we teach teams how to earn attention, create buyer confidence, diagnose real business problems, and engage buyers in a way that creates value long before a solution is discussed.

Our work goes beyond theory. We combine industry-defining thought leadership with a rigorous sales enablement operating system that turns ideas into execution. Through training, coaching, workshops, deal reviews, and leadership enablement, we operationalize problem-centricity across people, process, and culture—so it scales and sticks.

This isn't traditional sales training. It isn't motivational noise. And it isn't built on shortcuts, scripts, or brute-force activity. It's a fundamentally different way to sell—designed for modern buyers and the organizations that want durable, predictable growth.

To learn more about Gap Prospecting, Gap Selling, or how A Sales Growth Company helps organizations grow through Problem-Centric Enablement, visit **www.salesgrowth.com**.

CONNECT

GIVE US A SHOUT. WE'LL SHOUT BACK!

Keenan

- ✖ @KEENAN
- ⬜ @KEENAN_REDPLAID
- f FACEBOOK.COM/HEYKEENAN
- in LINKEDIN.COM/IN/JIMKEENAN
- ✉ INFO@SALESGROWTH.COM

- ✖ @JUSTWILLAITKEN
- ⬜ @JUSTWILLAITKEN
- ♪ @SALESFEED
- in LINKEDIN.COM/JUSTWILLAITKEN
- ▶ YOUTUBE.COM/@SALES_FEED

Will

NOTES

[1] It helps manage our emotions and connects: "Amygdala: What It Is and What It Controls," Cleveland Clinic, last reviewed 4/2023, https://my.clevelandclinic.org/health/body/24894-amygdala.

[2] Our brains' ability to perceive and interpret: Charlotte B.A. Sinke, Mariska E. Kret, Beatrice de Gelder, "Body Language: Embodied Perception of Emotion," in *Measurement With Persons: Theory, Methods, and Implementation Areas*, ed. B. Berglund, G. B. Rossi, J. T. Townsend, & L. R. Pendrill (Psychology Press, 2012) 335–352; http://beatricedegelder.com/documents/Bodylanguageembodiedperceptionofemotion.pdf, 2-3.

[3] Before we're aware that we've seen a face: Jonathan B. Freeman, Ryan M. Stolier, Zachary A. Ingbretsen, Eric A. Hehman, "Amygdala Responsivity to High-Level Social Information from Unseen Faces," *Journal of Neuroscience* 34, no. 32 (2014):10573-10581, DOI: 10.1523/JNEUROSCI.5063-13.2014.

[4] Through body language, even from a distance: Sinke, Kret, de Gelder, "Body Language," 2.

[5] Even when we're not fully paying attention: Sinke, Kret, de Gelder, "Body Language," 4.

[6] Body language is exceptionally good at spreading fear: Randolph E. Schmid, "Body Language Fuels the Spread of Fear," NBC News, November 15, 2004, https://www.nbcnews.com/id/wbna6495282.

[7] Responsible for triggering the body's protective fight or flight: Arlin Cuncic, MA, "Amygdala Hijack and the Fight or Flight Response," Verywell Mind, Updated on September 11, 2024, https://www.verywellmind.com/what-happens-during-an-amygdala-hijack-4165944#:~:text=The%20thalamus%20then%20relays%20that,with%20which%20we%20must%20contend.

[8] George C. Parker: Gabriel Cohen, "For You, Half Price," *The New York Times*, November 27, 2005, https://www.nytimes.com/2005/11/27/nyregion/thecity/for-you-half-price.html.

[9] Participants in a cruel "system of capitalism": Laura Linard, "Birth of the American Salesman," interviewed by Laura Linard, April 19, 2004, https://www.library.hbs.edu/working-knowledge/birth-of-the-american-salesman.

[10] 3.9%: Orum, Slack conversation with Will Aitken, January 2025.

[11] Eight in ten Americans: Colleen McClain, "Most Americans don't answer cellphone calls from unknown numbers," Pew Research Center, December 14, 2020, https://www.pewresearch.org/short-reads/2020/12/14/most-americans-dont-answer-cellphone-calls-from-unknown-numbers/.

[12] "phone phobia": John Dias, "Gen Z developing fear of phone calls, or 'phone phobia,'" CBS News, August 1, 2023, https://www.cbsnews.com/newyork/news/gen-z-developing-fear-of-phone-calls-or-phone-phobia/.

[13] According to a study out of UC Irvine: Gloria Mark, Victor M. Gonzalez, Justin Harris, "No Task Left Behind? Examining the Nature of Fragmented Work," *CHI '05: Take a Number,*

Stand in Line (Interruptions and Attention) (April 2005), 325, https://ics.uci.edu/~gmark/
CHI2005.pdf; UC Berkeley, "The Impact of Interruptions," People and Culture,
retrieved June 17, 2025, https://hr.berkeley.edu/grow/grow-your-community/wisdom-
caf%C3%A9-wednesday/impact-interruptions.

[14] Productivity expert: Laura Vanderkam, April 13, 2012, https://lauravanderkam.
com/2012/04/round-up-time-waste-deleting-email/?utm_source=chatgpt.com.

[15] Researchers found: Gloria Mark, Daniela Gudith, Ulrich Klocke, "The cost of interrupted work:
more speed and stress," *CHI '08: Proceedings of the SIGCHI Conference on Human Factors in Computing
Systems* (April 2008), 107–110, https://dl.acm.org/doi/proceedings/10.1145/1357054.

[16] In 2016, there were about fifty times as many items: Christopher Mims, "Why There Are
More Consumer Goods Than Ever," *Wall Street Journal*, April 25, 2016, https://www.wsj.
com/articles/why-there-are-more-consumer-goods-than-ever-1461556860.

[17] Technology like cloud computing: Michael Baxter, "The golden age of startups: Technology
is lowering barriers to entry, but increasing barriers to exit," *Information Age*, July 12, 2019,
https://www.information-age.com/golden-age-of-startups-technology-lowering-barriers-
to-entry-increasing-barriers-to-exit-14225/#:~:text=%E2%80%9CFor%20building%20
websites%2C%20creating%20brands,AI%20as%20a%20service%20product.

[18] There was a 1,200% increase in the number of SDRs: Dr. Howard Dover, *The Sales Innovation
Paradox: Harnessing Modern Methods for Optimal Sales Performance* (River Grove Books, 2022), 27.

[19] Sixty-five percent of sales leaders say: "THE STATE OF SALES DEVELOPMENT
2024," Orum, 2, https://8348499.fs1.hubspotusercontent-na1.nethubfs/8348499/
PDFs/State%20of%20Sales%20Report%202024%20-%2FINALpdf?__
hstc=120346455.0763abb079174d98bc5c12a1431f95ce.1761331357636.1761331357636.
1761331357636.1&__hssc=120346455.2.1761331357636&__hsfp=3571084072.

[20] More competition: Lucy J. Hopewell, Lisa A. Leaver, Stephen E.G. Lea, "Effects of competition
and food availability on travel time in scatter-hoarding gray squirrels (Sciurus carolinensis),"
Behavioral Ecology, 19, no.6 (December 2008) 1143-1149, https://doi.org/10.1093/beheco/
arn095.

[21] Spend more energy than they should: Steven L. Lima, Thomas J. Valone, Thomas Caraco,
"Foraging-efficiency-predation-risk trade-off in the grey squirrel," *Animal Behaviour*, 1985,
33, no.1 (February 1985) 155-165, https://doi.org/10.1016/S0003-3472(85)80129-9.

[22] The average sales position tenure: The Bridge Group, "Sales Development (SDR) Metrics and
Comp Report," March 2023, 21.

[23] 61% of buyers: "How B2B Buyers Want To Be Sold," A Salesgrowth Company, https://
salesgrowth.com/how-buyers-want-to-be-sold.

[24] A University of Pennsylvania study: Katie Delach, "To Encourage Physical Activity, Potential
to Lose a Financial Reward is More Effective Than Gaining One, Penn Study Shows,"
Penn Today, Penn University of Pennsylvania, February 16, 2016, https://penntoday.

upenn.edu/news/encourage-physical-activity-potential-lose-financial-reward-more-effective-gaining-one-penn-stu.

[25] Lieutenant Commander Michael Riley: Gary Klein, *Sources of Power: How People Make Decisions* (MIT Press, 1998), 35–39.

[26] Michael Riley initially couldn't explain: Klein, *Sources of Power*, 37.

[27] Subconsciously he saw a "deviation from a pattern": Klein, *Sources of Power*, 38–39.

[28] It will fixate on the missing pieces: "Zeigarnik Effect," Psychology Today, retrieved May 2025, https://www.psychologytoday.com/us/basics/zeigarnik-effect.

[29] "reflection yields:" Hannes Gustav Melichar, "Autonomy and Vulnerability: Elements of a Phenomenology of Reflection and Reason," *Human Studies* 48 (January 2025): 551, https://doi.org/10.1007/s10746-024-09775-w.

[30] reflection comes with human vulnerability: Melichar, "Autonomy and Vulnerability," 551.

[31] Reflection helps them see that there may be a reason for change: "Autonomy and Vulnerability," 558.

[32] Fear of vulnerability and the discomfort it brings: Kristen Robinson, "Critical reflection: a student's perspective on a 'pedagogy of discomfort' and self-compassion to create more flexible selves," *Reflective Practice* 22 no. 5, (2021): 642, DOI: 10.1080/14623943.2021.1948825.

[33] A sticky idea: Chip Heath and Dan Heath, *Made to Stick: Why Some Ideas Survive and Others Die* (Random House, 2007), 8.

[34] Sticky ideas consist of SUCCESs: Heath, *Made to Stick*, 16–18.

[35] Simplicity isn't the same thing as: Heath, *Made to Stick*, 27, 30.

[36] Every year, out of a pool of about 60,000 hopefuls: Martin E.P. Seligman, PhD, *Learned Optimism: How to Change Your Mind and Your Life* (Vintage Books, 2006), 96–106.

[37] There are three "dimensions": Seligman, *Learned Optimism*, 44–52.

[38] By repeatedly adding the single, powerful word "yet": GreatSchools, "Carol Dweck on the Power of 'Yet,'" YouTube, June 26, 2013, Length: 57 seconds, https://www.youtube.com/watch?v=ZyAde4nIIm8.

[39] Reframing rejection as a positive experience: Milka Waniak, *Viewing Rejection as a Positive Experience Helps People Perform Better and Motivates Them to Persist* (Thesis, University of California San Diego, 2024), DO- 10.13140/RG.2.2.11417.43366.

[40] "To complain is always nonacceptance of what is.": Eckhart Tolle, *The Power of Now: The Guide to Spiritual Enlightenment* (New World Library and Namaste Publishing, 1999), 43, https://www.hoopladigital.com/audiobook/the-power-of-now-eckhart-tolle/12025856.

[41] Grit is embodied by interest, practice, and hope tied to a sense of purpose: Shankar Vedantam, Maggie Penman, Max Nesterak, *Hidden Brain*, "The Power and Problem of Grit," podcast, NPR, 2016, https://www.npr.org/2016/04/04/472162167/the-power-and-problem-of-grit.

[42] A 3.9 percent connection rate: Orum.

[43] The vast majority of Americans: McClain, "Most Americans."

[44] The young generations: Dias, "Gen Z developing fear."

[45] Top performing reps are 2.5x: Leke Oyetoke, "Cold Calling Scripts That Actually Work," *Blog – SIIT*, Scholars Int'l Institute of Technology, accessed July 31, 2025, https://siit.co/blog/cold-calling-scripts-that-actually-work/44616?utm_source=chatgpt.com.

[46] In 2023, 69% of buyers: Erica Schultz, "Infographic: 3- Must-Know Sales Prospecting Stats and What They Mean for Sellers," RAIN Group, last updated March 15, 2023, https://www.rainsalestraining.com/blog/infographic-30-sales-prospecting-stats-and-what-they-mean-for-sellers.

[47] In 2013, the Italian: Jen Ortiz, "Pope Francis: Cold-Caller of the Year 2013," *GQ*, November 28, 2013, https://www.gq.com/story/pope-francis-men-of-the-year-cold-caller?utm_source=chatgpt.com.

[48] The voice on the other end: Elisabetta Povoledo and Dan Bilefsky, "The Pope Gets on the Line, and Everyone is Talking," *The New York Times*, September 9, 2013, https://www.nytimes.com/2013/09/10/world/europe/the-popes-on-the-line-and-everyones-talking.html.

[49] "I was speechless": Ortiz, "Pope Francis."

[50] He said that the call: Povoledo and Bilefsky, "The Pope."

[51] Italians nicknamed him: Povoledo and Bilefsky, "The Pope."

[52] Some sellers believe: Binal Raval: *The State of Cold Calling in 2024*, Cognism, accessed August 4, 2025, https://www.cognism.com/state-of-cold-calling?utm_content=SLS_MM_ICP_CNT_Static_BigRock_ColdCalling_ColdCallingReport_WantToKnowWhat; https://chrisritson.xyz/articles/3x-your-cold-call-conversions?utm_source=chatgpt.comThere's.

[53] Even when they can't see the person speaking: Amy Drahota, Alan Costall, Vasu Reddy, "The vocal communication of different kinds of smile," *Speech Communication* 50, no. 4 (2008): 278–287, https://doi.org/10.1016/j.specom.2007.10.001.

[54] Even "auditory smiles": Pablo Arias, et al, "Auditory smiles trigger unconscious facial imitation," *Current Biology* 28, no. 14, R782–R783, DOI: 10.1016/j.cub.2018.05.084.

[55] Emails that are crafted: Chelsea Castle, "Cold Email 101: How to Write Emails People Actually Read (and Reply To)" *Lavendar* (blog), March 23, 2023, https://www.lavender.ai/blog/cold-email-101?utm.

[56] Up to eight touchpoints: Mike Schultz, "How Many Touchpoints Does It Take to Make a Sale?" *RAIN Group Sales Blog*, RAIN Group, August 27, 2025, https://www.rainsalestraining.com/blog/how-many-touchpoints-does-it-take-to-make-a-sale.

[57] Dan Waldschmidt, a turnaround specialist: Stu Heinecke, *How to Get a Meeting with Anyone, Updated Edition: The Untapped Selling Power of Contact Marketing*, (BenBella Books, 2025), Chap. 8 accessed on bookshop.org, https://bookshop.org/ebooks.

[58] Data shows that if you book a meeting: Tito Bohrt, "Dear fellow SDR…you need to hit quota? Here's a tip," LinkedIn, 2022, https://www.linkedin.com/posts/titobohrt_sdrsmatter-activity-6960986362518900736-IZJk/?utm_source=share&utm_medium=member_

desktop&rcm=ACoAABcUAMwBLN-k3ddfcwiVyRixwzdLuEP21m8; Vlad Oleksiienko, "5 Tactics to Fight Demo No-Shows (+Ready-to-Use Sequence)," Reply, August 8, 2023, https://reply.io/fight-demo-no-shows.

59 Running "naked,": Kamilah Journét, "I Spent a Month Running Without a Smartwatch," Recreational Equipment, Inc., *Uncommon Path* (blog), July 17, 2023, retrieved September 22, 2025. https://www.rei.com/blog/run/running-without-a-smartwatch.

60 Willing to put in the extra hard work: Angela Duckworth, *Grit: The Power of Passion and Perseverance* (Scribner, 2016), 7–14, 19–34.

61 "Find [your] sources of motivation: Janet Levaux, "Packers' Aaron Rodgers on Leadership, Post-NFL Career: Pershing Insite," ThinkAdvisor, June 19, 2017, https://www.thinkadvisor.com/2017/06/19/packers-aaron-rodgers-on-leadership-post-nfl-career-pershing-insite.

62 Transactional leadership: Simone I. Flynn, "Transformational and Transactional Leadership," EBSCO, 2024, https://www.ebsco.com/research-starters/social-sciences-and-humanities/transformational-and-transactional-leadership.

63 "envision an appealing future goal state": Barbara Steinmann, Hannah J.P. Klug, Günter W. Maier, "The Path Is the Goal: How Transformational Leaders Enhance Followers' Job Attitudes and Proactive Behavior," *Frontiers in Psychology* 28, no. 9 (November 2018): 2338. https://doi.org/10.3389/fpsyg.2018.02338.

64 Transformational leaders exhibit: Chioma Ugochukwu, "Transformational Leadership Style: How To Inspire And Motivate," Simply Psychology, updated June 20, 2025, https://www.simplypsychology.org/what-is-transformational-leadership.html?utm_source=chatgpt.com.

65 Transformational leaders fuel the kind of energy and empowerment: Ronnie (Chuang Rang) Gao, William H. Murphy, Rolph E. Anderson, "Transformational leadership effects on salespeople's Attitudes, striving, and performance," *Journal of Business Research* 110 (March 2020): 237–245, https://doi.org/10.1016/j.jbusres.2020.01.023.

66 The American Psychological Association includes optimism: American Psychological Association, "Psychological capital: What it is and why employers need it now," August 21, 2023, https://www.apa.org/topics/healthy-workplaces/psychological-capital.

67 Psychologist Daniel Goleman: Herminia Ibarra, Ane Scoular, "The Leader as Coach," *Harvard Business Review*, November-December 2019, 60–61, https://hbr.org/2019/11/the-leader-as-coach.

68 Studies have shown: Ibarra, Scoular, "The Leader as Coach."

69 "Unlocking people's potential," Ibarra, Scoular, "The Leader as Coach;" John Whitmore, *Coaching for Performance*, 3rd ed. (Nicholas Brealey Publishing, 2002), 8, https://research-ebsco-com.atxlibrary.idm.oclc.org/linkprocessor/plink?id=90144759-d2ee-3423-91a9-fd5ef34d11bd.

70 Triggers people's stress response: "The Trier Social Stress Test as a paradigm to study how people respond to threat in social interaction," Johanna U. Frisch, Jan A. Häusser, Andreas Mojzisch, *Frontiers in Psychology* 6 (February 2015), https://doi.org/10.3389/fpsyg.2015.00014.

That's it.
Peace. We're out.

www.ingramcontent.com/pod-product-compliance
Lightning Source LLC
Chambersburg PA
CBHW031318280326
41949CB00042B/108/J